The Coming of the Nixon Court

The Coming of the Nixon Court

The 1972 Term and the Transformation of Constitutional Law

Earl M. Maltz

UNIVERSITY PRESS OF KANSAS

Published by the University Press of Kansas (Lawrence, Kansas 66045), which was organized by the Kansas Board of Regents and is operated and funded by Emporia State University, Fort Hays State University, Kansas State University, Pittsburg State University, the University of Kansas, and Wichita State University

Library of Congress Cataloging-in-Publication Data
Names: Maltz, Earl M., 1950–
Title: The coming of the Nixon court : the 1972 term and the transformation of constitutional law / Earl M. Maltz.
Description: Lawrence, Kansas : University Press of Kansas, [2016] | Includes bibliographical references and index.
Identifiers: LCCN 2016012021 | ISBN 9780700622788 (cloth : alk. paper) | ISBN 9780700622795 (ebook)
Subjects: LCSH: United States. Supreme Court—History—20th century. | Nixon, Richard M. (Richard Milhous), 1913–1994—Influence. | Constitutional history—United States—20th century. | Political questions and judicial power—United States—History—20th century. | United States—Politics and government—1969–1974.
Classification: LCC KF8742 .M2627 2016 | DDC 347.73/2609047—dc23
LC record available at http://lccn.loc.gov/2016012021.

British Library Cataloguing-in-Publication Data is available.

Printed in the United States of America

10 9 8 7 6 5 4 3 2 1

The paper used in this publication is recycled and contains 30 percent postconsumer waste. It is acid free and meets the minimum requirements of the American National Standard for Permanence of Paper for Printed Library Materials Z39.48-1992.

Contents

Preface

Typically, historical studies of the jurisprudence of the Supreme Court take one of a number of standard forms. Some are organized doctrinally, focusing either on a single case or a range of decisions that deal with a particular subject of interest to the author. Other studies cut across a variety of different areas of law, frequently dealing with either the constitutional jurisprudence of a single justice or the work of the Court under one chief justice.

This book has a different format. Rather than focusing on a single doctrinal area or the work of either a single justice or that of the Court as a whole over a long period, the book is an in-depth study of the Court's performance during a single term. The book is intended to situate that performance within the political and jurisprudential context of that period as well as to describe the approaches taken by the different members of the Court and to highlight the interactions that ultimately produced the pattern of decisions during the 1972 term.

I chose to focus on the 1972 term for a variety of reasons. First, the 1972 term was the first complete term that brought the participation of all of the justices who had been appointed by President Richard M. Nixon. Nixon had come into office in 1968 vowing to choose justices who would stem the tide of what he characterized as excessive liberal activism by the Warren Court and instead adopt a jurisprudence of judicial restraint. By the end of December 1971, Nixon had had the opportunity to replace four members of the Warren Court with justices of his own choosing. Although the Nixon justices had the opportunity to participate in some of the decisions of the 1971 term, the 1972 term provided a more complete picture of the judicial philosophies of Lewis F. Powell, Jr., and William H. Rehnquist, the last two Nixon appointees, and the impact that those two appointments in particular had on the evolution of constitutional doctrine.

Not surprisingly, the Nixon appointees substantially changed the ideological balance of the Supreme Court. The Court of the late Warren era was something of a historical anomaly—an institution dominated by progressives that also lacked any representation from true conservatives. The addition of the Nixon justices created a far more politically diverse Court, including not only committed progressives and conservatives but also justices with a wide variety of more moderate views. Thus, one could reasonably expect the behavior of such a Court to be fairly representative of that of the Court generally over time.

Moreover, one would be hard-pressed to find another term in the late twentieth century in which the Court dealt with so many issues with major implications for the future of constitutional law. The term is best remembered for the decision in *Roe v. Wade*, the abortion decision whose jurisprudential and political impact continues to be felt strongly more than forty years later.[1] However, the Court also handed down important rulings of lasting significance on a wide variety of other issues, including school desegregation, school finance, obscenity, the rights of the poor, gender discrimination, and aid to parochial schools.

On one level, the dynamic that produced the pattern of decisions in these cases can be described in relatively simple terms. Progressives could generally count on the votes of Justices William O. Douglas, William J. Brennan, Jr., and Thurgood Marshall. By contrast, Justice William H. Rehnquist was an equally reliable conservative vote and was usually joined by Chief Justice Warren E. Burger. Thus, the balance of power rested with holdover Justices Potter Stewart and Byron R. White and Nixon appointees Harry A. Blackmun and Lewis F. Powell, Jr., none of whom had views on constitutional law that could be described as either consistently progressive or consistently conservative. Instead, the political orientation of each of these justices depended on the particular issue being considered. Conservatives prevailed whenever they could attract the votes of three of the four centrist judges. Otherwise, the progressives emerged victorious.

Given this reality, any attempt to describe the political or jurisprudential orientation of the decisions of the 1972 term in general terms would be inherently misleading. Instead, the overall pattern of the decisions is nothing more or less than the sum of a number of individual decisions, each of which was produced by interactions among nine men with widely disparate worldviews. After coming to their own conclusions about the appropriate action to take in each case, the justices at times compromised with each other in the interest of generating majority opinions that would both establish strong precedents for the future and provide guidance to the lower courts.

Against this background, this book paints a picture of the 1972 term through a series of independent stories, each of which focuses on the Court's treatment of a specific area of constitutional law. Each chapter describes the political and doctrinal background of a particular set of disputes that came to the Court as well as the interaction among the justices themselves that ultimately produced the final resolution. In the book I will make no effort to evaluate the Court's actions against the hypothetical results that might be mandated by some overarching jurisprudential theory. Instead, the book is designed to provide the reader a sense of the complexity of the forces that shape the responses of a politically diverse Court to ideologically divisive issues.

I am deeply indebted to a number of people whose contributions greatly improved this book. Mark Tushnet read large portions of the manuscript and made a variety of useful suggestions. Rick Garnett, Mark Graber, John Jeffries, Serena Mayeri, and Mike Seidman also provided useful input. In addition, John Jacobs, the archivist of the Lewis F. Powell, Jr., Papers at Washington and Lee University, was unfailingly courteous and patient in dealing with what must have seemed endless requests to digitize Powell's case files.

The Coming of the Nixon Court

Chapter One

The Making of the Burger Court

The events of the 1972 term unfolded against the backdrop of the dramatic changes in US constitutional culture that had marked the tenure of Chief Justice Earl Warren. At the time Warren came to the Supreme Court on October 1, 1953, many progressives, haunted by the specter of the *Lochner* era jurisprudence, viewed the concept of judicial activism with deep suspicion. However, by the time Warren E. Burger succeeded Warren as chief justice on June 23, 1969, such activism was almost universally associated with the advancement of the progressive political agenda.[1]

The change began in 1954 with the landmark decision in *Brown v. Board of Education*, in which the Court unanimously held that state laws that required the maintenance of racially segregated schools violated the equal protection clause of the Fourteenth Amendment.[2] Although progressives won a number of significant victories during the early years of the Warren Court, they did not have a truly reliable majority on the Court until Arthur Goldberg took the seat previously occupied by Felix Frankfurter on September 28, 1962. Progressive control became even more complete when Thurgood Marshall replaced Tom C. Clark on October 2, 1967. Thus, during the two terms that followed Marshall's confirmation, progressive stalwart William J. Brennan, Jr., dissented from the judgment of the Court on a total of only seven occasions.[3]

During the late Warren era, a majority of the justices invoked the Constitution in support of the progressive agenda on a variety of different fronts. After some initial reticence, during the late 1960s the Court began to push back more aggressively against Southern efforts to resist the desegregation of public schools. Further, the justices sought to reshape the allocation of political power within the House of Representatives and the state legislatures and dramatically enhanced the protections required to be afforded to criminal defendants. In addition, as Warren's tenure as chief justice came to a close, the Court began to hint it was preparing to establish constitutional principles designed to substantially improve the lot of the poor in US society.[4]

The Warren Court also took an active role in the culture wars that wracked the nation during the 1960s. In hindsight, the decision to constitutionalize the right of married couples to use contraceptives would emerge as a critical turning point in the evolution of constitutional doctrine. However, during the Warren era itself, the cases that outlawed prayer in schools and provided significant protection for the right to distribute and possess sexually explicit materials were far more controversial and politically salient.[5]

These doctrinal developments provoked reactions from a variety of different quarters. By the late 1960s, progressive commentators, some of whom initially expressed concern about what they viewed as unprincipled judicial activism, had become increasingly supportive of the idea that the Court should move aggressively to support progressive ideals.[6] But at the same time, the Court's decisions also generated a political backlash in the populace at large.

The significance of this backlash became clear during the presidential campaign of 1968. As part of his effort to position himself as the "law-and-order" candidate during the campaign, Republican nominee Richard M. Nixon focused attention on the Warren Court decisions that expanded the rights of criminal defendants, criticizing the Court for giving the "green light" to "criminal elements in this country." Nixon pledged to appoint justices who were "judicial conservatives" and would not give expansive interpretations to constitutional limitations on government actions.[7]

For obvious reasons, this possibility was anathema to Chief Justice Warren. Fearing a Nixon victory and seeking to deprive Nixon of the potential opportunity to appoint the next chief justice, Warren resigned well in advance of the election, thereby providing President Lyndon Baines Johnson the opportunity to appoint Warren's successor. However, after Johnson's effort to elevate Associate Justice Abe Fortas to the chief justiceship was derailed by a Senate filibuster, and Nixon was in fact victorious in the November election, it became clear that the maneuver had backfired. Rather than paving the way for the selection of a like-minded successor, Warren's resignation provided the newly elected president the ability to immediately select a chief justice with a different jurisprudential perspective. Nixon quickly seized on this opportunity by appointing Warren E. Burger to succeed Warren.

By the end of his first term, Nixon was also able to fill three other seats on the Court. Soon after his nomination to succeed Warren was withdrawn, Fortas resigned in the face of new allegations of unethical behavior and was succeeded by Harry A. Blackmun.[8] In 1971, both John Marshall Harlan and Hugo Black left the Court under more conventional circumstances and were replaced by Lewis F. Powell, Jr., and William H. Rehnquist.

As a result of these changes, by 1972 the overall political orientation of the justices as a group was far more conservative than it had been only four years before. However, even after Nixon's appointments were confirmed, holdovers from the Warren era retained a majority of the seats on the Court. In addition, viewed from a distance at least, Nixon's own choices appear to have been less consistently conservative than they might have been. The relative moderation of the Nixon justices was the by-product of the interaction between two different factors.

First, despite his public attacks on the jurisprudence of the Warren Court progressives, Nixon plainly was not wedded to the idea that he should limit his judicial appointments to those with a demonstrable, unambiguous commitment to conservative ideology. To be sure, Nixon would not have considered appointing an identifiably progressive candidate to serve on the Court, and he appears to have been truly determined to make an effort to change the trajectory of the Warren Court's decisions on criminal procedure. Nonetheless, as Kevin J. McMahon has demonstrated, within those parameters Nixon's choices seem to have been driven as much by political concerns as by ideological imperatives.[9] Thus, among the four Nixon appointees ultimately confirmed by the Senate, only William H. Rehnquist and perhaps Warren E. Burger can appropriately be categorized as being consistent conservatives in the same sense that William O. Douglas, William Brennan, and Thurgood Marshall are generally characterized as consistent progressives. By contrast, although in general the political and jurisprudential orientations of both Harry Blackmun and Lewis Powell were to the right of the justices they replaced, both were perhaps best described as nondoctrinaire conservatives—men who quickly showed that on some issues, their views were more nearly akin to those of Douglas, Brennan, and Marshall than those of Burger and Rehnquist.

Nixon's decision to appoint at least some justices who ultimately agreed with their progressive colleagues on a number of critical issues also reflected the state of constitutional theory at the time he took office. During the late Warren era, John Marshall Harlan was generally viewed as the quintessential conservative on the Warren Court.[10] Yet with the possible exception of the conflict over the reapportionment and voting rights cases, in practical terms the differences between Harlan's approach and that of his more progressive brethren were largely ones of emphasis. Thus, for example, although he steadfastly opposed the idea that the Bill of Rights by its terms should be applied to the states, Harlan was willing to intervene in the contraception and school prayer cases in order to protect values he deemed fundamental and also derived significant protections for criminal defendants from the due process clauses of the Fifth and Fourteenth Amendments.[11] Against this background, it was not until the publication of a seminal article by Robert H. Bork in 1971 that a jurisprudential strategy based on the concept of originalism began to gain significant traction as a more conservative alternative to progressive constitutionalism.[12]

In any event, when combined with the holdovers from the Warren era, the Nixon justices created a Court with members whose views spanned the full spectrum of mainstream American politics and jurisprudence. Against this background, any attempt to explain the pattern of the Court's decisions in terms of voting blocs will almost inevitably be misleading. Instead, the pattern of decisions is best understood as reflecting the interaction among nine individuals, each of whom brought a unique perspective to the cases that came before the Court.[13]

Chief Justice Warren E. Burger

Nixon's choice of Warren Burger to succeed Earl Warren was no surprise to Washington insiders. Burger was in many ways a classic American success story—a self-made man who rose to the pinnacle of his chosen profession.[14] Born into a working-class family on September 17, 1907, by the time that Burger had graduated from high school, he had become something of a Renaissance man. Burger was not only a solid student and an athlete who earned letters in four sports but was also the president of the student council and editor of the school newspaper.

Although Burger was admitted to Princeton, the scholarship that he was offered was not large enough to defray the cost of his college education. Thus, Burger took a job as an insurance sales representative and for the next six years attended undergraduate and law school at night, graduating magna cum laude in 1931 from St. Paul College of Law. After completing law school, Burger joined the St. Paul law firm of Boyeson, Otis, and Farley. He became a partner in the law firm after five years and remained with the firm until he entered public service.

Burger was active in Republican politics, and after Dwight D. Eisenhower was elected president in 1952, Burger came to Washington to serve as head of what was to become the Civil Division of the Justice Department under Attorney General Herbert Brownell. After being nominated in 1955, Burger joined the US Court of Appeals for the District of Columbia in 1956. There he emerged as a leading conservative voice on a generally liberal court, becoming particularly well known for his criticism of the Warren Court's innovations in criminal procedure. Thus, given President Nixon's avowed distaste for these innovations, Burger was a logical choice to succeed Warren after Nixon took office. The confirmation process presented no real difficulties; conservatives were generally pleased with the nomination, while liberals were demoralized by the Fortas debacle and not disposed to attack a nominee whose only apparent vice was that he was relatively conservative. In this benign political climate, Burger was confirmed by the Senate with only three dissenting votes and sworn in as the fourteenth chief justice of the United States on June 23, 1969.

By the beginning of the 1972 term, Burger had already proved to be the generally reliable conservative voice that Nixon no doubt believed that he was appointing in 1969. However, the new chief justice was by no means either a great legal theorist or a gifted writer of opinions. Moreover, by the time Powell and Rehnquist joined the Court, it had already become clear that Burger lacked the skills necessary to become a true leader of an ideologically fractured Court.

William O. Douglas

William Orville Douglas was by far the most senior justice on the Court in the 1972 term.[15] Douglas was born on October 16, 1898, in Maine, Minnesota. In 1904, his family moved to a town fifty miles from Yakima, Washington. Douglas's father died shortly thereafter, and Douglas spent the remainder of his poverty-stricken childhood with his mother in Yakima.

After receiving his undergraduate degree from Walla Walla College in 1920, Douglas worked for two years as a schoolteacher before entering Columbia Law School, where he graduated second in his class in 1925. Douglas then worked for a major Wall Street law firm for two years before returning to the law school world as an academic, specializing in corporate law at Columbia and Yale from 1929 through 1934.

In 1934, Douglas left Yale to work at the newly formed Securities and Exchange Commission, becoming a commissioner in 1936 and chair in

1937. He also became a member of the New Deal inner circle and was appointed by President Franklin D. Roosevelt to succeed Louis D. Brandeis on the Court after Brandeis resigned in 1939. Ironically Douglas was chosen for the Court in part because he was viewed as more conservative than his primary competitor for the position, and the votes against his confirmation came from a small group of senators who accused Douglas of being a reactionary tool of Wall Street interests.

Douglas has been described as the "quintessential loner—a lover of humanity who did not like people."[16] In his interactions with both his staff and other justices, he often seemed to have almost no regard for the feelings of those with whom he was dealing. At the same time, from both political and jurisprudential perspectives, he was also clearly the most liberal of all of the justices on the Court during the 1972 term and the Burger era more generally, at times dissenting alone in cases in which the other justices who were typically characterized as progressives joined their more conservative colleagues.

William J. Brennan, Jr.

If asked to name the most important proponent of progressive constitutionalism during the 1972 term, most commentators would almost certainly nominate William J. Brennan, Jr.[17] The son of a respected labor leader who was also active in city government, Brennan was born on June 8, 1906, in Newark, New Jersey. He was an outstanding student both in high school and at the Wharton School of Finance of the University of Pennsylvania and in 1931 graduated from Harvard Law School, finishing in the top 10 percent of his class academically. He then joined an established labor law firm in Newark.

After being an important figure in a successful drive for constitutional reform of the New Jersey court system, Brennan was appointed to serve on the state trial court in 1949. He was elevated to the New Jersey Supreme Court three years later. When Sherman Minton retired from the US Supreme Court in 1956, President Eisenhower's political advisors saw an opportunity to reach out to the Catholic and labor union constituencies in the Northeast. Brennan was the perfect choice to advance this political agenda.

However, Eisenhower purportedly would later describe the appointment as the "biggest damn fool mistake that I ever made." Brennan quickly emerged as one of the Court's most consistent progressives and was frequently chosen by Chief Justice Warren to be the legal technician charged with the task of fashioning the doctrinal arguments necessary to attract and hold progressive majorities together. Indeed, during the late Warren era, Brennan's positions on controversial issues essentially defined those of the Court as a whole; during the last two terms of the Warren era, he dissented a total of only 6 times in the 322 cases in which the Court issued opinions.[18]

However, during the 1972 term, Brennan's position was quite different. The four Nixon appointments had shifted the balance of power, and he was far less likely to be in the majority in controversial cases. Thus, he dissented no fewer than 50 times in the 144 cases in which opinions were issued.[19] Moreover, even when Brennan was in the majority, in those cases in which the justices were closely divided, the task of writing the opinion of the Court more often fell to one of his centrist colleagues.

Thurgood Marshall

Even if he had not become the first African American to serve on the Supreme Court, Thurgood Marshall would have been known as one of the most important figures in twentieth-century American legal history.[20] Born Thoroughgood Marshall on July 2, 1908, in Baltimore, Maryland, he was raised by a schoolteacher mother and a father who worked both as a railroad porter and as a steward at a country club. Marshall received his early education in segregated public schools in Baltimore and at the equally segregated Lincoln University. After receiving his undergraduate degree, Marshall applied to the University of Maryland Law School but was rejected because of his race. He therefore chose to attend Howard University Law School, where he came under the tutelage of civil rights pioneer Charles Hamilton Houston and graduated first in his class in 1933.

Marshall began his career as a solo practitioner but in 1936 took a full-time position on the staff of the National Association for the Advancement of Colored People (NAACP). In 1940 he became the first president director of the NAACP Legal Defense Fund (LDF) and held that position until 1961. As the leader of the LDF, Marshall won a number of signal victories in civil rights litigation. However, he is best remembered for his role in *Brown v. Board of Education*, in which the Supreme Court outlawed racial segregation in public schools.

In 1961, Marshall left the LDF to take a position on the US Court of Appeals for the Second Circuit. At the request of President Johnson,

Marshall left the Second Circuit in 1965 to accept an appointment as the first African American solicitor general of the United States. Two years later, Johnson chose Marshall to succeed the retiring Clark on the Supreme Court. Despite stiff opposition from representatives of the Southern states, Marshall was confirmed and joined the Court on October 2, 1967.

At the time Marshall took his seat, the Court was already dominated by justices who shared his progressive instincts. He dissented only once during his first term and seven times during the 1968 term. However, as the Nixon appointees joined the Court, like Douglas and Brennan, Marshall found himself disagreeing with a majority of his brethren far more often. Thus, beginning in the 1972 term, Marshall delivered a number of passionate dissents in which he decried the Court's refusal to more aggressively deploy the Constitution to protect the interests of racial minorities and poor people more generally.

Potter Stewart

Potter Stewart was the only Republican holdover from the Warren Court.[21] Stewart was born while his family was on vacation south of Lansing, Michigan, on January 23, 1915, but spent his early childhood in Cincinnati, Ohio. His father was a prominent politician who served both as mayor of Cincinnati and as a justice on the Ohio Supreme Court. After attending a prestigious prep school in New England, Stewart received his undergraduate education at Yale University, graduating Phi Beta Kappa in 1937. He then went on to Yale Law School, where he became an editor on the *Yale Law Journal* before graduating in 1941.

After a short stint at a Wall Street law firm, Stewart served in the US Navy in World War II before joining a law firm in Cincinnati. There he was active in local politics and was elected to the city council. In 1954, President Eisenhower appointed Stewart to serve on the US Court of Appeals for the Sixth Circuit and four years later chose him to succeed Justice Harold H. Burton, who retired from the Supreme Court on October 13, 1958.

Eisenhower initially granted Stewart a recess appointment that allowed him to serve on the Court pending formal confirmation proceedings by the Senate. Although Stewart was not the first justice to receive a recess appointment from Eisenhower, some senators took the view that the device should not be used to fill a vacancy on the Supreme Court. In addition, Southern Democrats refused to support the nomination after Stewart endorsed the decision in *Brown v. Board of Education* during his confirmation hearings. Nonetheless, he was ultimately confirmed on a seventy-two to nineteen vote.

Stewart's role on the Court during the 1972 term was quite different than it had been during the late Warren era. In the late 1960s, on many issues Stewart was more conservative than a majority of his brethren and often dissented in cases that adopted the constitutional arguments advanced by progressives. Not surprisingly, after the Nixon appointees took their seats on the Court, Stewart became an integral part of majorities that limited the scope of some of the decisions with which he had disagreed. But in addition, Stewart not only provided indispensable support for some decisions that furthered the progressive agenda but also at times found himself in the unfamiliar position of dissenting in cases in which conservatives prevailed. In short, given the configuration of the Burger Court, Stewart's position was that of a true centrist.

Byron Raymond White

Even before his nomination to serve on the Supreme Court, Byron R. White was well known to much of the US public for reasons entirely unrelated to either law or politics.[22] White was born in Fort Collins, Colorado, on June 8, 1917, and spent his childhood in Wellington, Colorado, a tiny impoverished mining community in the north of the state, where his father ran a lumberyard. After attending public elementary and secondary schools in Wellington, White earned an academic scholarship to the University of Colorado, where he not only graduated first in his class in 1938 but also earned a total of ten letters in three different sports and was named an All American in football, acquiring the nickname "Whizzer."

After his graduation from college, White played professional football for one year with the Pittsburgh Pirates before spending a year at Oxford University in England as a Rhodes Scholar. Upon returning to the United States, White enrolled at Yale Law School in September 1939. In order to earn money, White left Yale at the end of his first year to return to the National Football League, this time playing for a year and a half with the Detroit Lions until being drafted to serve in the US Navy in the wake of the attack on Pearl Harbor. He returned to Yale at the end of World War II, graduating magna cum laude in 1946. White then spent a year as a law clerk to Chief Justice Frederick M. Vinson before entering private practice with a small law firm in Denver, Colorado. There, White quickly showed an interest in local politics and remained deeply involved in those politics throughout his time in private practice.

Although they were by no means close friends, White had met John F. Kennedy in Europe during White's tenure as a Rhodes Scholar, and they had renewed their acquaintance when both were in the Pacific during World War II. Later, White chaired Citizens for Kennedy, a national volunteer organization that was formed to support Kennedy's successful campaign for the presidency in 1960. After Kennedy's victory in the election, White served in the Justice Department as deputy attorney general, where he was charged with the task of evaluating the qualifications, experience, and fitness of potential nominees to the federal bench.

At the time White accepted the position in the Justice Department, he had expected to remain in Washington for only a relatively short time before returning to private practice in Denver. However, his plans changed radically after Justice Charles E. Whitaker resigned from the Supreme Court in 1962, and Kennedy chose White to succeed Whitaker. The nomination was uncontroversial, and White took his seat on the Court after being confirmed by the Senate on a voice vote.

Based only on raw numbers, one might well characterize White's voting pattern during the 1972 term as that of a moderate conservative. Only Lewis Powell dissented less frequently than White did during the term, and White was considerably more likely to have voted with the Nixon appointees than with either Potter Stewart or any of the committed progressives on the Court.[23] However, White's dissents often came in the most politically contentious cases decided by the Court, and in a number of those dissents his position differed from that of the Nixon appointees and closely resembled that of Justices Douglas, Brennan, and Marshall. Thus, although his voting pattern was significantly different from Stewart's, White is also best described as a centrist.

Harry Andrew Blackmun

Harry A. Blackmun was not Richard Nixon's first choice to succeed Abe Fortas after Fortas was forced to resign from the Court in 1969. Instead, making a conscious decision to attempt to replace Fortas with a Southerner, Nixon nominated Clement Haynsworth of South Carolina, an experienced member of the US Court of Appeals for the Fourth Circuit. Although

Haynsworth was initially expected to be confirmed with relative ease, the nomination was undone by a combination of two different forces. First, because Haynsworth had a relatively conservative voting record, his nomination was predictably opposed by civil rights groups and representatives from organized labor. In addition, some aspects of Haynsworth's record left him vulnerable to charges of unethical behavior. Democrats, still smarting from the defeat of Fortas in 1968, seized on these incidents to charge that Haynsworth lacked the requisite integrity to serve on the Court, and the nomination was ultimately defeated on a fifty-five to forty-five vote.[24]

Nixon then turned to G. Harold Carswell of Georgia, who sat on the US Court of Appeals for the Fifth Circuit. It soon became apparent that the Carswell nomination faced difficulties not with ideology or integrity but rather with simple competence. The high point of the Senate debate was the declaration by one Carswell supporter that mediocre people deserved representation on the Supreme Court. Against this background, a bipartisan coalition united to defeat the Carswell nomination as well.[25]

Publicly complaining about the unwillingness of the Senate to confirm a Southerner, at this point Nixon turned to Blackmun.[26] Born in Nashville, Illinois, on November 12, 1908, Blackmun grew up in a working-class neighborhood of St. Paul, Minnesota, where he was a childhood friend of Warren Burger and later served as best man at Burger's wedding. Blackmun attended college and law school at Harvard, graduating from law school in 1932. He then joined a prominent Minneapolis law firm, where he specialized in tax law and estate planning until he became the general counsel of the Mayo Clinic in 1950. In 1959, President Eisenhower appointed Blackmun to the US Court of Appeals for the Eighth Circuit, and Blackmun remained on that court until his nomination to replace Fortas.

In the wake of the protracted struggle over the Haynsworth and Carswell nominations, the quiet, mild-mannered Blackmun seemed to be a godsend. Generally perceived to be a moderate conservative, he was described by one popular publication as "a judicial superblend of intelligence, industry, fairness, excellence, and probity." Even the executive director of the progressive American Civil Liberties Union praised Blackmun effusively, declaring that the nominee possessed a "capacity for objectivity and fairness in the highest degree, combined with a high intellect and sharply honed legal mind."[27] Against this background, Blackmun was confirmed unanimously by the Senate.

Standard accounts of Blackmun's career describe him as coming to the Court as one of the so-called Minnesota Twins—a generally reliable ally of Warren Burger—who would subsequently move to the left in reaction to the strident conservative reaction to his position on abortion. Although generally accurate, such characterizations tend to obscure subtle differences between Burger and Blackmun that had begun to emerge even before the issue of abortion took on such prominence. To be sure, during the 1972 term, Blackmun was a reliably conservative voice on issues such as criminal procedure and obscenity and joined the chief justice in taking less conservative positions in cases involving sex discrimination and aid to parochial schools. However, at the same time, Blackmun also abandoned Burger to join Douglas, Brennan, and Marshall in significant cases involving school desegregation and welfare rights. In short, although he rejected many of the tenets of progressive constitutionalism, Blackmun was at least marginally less conservative than some of the other Nixon appointees.

Lewis Franklin Powell, Jr.

Lewis F. Powell, Jr., was the only member of the Burger Court to have spent his entire career in private practice before his appointment to the Court.[28] Powell was born into an affluent family in a suburb of Norfolk, Virginia, on September 19, 1907. Soon after his birth, Powell's family moved to Richmond, where he attended a series of public and private schools before entering Washington and Lee University in 1925. Powell spent six years at Washington and Lee, graduating Phi Beta Kappa and president of his undergraduate class in 1929 before completing law school in 1931.

Powell subsequently spent a year at Harvard Law School before returning to Richmond to enter private practice. After spending a short time practicing in a small firm, Powell joined Hunton and Williams, the most prestigious firm in the city. Except for a hiatus when he served in the US Army during World War II, Powell remained with the same firm from 1935 through 1971, becoming a named partner in 1954.

During his time in private practice, Powell also devoted considerable time and energy to public service. He was the chair of the Richmond School Board during the tumultuous period immediately following the Supreme Court's decision in *Brown v. Board of Education* and also served on the state board of education. Subsequently, he achieved national prominence as president of both the American Bar Association and the American College of Trial Lawyers. Powell also served on President Johnson's Crime Commission and President Nixon's Defense Panel.

Unbeknownst to Powell, he was apparently Richard Nixon's first choice to succeed Abe Fortas in 1969 before writing a letter asking not to be considered. However, in 1971, after some hesitation, Powell agreed to accept a nomination to serve on the Court. Although Powell faced some opposition from civil rights leaders, the simultaneous nomination of William Rehnquist drew most of the fire from liberal activists, and Powell was ultimately confirmed by the Senate with only one negative vote.

Like that of Harry Blackmun, Powell's overall voting record was that of a moderate conservative. During the 1972 term, he was more likely to be in the majority than any other member of the Court.[29] On some issues, Powell's views plainly reflected those held generally by the Southern white aristocracy of which he was a member. For example, he complained bitterly to his colleagues about the preclearance requirement that had been imposed on many of the Southern states by the Voting Rights Act of 1965[30] and had a fierce belief in the efficacy of the basic structures of American government. However, despite his conservative instincts, like Blackmun, Powell showed at least some willingness to support his more progressive colleagues in cases that he viewed as involving profoundly unjust treatment of individual citizens.

William Hobbes Rehnquist

On the Burger Court, William H. Rehnquist stood at the opposite end of the ideological spectrum from William O. Douglas.[31] Rehnquist was born on October 1, 1924, in Milwaukee, Wisconsin. After spending his childhood in a middle-class suburb of Milwaukee, Rehnquist briefly attended Kenyon College before joining the US Army and serving for three years during World War II. After leaving the army, he received bachelor of arts and master of arts degrees from Stanford University as well as a master of arts from Harvard University. Rehnquist then returned to Stanford for law school, graduating as the class valedictorian in 1952.

After serving as a law clerk to Justice Robert H. Jackson, Rehnquist entered private practice in Phoenix, Arizona. There he became known as an outspoken, politically active conservative, criticizing the Warren Court for "extreme solicitude for the claims of Communists and other criminal defendants" and at one point asserting that open housing laws were an unjustifiable infringement on private property rights. After Richard Nixon was elected president, he chose Rehnquist to head the Office of Legal Counsel in the Justice Department. While serving in that capacity, Rehnquist often served as the administration spokesperson on controversial legal issues.

Rehnquist's nomination to succeed John Marshall Harlan on the Supreme Court in 1971 was strongly opposed by progressives who were disturbed by his views on civil rights. In particular, opponents of the nomination focused on two aspects of Rehnquist's record. The first was a memorandum Rehnquist had written to Justice Jackson in connection with the Court's consideration of *Brown v. Board of Education* that argued *Plessy v. Ferguson* "was right and should be reaffirmed." The second was Rehnquist's participation in a Republican poll-watching project that challenged voting credentials in Hispanic and African American neighborhoods. Rehnquist responded that Jackson himself had requested a defense of *Plessy* and that he had engaged in no wrongdoing during the poll-watching project. Ultimately, Rehnquist emerged victorious when the opponents of the nomination could only muster twenty-six votes in opposition.

Rehnquist's performance as a justice largely vindicated both the hopes of his conservative supporters and the fears of those who had opposed him. He argued for an originalist approach to constitutional interpretation and was at times characterized as a champion of judicial restraint. In later years, Rehnquist showed a willingness to actively deploy the Constitution in support of conservative values.[32] However, during the 1972 term, disputes that came before the Court involved only efforts to enshrine progressive values in constitutional law. In those cases, Rehnquist was less likely than any other member of the Court to vindicate a constitutional challenge to governmental action.

However, Rehnquist did not have the power to unilaterally determine the outcome of the cases that came before the Court. In order to prevent the progressives on the Court from achieving their objectives, in each case those advocating conservative positions needed to attract the votes of at least four other justices. The chief justice was Rehnquist's most frequent ally in his campaign against progressive constitutionalism. In addition, Burger and Rehnquist often gained the support of the other Nixon appointees.

Throughout the 1972 term, the balance of power was held by Nixon appointees Harry Blackmun and Lewis Powell and holdovers Potter Stewart and Byron White. The positions taken by Justices Blackmun and Powell were not uniformly more conservative than those of Justices Stewart and White. Indeed, in cases involving constitutional challenges to government aid to parochial schools and limitations on access to abortion, White's views were to the right of those of both Blackmun and Powell. Nonetheless, during the 1972 term, the Court adopted the progressive position in almost every significant case in which either Blackmun or Powell chose to vote with Douglas, Brennan, and Marshall rather than joining with Burger and Rehnquist. Conversely, the conservative position typically prevailed only in cases where the four Nixon appointees voted together and were joined by either Justice Stewart or Justice White. The result was an overall pattern of decisions that defied easy ideological characterization and whose political orientation varied greatly depending on the specific issues being decided by the Court. The outlines of this dynamic began to emerge almost immediately after Powell and Rehnquist were sworn in as justices.

Chapter Two

Prelude: The 1971 Term

Although the 1972 term was the first complete term in which the full complement of Nixon appointees participated, Lewis Powell and William Rehnquist actually took their seats midway through the term that had begun in October 1971. At the time, their confirmation was heralded as a "major event with important political consequences for [President Nixon], for the Supreme Court, and for the nation." Some commentators declared that the addition of Powell and Rehnquist gave the Court a "strongly conservative flavor" and that the "philosophy of judicial restraint espoused by [Nixon now has] a working majority."[1] Although some of the actions taken during the 1971 term were consistent with this perspective, others pointed to a more complex reality.

Conservatives clearly scored a number of important victories soon after the confirmation process was completed. In *Moose Lodge v. Irvis*, for example, the Court revitalized the state action doctrine as a limitation on the authority of the Court to act against racial discrimination.[2] The defendant in *Moose Lodge* was the local branch of a national fraternal organization whose bylaws limited membership to white males. The branch was also the holder of a license to sell alcoholic beverages that had been granted by the Pennsylvania Liquor Control Board. After having been denied beverage service because of his race, the plaintiff, who had been a guest at the Moose Lodge, argued that the equal protection clause required the state to revoke the license unless and until the lodge abandoned its racially discriminatory policies. Speaking for a six-justice majority, Rehnquist concluded that the Constitution did not require the revocation of the license.

Both Rehnquist and the plaintiff himself defined the critical question in *Moose Lodge* as whether the decision to deny service should be considered "state action" for constitutional purposes.[3] Although all agreed that, in theory at least, purely private actions were not subject to the constraints of the Fourteenth Amendment, in cases such as *Burton v. Wilmington Housing Authority* and *Reitman v. Mulkey* the Warren Court had concluded that in some cases, decisions by private parties could be attributed to the state and thereby made subject to the constitutional prohibition on racial discrimination.[4] However, noting that in *Burton* the Court had emphasized what it described as a symbiotic relationship between the government and the restaurant that had denied service to an African American, Rehnquist argued that no such relationship existed in *Moose Lodge*. In reaching this conclusion, he noted that, unlike the restaurant in *Burton*, the Moose Lodge was a purely private club owning the land and building in which it was located and that as such was not performing a function that would otherwise be performed by the state itself. Thus, while acknowledging the invalidity of a provision in the liquor license that essentially required the lodge to honor the racial restrictions in its bylaws, the majority concluded that the removal of this requirement would obviate all constitutional difficulties in the case.[5]

Dissenting, Justices William O. Douglas, William Brennan, and Thurgood Marshall characterized the central issue in *Moose Lodge* somewhat differently. Rather than focusing on the question of whether the decision of the club to refuse service could be attributed to the government, they argued that the issuance of the liquor license itself had "intertwine[d] the State with the operation of the Lodge bar in a 'significant way [and] len[t] [the State's] authority to the sordid business of racial discrimination.'" In reaching this conclusion, Douglas emphasized the limits on the number of licenses available, whereas Brennan focused primarily on the detailed conditions that were often attached to the licenses.[6] Both implicitly took the view that, against this background, the state could not grant a liquor license to a private club without affirmatively banning the club from engaging in racial discrimination.

More often, conservative victories in early 1972 involved issues of criminal procedure. *Kirby v. Illinois* illustrated both the impact of the Nixon appointments and the complexity of the forces that shaped the Court's decision-making process in the early 1970s.[7] *Kirby* was a challenge to the conviction of a man who had been arrested after having been found in the possession of traveler's checks and a Social Security card bearing the name of Shard, a person who had reported being robbed two days before. Shard was called to the police station and immediately identified the defendant as the man who had robbed him. However, the defendant was not advised of his right to counsel until after his arraignment on charges for robbery more than six weeks later. The defendant was convicted after Shard once again identified him at trial as the man who had committed the robbery. The conviction was challenged on the theory that both the original identification and Shard's testimony should have been excluded from evidence at the trial.

The challenge to the conviction was based primarily on the 1967 decisions in *United States v. Wade* and *Gilbert v. California*.[8] In those cases, over the dissents of Justices John Marshall Harlan, Potter Stewart, and Byron White, the Court had held that indicted defendants had a Sixth Amendment right both to have an attorney present at pretrial lineups and to be informed of that right. The majority reasoned in *Wade* that "since it appears that there is grave potential for prejudice, intentional or not, in the pretrial lineup, which may not be capable of reconstruction at trial, and since presence of counsel itself can often avert prejudice and assure a meaningful confrontation at trial, there can be little doubt that, for Wade, the post-indictment lineup was a critical stage of the prosecution at which he was 'as much entitled to such aid [of counsel] . . . as at the trial itself.'" Moreover, in *Gilbert*, the majority concluded that a participant in an illegal lineup was also barred from giving testimony identifying the defendant at trial, with Justice Brennan insisting that "only a per se exclusionary rule as to such testimony can be an effective sanction to assure that law enforcement authorities will respect the accused's constitutional right to the presence of his counsel at the critical lineup."[9] Noting that in *Escobedo v. Illinois* the Court had held that the Sixth Amendment right to counsel attached at the time a suspect was detained, the defendant in *Kirby* contended that the case was indistinguishable from *Wade* and *Gilbert*.[10]

Kirby was initially argued before a seven-member Court on November 11, 1971. At the conference that followed the argument, Chief Justice Warren Burger broached the possibility of explicitly overruling *Wade* and *Gilbert*. However, notwithstanding the fact that they had dissented in 1967, neither Justice Stewart nor Justice White was willing to consider this course of action in *Kirby*. Against this background, White took the view that *Kirby* was indistinguishable from the earlier decisions and joined Justices Douglas, Brennan, and Marshall in voting to reverse the conviction in *Kirby*. By contrast, Justices Stewart and Blackmun joined Burger in voting to affirm the judgment of the lower court.[11]

Justice Brennan, who was assigned the task of writing the majority opinion, realized that time was of the essence. With Powell and Rehnquist already having been nominated to replace John Marshall Harlan and Hugo Black, Brennan knew that if the decision in *Kirby* was not handed down prior to the confirmation of the two new justices, then Burger would move to have the case reargued before a full nine-member Court. Thus, only four days after the conference and five days after the case was argued, Brennan distributed the draft of his majority opinion on November 16, 1971. One week later, Stewart circulated a draft dissent, and White followed suit with a brief statement concurring in the result.[12]

However, after first indicating on November 16 that he was contemplating writing a separate dissent, Burger remained silent until January 17—ten days after Rehnquist and Powell were sworn in—thus preventing the announcement of the Court's judgment in *Kirby*. Although observing that he agreed with much of what Stewart had written, Burger also claimed that the reason he had not formally joined Stewart was that he "had been working on a [separate] dissent." Burger then moved to have *Kirby* reargued before the full Court, and this motion carried over the objections of Justices Douglas, Brennan, and Marshall.[13]

The reargument took place on March 20 and 21. At the conference that followed Justices Powell and Rehnquist joined the former dissenters in voting to affirm the judgment of conviction. Potter Stewart was then assigned the task of preparing the opinion for the Court, and on May 2, Stewart circulated a draft that, with only a few minor stylistic changes, would eventually become the plurality opinion in *Kirby*.[14]

Stewart observed that the Sixth Amendment by its terms provided that a right to counsel was triggered only by "criminal prosecutions" and that *Kirby* itself involved an "identification that took place long before the commencement of any prosecution whatever." Stewart also asserted that, with the exception of *Escebedo*, the case law had consistently taken the view that the right to counsel attached only at the time judicial proceedings had been initiated against the accused. Stewart also argued that subsequent decisions had limited *Escebedo* to its facts and that those facts "are not remotely akin to the facts of [*Kirby*]." Finally, Stewart emphasized that *Kirby* involved only the claim that the identification was subject to a per se exclusionary rule and that the defendant remained free to argue that the identification had taken place under the general due process principles established in cases such as *Stovall v. Denno*.[15] Four days later, Brennan circulated the draft of a dissent that argued that the same practical considerations the Court had cited in establishing the per se exclusionary rule in *Gilbert* applied equally to identifications made before formal arraignments.[16]

By May 10, Chief Justice Burger and Justices Blackmun and Rehnquist had signed on to Stewart's opinion, with Burger also adding a short concurring statement. Conversely, Justices Douglas and Marshall had joined in Brennan's dissent, and Justice White had submitted a terse dissenting statement observing simply that, in his view, *Kirby* was controlled by *Gilbert* and *Wade*.[17] Against this background, Lewis Powell provided the fifth vote to affirm the judgment of the state court.

Powell had a strong distaste for per se exclusionary rules generally and wrote privately that he would have joined the dissenters in *Wade* and *Gilbert*. But at the same time, Powell found Stewart's effort to distinguish those cases in *Kirby* unconvincing. Moreover, Powell also believed the identification process employed by the police in *Kirby* might well be characterized as inherently unfair under the principles articulated in *Stovall v. Denno*.[18]

However, with the 1971 term rapidly coming to a close, Powell decided he would not use *Kirby* as the vehicle for a wide-ranging discussion of his views on the use of exclusionary rules generally. Instead, his primary goal was "keeping [his] options open for the future." Thus, after circulating a memorandum on May 8 indicating that he agreed the conviction should not be overturned, Powell concurred only in the result and filed a brief statement averring simply that he would not extend the *Wade/Gilbert* per se exclusionary rule.[19]

The same forces that generated the result in *Kirby* would determine the outcome of a wide variety of constitutional disputes during the early Burger era.[20] First, and most obviously, *Kirby* reflected the significance of the appointments of Powell and Rehnquist in shifting the ideological center of gravity of the Court. If Hugo Black had survived and not been replaced by Powell, Black would almost certainly have voted to overturn the judgment of the lower court and thereby created a majority in favor of extending the *Wade/Gilbert* exclusionary rule to preindictment identifications. Indeed, even after Black's departure from the Court, the progressives would have prevailed if *Kirby* had been decided prior to the confirmation of Powell and Rehnquist.

However, in some respects, the dynamics that produced the conservative victory in *Kirby* also suggested the limits of this ideological reorientation. The addition of Powell and Rehnquist did not by any means create an institution that was the conservative mirror image of the progressive-dominated Court of the late Warren era. Three committed progressives remained on the Court. Thus, even in cases in which the Nixon justices were united in advocating a more conservative position, that position could only prevail if it also attracted the support of either Potter Stewart or Byron White. Admittedly, that support was forthcoming in the majority of the criminal procedure cases that came before the Court during the early Burger era. Nonetheless, in what was perhaps the most widely publicized case of the 1971 term, the Nixon appointees suffered a spectacular defeat in *Furman v. Georgia*.[21]

In *Furman*, the justices were faced with the claim that the imposition of the death penalty ran afoul of the Eighth Amendment prohibition on cruel and unusual punishment.[22] Those who opposed the use of the death penalty hoped that a favorable ruling in *Furman* would be the culmination of a long campaign against capital punishment that was being conducted on a number of different fronts. By the late 1960s, there were clear indications that this campaign was making considerable progress in the court of public opinion. The number of executions conducted annually in the United States was dropping dramatically, and a 1966 Gallup poll found that, for the first time, a majority of Americans were opposed to the use of the death penalty. Although public support for capital punishment increased slightly in the wake of the widespread social unrest of 1967 and 1968, death penalty opponents still had good reason to believe they could continue to make headway through the political process in their efforts to have capital punishment abolished.[23]

However, in making their constitutional arguments, the opponents of capital punishment faced difficulties that were of less significance in ordinary political discourse. They were forced to confront the reality that use of the death penalty not only had a long historical pedigree but also was explicitly recognized in the text of the Constitution itself. Moreover, a number of the Court's own decisions seemed to assume the Constitution did not prohibit either the federal government or the states from imposing the death penalty. Thus, for example, in the 1958 decision in *Trop v. Dulles*, although concluding that the deprivation of citizenship did in fact violate the Eighth Amendment, Earl Warren took pains to distinguish that penalty from capital punishment, declaring:

> [We must] put to one side the death penalty as an index of the constitutional limit on punishment. Whatever the arguments may be against capital punishment, both on moral grounds and in terms of accomplishing the purposes of punishment—and they are forceful—the death penalty has been employed throughout our history, and, in a day when it is still widely accepted, it cannot be said to violate the constitutional concept of cruelty.[24]

Death penalty opponents sought to downplay the significance of this historical record by emphasizing the fact that the Court's Eighth Amendment decisions had consistently maintained that the scope of the cruel and unusual punishment clause was not to be viewed in static terms. Instead, the justices had maintained that the constitutionality of any particular punishment could only be determined by reference to "evolving standards of decency."[25] The constitutional assault on capital punishment was based on the theory that declining public support for capital punishment and the fact that the death penalty was only infrequently carried out indicated that its use was inconsistent with contemporary standards of morality.

As early as 1963, there were signs this argument was gaining some traction with at least some of the justices, as Justices Douglas and Brennan joined Arthur Goldberg in arguing that the Court should give plenary consideration to the claim that the imposition of the death penalty for rape constituted cruel and unusual punishment.[26] Five years later, the anti-capital-punishment forces won a significant victory in *Witherspoon v. Illinois*, in which the Court struck down an Illinois statute that provided that potential jurors who exhibited "conscientious scruples against capital punishment" could be dismissed for cause in cases in which the prosecution sought to have the death penalty imposed by the jury.[27] Speaking for a six-justice majority, Potter Stewart concluded that the statute violated the due process clause. In his opinion, Stewart declared, "in a nation less than half of whose people believe in the death penalty, a jury composed exclusively of such people cannot speak for the community. Culled of all who harbor doubts about the wisdom of capital punishment—of all who would be reluctant to pronounce the extreme penalty—such a jury can speak only for a distinct and dwindling minority."[28]

However, less than three years later, Stewart joined the three *Witherspoon* dissenters and the newly appointed Chief Justice Burger and Justice Blackmun to deal a major blow to the opponents of capital punishment in *McGautha v. California*.[29] *McGautha* was a due process challenge to the sentencing regime established by the state of California, which, like Illinois, vested the jury with the authority to decide whether the death penalty should be imposed on one found guilty of a capital crime without providing any standards to guide the exercise of the jury's discretion. The defendants argued that "to leave the jury completely at large to impose or withhold the death penalty as it sees fit is fundamentally lawless and therefore violates the basic command of the Fourteenth Amendment" and that vesting uncontrolled sentencing discretion in the jury was particularly offensive in an era in which the death penalty was in fact imposed only in "extraordinary" cases. Speaking for the three dissenters, Justice Brennan endorsed this view in the strongest terms, asserting that "the rule of law . . . is fundamentally inconsistent with capital sentencing procedures that are purposely constructed to allow the maximum possible variation from one case to the next, and provide no mechanism to prevent that consciously maximized variation from reflecting merely random or arbitrary choice." However, Justice Harlan's majority opinion rejected these arguments, declaring, "In light of history, experience, and the present limitations of human knowledge, we find it quite impossible to say that committing to the untrammeled discretion of the jury the power to pronounce life or death in capital cases is offensive to anything in the Constitution."[30]

After *McGautha* was handed down, the justices turned to the problem of disposing of the death penalty cases that had been held pending that decision. Justice Brennan believed capital punishment constituted cruel and unusual punishment and thus violated the Eighth Amendment. Nonetheless, fearing that if squarely faced with the issue a majority of the justices would conclude that the use of the death penalty was not inconsistent with constitutional norms, he argued that certiorari should be denied in all of the cases that had been held for *McGautha*. However, Harry Blackmun argued that the Court should definitively resolve the basic constitutional issue, and his views prevailed at the conference that considered the matter in June 1971. Thus, Justices Brennan and Stewart were given the task of choosing two rape cases and two murder cases to serve as the vehicles for the Court's consideration of the constitutionality of capital punishment, and *Furman* and its companion cases were argued in January 1972.[31]

At the conference that followed the oral arguments on January 21, it became clear Brennan had underestimated the strength of the sentiment against the death penalty on the Court. With Justice Blackmun initially declining to vote, only Chief Justice Burger and Justices Powell and Rehnquist stated that they were firmly committed to rejecting the constitutional challenges. By contrast, Justices Douglas, Brennan, Stewart, White, and Marshall all indicated that they were at least tentatively inclined to strike down the use of capital punishment as it was then being applied.[32] Although Blackmun would resolve his doubts in favor of voting to reject the constitutional challenges, after some anxious moments all of the remaining justices adhered to the positions they had taken in conference, thus creating a five-justice majority that essentially invalidated all existing death penalty statutes in the United States.

Each of the nine justices eventually wrote a separate opinion in *Furman*. Each member of the majority spoke only for himself, and the five opinions relied on a wide variety of different arguments in concluding that existing capital punishment schemes were unconstitutional. Whereas Justices Brennan and Marshall argued that the imposition of the death penalty would invariably constitute cruel and unusual punishment, the opinions of Justices Douglas, Stewart, and White took more equivocal positions on the constitutionality of capital punishment generally.[33]

After reviewing the relevant precedents, Brennan asserted, "The test [is whether] it is a denial of human dignity for the State arbitrarily to subject a person to an unusually severe punishment that society has indicated it does not regard as acceptable, and that cannot be shown to serve any penal purpose more effectively than a significantly less drastic punishment." Against this background, Brennan contended that the "deliberate extinguishment of human life by the State is uniquely degrading to human dignity." He also emphasized the rarity of executions in the United States at the time *Furman* was decided, declaring, "When a country of over 200 million people inflicts an unusually severe punishment no more than 50 times a year, the inference is strong that the punishment is not being regularly and fairly applied." In addition, Brennan asserted that the "objective indicator of society's view of an unusually severe punishment is what society does with it, and today society will inflict death upon only a small sample of the eligible criminals. Rejection could hardly be more complete without becoming absolute."[34]

The infrequency with which the death penalty was administered also figured prominently in Brennan's rejection of the claim that the existence of capital punishment served a valuable function by deterring crimes such as murder and expressing the moral outrage of the community at the commission of those crimes. He argued that the "risk of death is remote and improbable; in contrast, the risk of long-term imprisonment is near and great. In short, whatever the speculative validity of the assumption that the threat of death is a superior deterrent, there is no reason to believe that, as currently administered, the punishment of death is necessary to deter the commission of capital crimes." In addition, Brennan insisted that "if capital crimes require the punishment of death in order to provide moral reinforcement for the basic values of the community, those values can only be undermined when death is so rarely inflicted upon the criminals who commit the crimes."[35]

Marshall's formulation of the appropriate test to be applied in Eighth Amendment cases was similar to that elaborated by Brennan. Marshall declared that a "penalty may be cruel and unusual because it is excessive and serves no valid legislative purpose" and that "where a punishment is not excessive and serves a valid legislative purpose, it still may be invalid if popular sentiment abhors it." After an extensive discussion of the statistical evidence, Marshall concluded that those who opposed the death penalty had demonstrated by "clear and convincing evidence" that the prospect of capital punishment deterred crime no better than the imposition of lengthy prison sentences. However, perhaps the most striking feature of Marshall's opinion was his defense of the claim that the use of the death penalty would in any event be unconstitutional because it "is morally unacceptable to the people of the United States at this time in their history."[36]

In making this claim, Marshall seemed to implicitly concede that, if asked, a majority of the public at large would have expressed support for the use of the death penalty in at least some circumstances. However, he rejected the argument that majority support per se was sufficient to refute the assertion that capital punishment was "morally unacceptable to the people." Instead, he argued that "whether or not a punishment is cruel and unusual depends not on whether its mere mention 'shocks the conscience and sense of justice of the people,' but on whether *people who are fully informed as to the purposes of the penalties* [*sic*] *and its liabilities* would find the penalty shocking, unjust, and unacceptable." Observing that "it has often been noted that American citizens know almost nothing about capital punishment," Marshall asserted that, if widely disseminated and understood, the information available on the efficacy of capital punishment as a deterrent "would almost surely convince the average citizen that the death penalty was unwise."[37]

Marshall conceded that, in theory, even well-informed people might find the use of the death penalty morally unobjectionable simply as retribution for particularly heinous crimes. Nonetheless, he declared that "I cannot believe that at this stage in our history, the American people would ever knowingly support purposeless vengeance," particularly if they were aware that "it is usually the poor, the illiterate, the underprivileged, the member of the minority group—the man who, because he is without means, and is defended by a court-appointed attorney—who becomes society's sacrificial lamb" and that innocent people were at times sentenced to death. Thus, Marshall concluded by asserting confidently that "assuming knowledge of all the facts presently available regarding capital punishment, the average citizen would . . . find it shocking to his conscience and sense of justice" and that this fact alone was sufficient to condemn the death penalty under the Eighth Amendment.[38]

Douglas, Stewart, and White joined Brennan and Marshall in concluding that the imposition of the death penalty under then-existing statutes was unconstitutional. However, each of their separate opinions left open at least the possibility that they might find capital punishment constitutionally unobjectionable under other circumstances. Douglas in particular had dramatically changed his position since the previous term when the Court had considered the question of how to proceed in the wake of the decision in *McGautha.* After the justices had decided to grant the petitions for certiorari in *Furman* and its companion cases, Douglas had circulated a draft dissent in which he asserted that none of the cases presented a substantial federal question. Although the opinion explicitly stated, "I personally think it is monstrous for society to take [a] life because the defendant took one," Douglas also made an uncharacteristic appeal to the concept of judicial restraint, declaring, "I do not see any mandate under the Constitution for judges to be the arbiters of the wisdom or folly, the ethics or barbarity of capital punishment. These are issues with which the people must wrestle. . . . Indeed, I can think of no class less qualified than judges to bring light to these problems."[39] Despite the fact that this opinion was never actually filed, its import for constitutional challenges to the death penalty could hardly have been clearer. Nonetheless, at the conference in January 1972 Douglas voted to hold that the imposition of the death penalty in the cases before the Court violated the Eighth Amendment.

Douglas's change of heart was apparently a by-product of his continuing frustration with the decision in *McGautha.* At the conference on *Furman,* Douglas asserted that because of *McGautha,* the Court was "locked into a position where [the conclusion that the imposition of the death penalty under existing conditions was unconstitutional] was almost compelled," and in his opinion in *Furman* he declared that the Court was "imprisoned" in the *McGautha* holding. Like Marshall, Douglas emphasized the disparities in the use of capital punishment, averring that "in a Nation committed to equal protection of the laws there is no permissible 'caste' aspect of law enforcement" and observing that "we know that the discretion of judges and juries in imposing the death penalty enables the penalty to be selectively applied, feeding prejudices against the accused if he is poor and despised, and lacking political clout, or if he is a member of a suspect or unpopular minority, and saving those who by social position may be in a more protected position."[40] Thus, although explicitly reserving judgment on the constitutional issues that might be raised by statutes that made the imposition of the death penalty for specified crimes mandatory, Douglas concluded that the existing system violated strictures of the Eighth Amendment.

The opinions of Justices Stewart and White were by-products of a more complicated dynamic. Stewart had not been in favor of granting the petitions for certiorari and initially did not believe that the imposition of capital punishment was unconstitutional—a view seemingly foreshadowed by his decision to join the majority opinion in *McGautha* less than a year before *Furman* was argued. However, by the time that *Furman* was argued, Stewart had come to the conclusion that he could not in good conscience vote to uphold the death penalty. Thus, at the January 21 conference, emphasizing the infrequency with which the death penalty was actually imposed, Stewart cast his lot with Douglas, Brennan, and Marshall. Moreover, after Brennan provided him the first draft of his opinion in March, Stewart indicated that he was willing to join in a broader critique of the constitutionality of the death penalty, observing that "it was enough for him that the death penalty treated people as things."[41]

However, at this point Stewart's approach became entangled with that of Byron White. Once Harry Blackmun committed himself to vote to reject the constitutional challenge to the death penalty, it became clear that White would be the swing vote in *Furman*. At the initial conference on *Furman*, White had tentatively voted to hold that the imposition of the death penalty under existing statutes was unconstitutional, at the same time making it clear that he was uncertain about the appropriate course of action. The following week, he had withdrawn his vote, initially giving no indication about which way he was leaning. However, after Justices Douglas, Brennan, Marshall, and Powell had circulated drafts of their opinions, White told Stewart that unless some narrower ground for invalidating the existing statutes was articulated, White would join Powell's opinion and create a majority in favor of rejecting the constitutional challenges.[42]

Faced with this prospect, after lengthy discussions Stewart was able to persuade White to accept a different solution. On June 9, Stewart and White agreed that each would publish a separate opinion that concluded that capital punishment was unconstitutional when imposed under the existing legal regime but also clearly recognized the possibility that the death penalty might constitutionally be imposed if the structure of the sentencing process was changed. Thus, although characterizing the case for holding that the imposition of capital punishment invariably constituted cruel and unusual punishment as a "strong one," Stewart's opinion also argued that the Court should not reach that issue in *Furman* and its companion cases and should instead dispose of those cases on the narrower ground that, as administered immediately prior to 1972, the death penalty was not only rare but also "so wantonly and so freakishly imposed" as to be "cruel and unusual in the same way that being struck by lightning is cruel and unusual." Similarly, despite conceding that under some circumstances the existence of the death penalty might deter crime or serve a retributive function, White observed that the "death penalty is exacted with great infrequency even for the most atrocious crimes, and that there is no meaningful basis for distinguishing the few cases in which it is imposed from the many cases in which it is not." He concluded that, under these circumstances, the imposition of capital punishment constituted the "pointless and needless extinction of life with only marginal contributions to any discernible social or public purposes" and thus violated the Eighth Amendment.[43]

In sharp contrast to the deeply divided majority, the dissenters were far more united in their views. Although because of the very personal nature of his opinion Justice Blackmun spoke only for himself, all of the dissenters joined each of the other dissenting opinions written by their colleagues. Not surprisingly, a number of common threads ran through the dissents. In part, the dissenters focused on what they saw as evidence that refuted the claim that the imposition of the death penalty was inconsistent with "evolving standards of decency." Thus, Burger and Powell in particular detailed the long historical pedigree of capital punishment, the language in the Constitution that appeared to implicitly vindicate the use of the death penalty, and the fact that the efforts to abolish the death penalty by statute at both the state and federal levels had been largely unavailing.[44]

In addition, the dissenters contended that institutional considerations mitigated strongly against the majority's decision to enter the debate over capital punishment. Declaring that *Furman* "necessarily brings into sharp relief the fundamental question of the role of judicial review in a democratic society," Justice Rehnquist asserted that the "very nature of judicial review . . . makes the courts the least subject to Madisonian check in the event that they shall, for the best of motives, expand judicial authority beyond the limits contemplated by the Framers. It is for this reason that judicial self-restraint is surely an implied, if not an expressed, condition of the grant of authority of judicial review." Thus, Rehnquist averred that the "task of judging constitutional cases imposed by Art. III cannot . . . be avoided, but it must surely be approached with the deepest humility and genuine deference to legislative judgment" and asserted that "today's decision to invalidate capital punishment is . . . significantly lacking in those attributes." Similarly, Chief Justice Burger noted that even those challenging the death penalty had conceded that "'both in constitutional contemplation and in fact, it is the legislature, not the Court, which responds to public opinion and immediately reflects the society's standards of decency.'" In addition, responding specifically to the opinions of Justices Stewart and White, Burger declared that "it seems remarkable to me that with our basic trust in lay jurors as the keystone in our system of criminal justice, it should now be suggested that we take the most sensitive and important of all decisions away from them."[45]

Justices Blackmun and Powell were, if anything, even more emphatic in emphasizing the importance of recognizing the institutional competence of other branches of government. Blackmun minced no words in expressing his personal opposition to capital punishment, asserting, "I yield to no one in the depth of my distaste, antipathy, and, indeed, abhorrence, for the death penalty" and declaring that "were I a legislator, I would vote against the death penalty for the policy reasons argued by counsel for the respective petitioners and expressed and adopted in the several opinions filed by the Justices [in the majority]." He also observed that "it [would be] comforting to relax in the thoughts—perhaps the rationalizations—that this is the compassionate decision for a maturing society; that this is the moral and the 'right' thing to do; that thereby we convince ourselves that we are moving down the road toward human decency; that we value life even though that life has taken another or others or has grievously scarred another or others and their families; and that we are less barbaric than we were [when *McGautha* and other cases were decided]." But at the same time, Blackmun contended that the arguments against the death penalty made sense "only in a legislative and executive way, and not as a judicial expedient" and that "on the Legislative Branch of the State or Federal Government, and secondarily, on the Executive Branch—is where the authority and responsibility for this kind of action lies. The authority should not be taken over by the judiciary in the modern guise of an Eighth Amendment issue."[46]

Although Justice Powell's opinion was less overtly personal, he was no less passionate than Blackmun was in his appeal to the principles of separation of powers. Powell proclaimed that *Furman* "encroaches upon an area squarely within the historic prerogative of the legislative branch—both state and federal—to protect the citizenry through the designation of penalties for prohibitable conduct" and decried what he characterized as the "shattering effect [the judgment of the majority] has on the root principles of stare decisis, federalism, judicial restraint, and—most importantly—separation of powers." Declaring that "I can recall no case in which, in the name of deciding constitutional questions, this Court has subordinated national and local democratic processes to such an extent," Powell also emphasized what he viewed as the practical downside of constitutionalizing the law of capital punishment, observing that the "sobering disadvantage of constitutional adjudication of this magnitude is the universality and permanence of the judgment," whereas the "enduring merit of legislative action is its responsiveness to the democratic process, and to revision and change: mistaken judgments may be corrected and refinements perfected."[47]

The reaction of the nation as a whole to *Furman* was as divided as the Court itself. Progressives were exultant. For example, describing the decision as "one of the great judicial milestones in American history," Senator Edward M. Kennedy of Massachusetts asserted that the *Furman* Court "has ruled for life, and it has thereby given new life to our democracy and to the quality of American justice." Similarly, the director of the NAACP LDF declared that *Furman* was "comparable in importance only to the victory we won in [*Brown v. Board of Education*]." By contrast, Lieutenant Governor Lester Maddox of Georgia characterized the decision as a "license for rape, anarchy, and murder," and the state attorney general of Nevada denounced *Furman* as an "insult to Nevada, to its laws, and to its people."[48]

Reactions such as these presaged a dramatic change in the dynamic of the political struggle over the future of the death penalty in the United States. By striking down all existing capital punishment statutes while at the same time leaving the door open for reinstatement of the death penalty under differently constructed statutes, the *Furman* Court virtually guaranteed an intense, protracted political battle between those who wished to have the death penalty reinstated for some combination of practical and symbolic reasons and those who strongly opposed capital punishment on principle. This battle largely displaced the dispute over the Warren Court's procedural rulings as the centerpiece of the constitutional and political conflict between those who saw themselves as champions of law and order and those who were strongly committed to protecting the interests of criminal defendants.

In any event, *Furman* was not the only progressive victory of the 1971 term. Although much less widely discussed in the media than *Furman*, *Weber v. Aetna Casualty and Surety Co.* was in many respects far more significant in doctrinal terms.[49] *Weber* was a challenge to a Louisiana statute that distinguished sharply between legitimate children and unacknowledged illegitimate children in determining eligibility for workmen's compensation benefits for the death of their biological father. Under the statute, legitimate and acknowledged illegitimate children were treated equally for purposes of determining their rights to recover benefits. By contrast, unacknowledged children born out of wedlock were relegated to the status of "other dependents" and thus could recover only if the claims of their legitimate and acknowledged counterparts had not exhausted the maximum amount of benefits provided by law. In *Weber* itself, the situation was further complicated by the fact that the father had been prohibited by law from legitimating the children borne out of wedlock because at the time of his death he had still been married to the mother of his legitimate children. The illegitimate children argued that, in these circumstances, treating them less favorably than the legitimate offspring of the deceased violated the equal protection clause.

The justices were called upon to evaluate this claim against the background of two other recent decisions in which illegitimate children had mounted equal protection challenges. In 1968, over the objections of Justices Harlan, Black, and Stewart, in *Levy v. Louisiana* the Court had invalidated a state statute that denied children born out of wedlock the right to recover damages for the wrongful death of their mother. Speaking for the majority, Justice Douglas observed that "these children, though illegitimate, were dependent on [the mother]; she cared for them and nurtured them; they were indeed hers in the biological and in the spiritual sense; in her death they suffered wrong in the sense that any dependent would" and concluded that "it is invidious to discriminate against them when no action, conduct, or demeanor of theirs is possibly relevant to the harm that was done the mother."[50] By contrast, three years later, in *Labine v. Vincent*, the newly appointed Warren Burger and Harry Blackmun joined the *Levy* dissenters in rejecting a constitutional challenge to a statute that did not allow illegitimate children to inherit intestate from their biological father. Hugo Black's majority opinion in *Labine* asserted that the "State does not need biological or social reasons for distinguishing between ascendants and descendants" and concluded that "in the circumstances presented in this case, there is nothing in the vague generalities of the Equal Protection and Due Process Clauses Page which empowers this Court to nullify the deliberate choices of the elected representatives of the people of Louisiana."[51]

In *Weber* itself, William Rehnquist took the opportunity to articulate the approach to equal protection analysis that would characterize his entire tenure on the Court. He asserted that, except in cases involving racial discrimination, the Court should reject equal protection challenges unless the challenger demonstrated that the classification at issue lacked a rational basis. Arguing that the policy judgments reflected in the Louisiana statute could plausibly be viewed as embodying reasonable presumptions about the intentions of the deceased and also be defended as efforts to avoid difficult problems of proof, Rehnquist had no difficulty in concluding that the treatment of unacknowledged illegitimate children passed constitutional muster.[52]

However, Rehnquist stood alone in voting to reject the constitutional challenge in *Weber*. The three remaining Nixon appointees joined the five holdovers from the Warren Court in concluding that the Louisiana statute ran afoul of the equal protection clause. Whereas Harry Blackmun would have focused only on the fact that the biological father was powerless to remove the disability under which his illegitimate children suffered, Lewis Powell spoke for seven justices in a majority opinion that swept more broadly. Noting that the "status of illegitimacy has expressed through the ages society's condemnation of irresponsible liaisons beyond the bonds of marriage," Powell declared that "visiting this condemnation on the head of an infant is illogical and unjust" and also averred that "imposing disabilities on the illegitimate child is contrary to the basic concept of our system that legal burdens should bear some relationship to individual responsibility or wrongdoing. Obviously, no child is responsible for his birth, and penalizing the illegitimate child is an ineffectual—as well as an unjust—way of deterring the parent."[53]

The significance of the decision in *Weber* might be evaluated from a variety of different perspectives. Considered in isolation, the impact of the case was quite limited, affecting the rights of a relatively small number of children under an idiosyncratic state statutory scheme. Nonetheless, in doctrinal terms, *Weber* proved to be an important harbinger of things to come. The case demonstrated that with the exception of Justice Rehnquist, none of the Nixon appointees were strongly committed to a formal or quasiformal approach to constitutional adjudication. Instead, despite their innate conservative instincts, all of the other Nixon justices were at times willing to embrace a relatively expansive view of constitutional protections in order to redress what they saw as grave injustices.

The decisions of the following term showed much the same pattern. On one hand, the Nixon justices were in many cases united in opposition to progressive initiatives and in those cases were often successful in attracting support from Justice Stewart, Justice White, or both. However, in other cases, Justice Rehnquist was abandoned by one or more of the other recent appointees, who thereby often provided crucial support for majority opinions that embraced the precepts of progressive constitutionalism.

Chapter Three

Reapportionment and Voting Rights

Of all the many doctrinal innovations of the Warren Court, none was more revolutionary or had a greater lasting impact on the nation than the change in the Court's approach to the constitutional analysis of legislative apportionment and voting rights generally.[1] Prior to the mid-1960s, with the sole exception of laws that discriminated on the basis of race or sex, the states had been viewed as having almost unlimited leeway in determining the structure of their respective state legislatures, the shape of the districts from which their members of the US House of Representatives were chosen, and the qualifications required of voters in state and federal elections. However, in a series of late Warren Court decisions, a majority of the justices concluded that the Fourteenth Amendment imposed stringent constraints on state authority to regulate the process of electing public officials. During the 1972 term, the Court was called upon to decide a number of important cases that tested the limits of these constraints.

In the pre-Warren era, constitutional challenges to legislative apportionment decisions rarely even came to the Court. To be sure, the justices were at times actively involved in interpreting the import of federal statutes that established the procedures for selecting senators or members of the House of Representatives.[2] However, in the 1946 decision in *Colegrove v. Green*, over the objections of Justices Hugo Black, William O. Douglas, and W. Frank Murphy, a majority of the justices concluded that the Court should not even consider the merits of constitutional challenges to the manner by which members of Congress were chosen under Illinois law.[3]

By contrast, even before the Warren Court entered the fray, the Court had regularly considered and rejected a variety of Fourteenth Amendment challenges to state rules that limited access to the right to vote. Unless race was involved, the justices had uniformly rejected these challenges. Justice

Rufus Peckham's 1911 opinion in *Pope v. Williams* aptly summarized the Court's attitude toward these cases.[4] Speaking for a unanimous Court in rejecting a challenge to a Maryland law that required a person coming into the state to have declared his intention to become a Maryland citizen one year before registering to vote, Peckham asserted:

> The privilege to vote in any state is not given by the federal Constitution, or by any of its amendments. It is not a privilege springing from citizenship of the United States. It may not be refused on account of race, color, or previous condition of servitude, but it does not follow from mere citizenship of the United States. In other words, the privilege to vote in a state is within the jurisdiction of the state itself, to be exercised as the state may direct, and [generally] upon such terms as to it may seem proper.[5]

Indeed, as late as 1959, the Warren Court itself expressed similar sentiments in *Lassiter v. Northampton County Board of Elections,* in which it concluded without dissent that the state of North Carolina could constitutionally limit the right to vote to those adults who could pass a literacy test.[6] Although declining to hold unequivocally that *no* restriction on the right to vote would ever be held to violate the Constitution, Justice Douglas cited *Pope* for the proposition that the "States have long been held to have broad powers to determine the conditions under which the right of suffrage may be exercised" and explicitly reaffirmed the principle that "there is wide scope for exercise of [the state's] jurisdiction" to establish its qualifications for voters.[7]

Three years later, however, the decision in *Baker v. Carr* signaled the beginning of a dramatic change in course.[8] *Baker* was a constitutional challenge to the apportionment of the legislature of the state of Tennessee. The Tennessee constitution required seats in the legislature to be allocated according to population. Nonetheless, despite major changes in the distribution of the state's population, the apportionments of seats had not been altered since 1901. Over the vigorous dissents of Justices Felix Frankfurter and John Marshall Harlan, Justice William J. Brennan, Jr.'s opinion for the majority concluded that, notwithstanding the disposition of *Colegrove v. Green,* the federal courts did in fact have authority to reach the merits of a claim that the Tennessee scheme violated the equal protection clause.

Baker did not by its terms establish any standard for determining the constitutionality of the apportionment of state legislatures or the distribution of the members of the House of Representatives allocated to each state. However, it soon became clear that a majority of the justices had a very specific conception of the types of apportionment that should be deemed constitutionally permissible. In its 1964 decision in *Wesberry v. Sanders,* over the dissents of Justices Harlan, Tom Clark, and Potter Stewart, the Court relied on the Article I requirement that members of the House of Representatives be chosen by "the People of the several States" to hold that the members of the House must be chosen from districts of equal population.[9] The following year, in *Reynolds v. Sims,* a majority of the justices concluded that the equal protection clause imposed the same basic requirement on state legislatures.[10] Chief Justice Earl Warren declared that "legislators represent people, not trees or acres. Legislators are elected by voters, not farms or cities or economic interests. As long as ours is a representative form of government, and our legislatures are those instruments of government elected directly by and directly representative of the people, the right to elect legislators in a free and unimpaired fashion is a bedrock of our political system" and that "full and effective participation by all citizens in state government requires, therefore, that each citizen have an equally effective voice in the election of members of his state legislature. Modern and viable state government needs, and the Constitution demands, no less."[11] The majority opinion also emphasized that the apportionment of both houses of the state legislature was subject to the same constitutional constraints.

Four years later, the decision in *Kirkpatrick v. Preisler* illustrated the extent of the Warren Court's commitment to the principle of mathematical equality in apportionment decisions.[12] *Kirkpatrick* was a challenge to the reapportionment scheme the Missouri state legislature had adopted in 1967 in response to lawsuits that had been filed in an effort to force the state to comply with the principles established in *Wesberry v. Sanders.* Based on the figures from the 1960 census—the most recent authoritative numbers available in 1967—if the state's ten-member congressional district had been divided among districts of precisely equal population, each such district would have had a population of 431,981 persons. None of the districts established by the state legislature would have deviated from this population by more than 3.13 percent.

As a number of the justices pointed out in *Preisler,* even if the districts had been of precisely equal population according to the 1960 figures, by 1967 the actual populations of some might easily have varied from mathematical equality by well more than 3.13 percent. Nonetheless, the Court concluded that the Missouri plan did not pass constitutional muster. Speaking for five justices, Justice Brennan rejected the claim that the deviation from population equality should have been found unobjectionable because it was de minimis, declaring instead that the Constitution "requires that the State make a good faith effort to achieve precise mathematical equality. Unless population variances among congressional districts are shown to have resulted despite such effort, the State must justify each variance, no matter how small."[13] Because alternative plans would have divided the state into districts that had an even smaller variation in population according to the 1960 figures, the majority concluded that the plan adopted by the Missouri state legislature violated the strictures of the equal protection clause.

The same basic political theory that underlay the reapportionment decisions also impelled a majority of the Warren-era justices to abandon the approach of *Lassiter* in favor of close scrutiny of state laws that limited access to the right to vote. The trend began in 1966 with *Harper v. Virginia State Board of Elections*, in which a majority of the justices voted to overrule *Breedlove v. Suttles* and strike down a Virginia statute that required otherwise qualified citizens to pay a small tax in order to be allowed to vote.[14] In concluding that the imposition of the poll tax was unconstitutional, Justice Douglas emphasized the fact that the statute discriminated against the poor as well as presenting a barrier to the exercise of voting rights. However, three years later, the decision in *Kramer v. Union Free School District* focused exclusively on suffrage.[15]

Kramer was a challenge to a New York statute that limited the right to vote in elections for local school boards to those who either had children in the public schools or possessed real property within the relevant school district. Noting that the school board could levy taxes only on real property, the state argued that the requirements did nothing more than ensure that the right to vote for school board members was limited to those who were "substantially interested in and affected by" the decisions of the school board. However, the Court found this justification insufficient and concluded that the limitation was unconstitutional.

Speaking for the six-member majority, Chief Justice Warren gave short shrift to the state's argument. Declaring that because the "right to exercise the franchise in a free and unimpaired manner is preservative of other basic civil and political rights, any alleged infringement of the right of citizens to vote must be carefully and meticulously scrutinized." Warren apparently accepted the contention that "all members of the community have an interest in the quality and structure of public education." Asserting that there was no compelling state interest for denying childless, propertyless adults the right to vote in school board elections, he concluded that the New York statute denied equal protection of the laws to that group.[16]

The departure of Warren at first had little effect on the Court's approach to reapportionment and voting rights cases. In the interim between the resignation of Abe Fortas and the seating of Harry Blackmun, the Court reemphasized the broad scope of the principles initially enunciated in *Reynolds v. Sims* in *Hadley v. Junior College School District*.[17] *Hadley* focused on a Missouri statute that defined the mechanism by which separate school districts could vote by referendum to establish a consolidated junior college district and elect six trustees to conduct and manage the necessary affairs of that district. Following the procedures established by the statute, the Kansas City School District had joined with seven other school districts to form such a junior college district. Under the terms of the statute, if one of the separate school districts contained between 50 percent and 66.66 percent of the "enumerated school population" of the consolidated junior college district, three of the trustees were to be elected from that separate district, whereas the remaining three trustees were to be elected at large from the other constituent school districts. Because the Kansas City district contained 60 percent of the enumerated population of the consolidated district, voters in Kansas City were allowed to vote for three of the six trustees. A group of Kansas City voters argued that this arrangement violated the equal protection clause because it left 60 percent of the population of the junior college district with the ability to choose only 50 percent of the members of the board of trustees of the district.

Over the objections of Chief Justice Warren Burger and Justices Stewart and Harlan, five justices concluded that the apportionment of the trustees violated the equal protection clause. Observing that the trustees of the junior college district had the power to levy and collect taxes, issue bonds with certain restrictions, hire and fire teachers, make contracts, collect fees, supervise and discipline students, pass on petitions to annex school districts, acquire property by condemnation, and in general manage the operations of the junior colleges, Justice Black's majority opinion rejected the argument that *Hadley* was distinguishable from *Reynolds* and its progeny because of the narrow purpose of the consolidated district. Instead, Black argued that because the trustees of the consolidated district performed "important governmental functions," the apportionment of the trustees was constrained by the same constitutional principles that governed the elections for state officials more generally and that the statutory allocation of the trustees in *Hadley* was inconsistent with these principles.[18]

Similarly, at first, the seating of Justice Blackmun did little to limit the Court's aggressiveness in pursuing the expansion of the right to vote. *Dunn v. Blumstein* provided the newly appointed Blackmun his first opportunity to deal with the issue.[19] *Dunn* was a challenge to a Tennessee statute that required citizens to be residents of the state for one year and of their county for three months before being allowed to vote. On its face, the issue presented by the case was almost identical to that which the Court had faced in *Pope v. Williams* almost seventy years earlier. Chief Justice Burger argued that *Dunn* should be controlled by *Pope* and declared, "It is no more a denial of equal protection for a State to require newcomers to be exposed to state and local problems for a reasonable period such as one year before voting, than it is to require children to wait 18 years before voting."[20] However, the remaining six participating justices disagreed, concluding that the Tennessee requirement violated the equal protection clause.

Speaking for five justices, Thurgood Marshall sought to characterize *Pope* as a case in which the state of Maryland had simply been requiring that potential voters be bona fide residents of the state in order to have the right to vote. Relying on *Kramer*, he averred that the durational residency requirement in *Dunn* could only survive constitutional scrutiny if the requirement was "'drawn with precision'" to serve a compelling governmental interest.

The state of Tennessee argued that the restriction was necessary to guarantee that those who sought to vote in Tennessee were not fraudulently claiming to be bona fide residents of the state. However, Marshall rejected this argument, observing that the state had introduced no evidence to support this claim, that the asserted interest was adequately served by the requirement that residents formally register in order to be allowed to vote, and that residents were allowed to register to vote as late as thirty days before the date of the election itself.[21]

The tone of the analysis in *Dunn* was much like that in cases such as *Preisler* and *Hadley*. By contrast, the 1972 term brought a significant change in the tenor of the Court's decisions on voting rights and reapportionment. During the term, those advocating the imposition of increasingly stringent constitutional limitations on state authority suffered defeats in a variety of cases. However, none of the Court's opinions challenged the basic principles that had been established in the late 1960s and early 1970s. Instead, operating at the margins the decisions simply preserved a small measure of state autonomy in the regulation of the electoral process.

Marston v. Lewis and *Burns v. Fortson* provide typical examples of this phenomenon.[22] *Marston* and *Burns* arose from challenges to limitations that had been imposed on voter registration in Arizona and Georgia, respectively. In both states, voters were required to register to vote no later than fifty days prior to actually casting a vote in an election. In addition, Arizona explicitly imposed a fifty-day durational residency requirement on those who wished to vote. The constitutionality of these requirements was challenged by prospective voters who insisted that the time limitations violated the principles that had been established in *Dunn*.

The consideration of *Marston* and *Burns* necessarily implicated issues that were implicit in the invocation of strict scrutiny by the Court in cases such as *Dunn* and *Kramer* but not fully addressed by the majority opinion in either case. As developed in the context of cases involving racial discrimination, the compelling governmental interest test had been viewed as establishing a standard that was for all intents and purposes impossible for the state to meet. Thus, in 1972, one commentator famously described the standard as "'strict' in theory but fatal in fact."[23]

This version of strict scrutiny could not plausibly be applied in cases involving challenges to restrictions on voting rights. Although it would certainly be possible to create a legal regime in which no classifications based on race could pass constitutional muster, no one would argue that a state was required to allow all people who appeared at polling stations to participate in state elections. For example, the majority opinion in *Dunn* explicitly conceded that the state could limit the right to vote to permanent residents, and the *Kramer* Court implicitly acknowledged the right of the state to require that residents reach the age of majority before being allowed to participate in elections. Thus, as Justice Blackmun observed in his concurring opinion in *Dunn,* voting rights cases often involved issues of line drawing rather than absolute rules. *Marston* and *Burns* required the justices to determine precisely where those lines were to be drawn in cases involving durational residency requirements for voting.

In both cases, Justices Douglas and Brennan joined opinions by Justice Marshall that insisted *Dunn* had established the proposition that thirty days was sufficient for the government to investigate the qualifications of new registrants in order to ensure that they were in fact eligible to vote and that any rule that required registration more than thirty days before an election was therefore an unconstitutional restriction on the right to vote.[24] However, a majority of the justices disagreed and in a pair of brief, per curiam opinions authored by Justice Byron White concluded that neither the Arizona nor the Georgia statute ran afoul of the equal protection clause. In *Marston,* the majority relied on evidence regarding special circumstances in

Arizona in finding that the fifty-day period was constitutionally justifiable, whereas in *Burns* the Court simply relied on *Marston* in rejecting the constitutional challenge to the fifty-day waiting period in Georgia.

The same justices who formed the majority in *Marston* and *Burns* established limits on the scope of the reapportionment and voting rights decisions in other contexts as well. For example, in *Salyer Land Co. v. Tulare Lake Basin Water District,* the Court held that the principles established in *Reynolds* and *Kramer* did not require the state of California to follow the principle of one person, one vote in elections to the board of directors of a government body charged with planning and executing projects "for the acquisition, appropriation, diversion, storage, conservation, and distribution of water" within the relevant district.[25] Justices Douglas, Brennan, and Marshall argued that the case was governed by *Reynolds* and *Kramer* because of the importance of the functions performed by the water district and the impact its decision would have on the populace as a whole. However, the remainder of the justices disagreed, joining an opinion by Justice William Rehnquist that concluded that the state could constitutionally limit the right to vote in water district elections to landowners and to have the votes weighted according to the assessed value of the voter's property. Rehnquist noted that even the one person, one vote cases themselves had observed that "'there might be some case in which a State elects certain functionaries whose duties are so far removed from normal governmental activities and so disproportionately affect different groups that a popular election in compliance with *Reynolds* . . . might not be required'" and concluded that the government body at issue in *Salyer* fell within that category.[26]

Although the voting pattern was slightly different, progressives suffered another defeat in *Rosario v. Rockefeller.*[27] *Rosario* was a challenge to a New York statute that described the conditions under which voters were allowed to vote in the primary elections in which each party chose its candidates for upcoming general elections. Basically, the statute provided that a person could vote in a primary election only if he or she had enrolled as a member of the appropriate party at least thirty days prior to the general election that preceded the primary in which he or she sought to participate. In practical effect, this requirement limited participation to those who had registered eight months before a presidential primary and eleven months before a nonpresidential primary.

Speaking for himself and Justices Douglas, Brennan, and Marshall, Justice Lewis Powell contended that the New York statute was unconstitutional. Observing that a number of decisions had established the principle that, for constitutional purposes, the right to vote in a primary was entitled to the same level of protection as the right to vote in a general election, he argued that the statute should be subject to strict scrutiny because it in essence imposed the same type of durational requirement condemned in *Dunn*. Powell appeared to concede that some time limitation on the declaration of party affiliation was appropriate. Nonetheless, he asserted that the New York statute imposed "substantial and unnecessary restrictions" on the right to vote and therefore ran afoul of the equal protection clause.[28]

However, the remaining five justices took a different view of the issues presented by *Rosario*. Justice Stewart's majority opinion rejected the analogy to *Dunn*, arguing that although the durational residency in that case had completely disqualified newly arrived residents from voting in Tennessee, the plaintiffs in *Rosario* could have, if they had so chosen, participated in a primary election by the simple expedient of enrolling in the party before the statutory deadline. The majority contended that the New York requirement served the state interest in "inhibit[ing] party 'raiding,' whereby voters in sympathy with one party designate themselves as voters of another party so as to influence or determine the results of the other party's primary."[29] Thus, the *Rosario* majority concluded that the New York requirement did not run afoul of the Fourteenth Amendment.

The results of the cases dealing specifically with the issue of reapportionment were more mixed. In cases in which the Warren Court decisions could be plausibly distinguished, a majority of the justices demonstrated a willingness to allow at least marginal departures from the principle of one person, one vote. This point emerged clearly in *Mahan v. Howell*.[30] *Mahan* arose from a challenge to the manner by which the Virginia state legislature sought to reapportion itself in 1971 following the adoption of a new state constitution. Under the plan adopted by the legislature, the 100 members of the state's House of Delegates were to be selected from 52 single-member, multimember, and "floater" districts that almost universally followed the preexisting jurisdictional lines of cities and counties within the state. According to the terms of the legislature's plan, the maximum deviation in the population of any district from the ideal mean was 9.6 percent, and the maximum percentage variation between any two districts was 16.4 percent. Speaking for himself and Justices Douglas and Marshall, Justice Brennan argued vigorously that the principles established in *Kirkpatrick v. Preisler* required that this apportionment be held unconstitutional.[31] However, with Justice Powell not participating, the five remaining justices concluded that the Virginia plan did not violate any constitutional norms.

Speaking for the majority, Justice Rehnquist argued that *Preisler* was not controlling because the standards for evaluating the makeup of state legislatures should be different from those that governed the creation of congressional districts. He emphasized the fact that the opinion in *Reynolds v. Sims* itself had explicitly recognized both the possibility that the state might be given more flexibility in apportioning its own legislature and the legitimacy of pursuing a policy of maintaining the integrity of jurisdictional lines.[32] Several months later, in *Gaffney v. Cummings* and *White v. Regester*, Justice Powell added his vote to those of the members of the *Mahan* majority in concluding that state legislative districts could differ in population by as much as 9.9 percent without running afoul of the equal protection clause.[33] Although Powell expressed private misgivings, the *Gaffney* majority also rejected the contention that states could not constitutionally make a conscious effort to ensure that the makeup of the state legislature would accurately reflect the relative strengths of the Republican and Democratic Parties in the state.[34]

Like the voting rights decisions, *Mahan* was clearly a defeat for the most ardent defenders of the principle of one person, one vote. However, the significance of decisions such as these should not be overstated. Although the apportionment and voting rights decisions of the 1972 term obviously softened the basic principles established by *Reynolds*, *Kramer*, and their progeny at the margins, the basic structure established by the late Warren Court cases dealing with the right to participate in the political process remained generally intact.

Indeed, at times the more conservative justices on the Court seemed to almost go out of their way to emphasize their fidelity to existing precedent. For example, nothing in the majority opinions in *Marston* or *Burns* even suggested that the justices were disavowing the holding in *Dunn*. Instead, in *Burns*, over the objection of Justice Blackmun, five justices indicated that fifty days "approaches the outer constitutional limits in this area."[35] Similarly, although one can hardly imagine Justice Rehnquist having concurred in *Reynolds* at the time the case was decided, his majority opinion in *Mahan* invalidated a small portion of the Virginia plan on the ground that the makeup of the districts in question violated the principles established by the original reapportionment decisions.[36] The principles established by *Wesberry v. Sanders* and *Kirkpatrick v. Preisler* were reaffirmed even more emphatically in *White v. Weiser*.[37]

In *Weiser*, the justices were faced with a challenge to the constitutionality of a redistricting plan adopted by the Texas state legislature that would have created a set of districts with a maximum deviation from the average population of 2.41 percent and a difference of 4.13 percent between the population of the largest district and that of the smallest district. Although this deviation was considerably smaller than that which the Court had rejected in *Preisler*, it was nonetheless larger than the deviation envisioned by two other plans presented to the district court that considered the challenge.

At the initial conference on *Weiser*, it appeared that five justices were in favor of rejecting the constitutional attack on the Texas plan, as Justice White joined the four Nixon appointees in voting to uphold the plan. Although White had dissented in *Preisler*, he did not propose to overrule the 1969 decision but instead to distinguish it and establish a maximum deviation that would be viewed as constitutionally acceptable without further justification. Although tentatively voting to strike down the Texas plan, Stewart also indicated that he might be willing to endorse an opinion that adequately distinguished *Preisler*.[38]

However, after being assigned to write the opinion on March 1, White changed his mind. Apparently believing he would be unable to craft an opinion that satisfactorily distinguished *Preisler* and unwilling to vote to overrule a decision cited with apparent approval earlier in the 1972 term itself, on March 5 he circulated a memorandum declaring that upon further reflection, he had come to the conclusion that the redistricting plan adopted by the Texas state legislature should be found unconstitutional.[39] He ultimately produced an opinion that simply relied on *Preisler* and rejected the plan approved by the state legislature because the "districts were not as mathematically equal as reasonably possible."[40]

None of the Nixon justices formally dissented from the disposition of *Weiser*. However, Chief Justice Burger and Justice Rehnquist joined a concurring opinion by Justice Powell describing *Weiser* as "virtually indistinguishable" from *Preisler* but at the same time clearly indicating that they would be willing to cast their votes to overturn the 1969 decision if a majority could be assembled in support of that course of action.[41]

Weiser thus stands as a monument to the impact of the concept of precedent on the judicial decision-making process during the 1972 term. Given the fact that Justices Stewart and White had dissented in *Preisler*, if they had viewed *Weiser* as a case of first impression, they would have almost certainly joined Chief Justice Burger and Justices Powell and Rehnquist in voting to reject the constitutional challenge to the districting plan that had been adopted by the Texas legislature. Based on his comments at the conference on *Weiser*, Justice Blackmun would very likely have taken the same position. However, because they were operating in the shadow of the majority opinion in *Preisler,* Stewart and White felt compelled to conclude that the legislatively approved plan should be found unconstitutional.

In short, the decision in *Weiser* reflected the continuing impact of institutional considerations on the Court's actions during the 1972 term. However, on issues where political pressures were stronger and the existing legal standards were more amorphous, the decisions were clearly more driven by ordinary ideological considerations. The Court's treatment of the obscenity cases provides a classic example of this phenomenon.

Chapter Four

The Battle over Obscenity

During the late Warren era, the Supreme Court moved aggressively to expand the scope of First Amendment protections for freedom of speech and freedom of the press in a variety of different contexts. For example, in the 1964 decision in *New York Times Co. v. Sullivan*, the justices held for the first time that the First Amendment imposed substantial constraints on the ability of the states to allow recovery for defamatory statements.[1] Similarly, in 1969, *Tinker v. Des Moines Community Independent School District* established the principle that students possessed First Amendment rights to protest in public schools.[2] Admittedly, not all of the Court's First Amendment decisions during the late 1960s were consistent with this pattern. Nonetheless, on the whole, progressives had good reason to be satisfied with the performance of the Warren Court justices in speech and press cases.

By the end of the 1972 term, it had become clear that the Burger Court would in general take a less expansive view of speech and press rights. To be sure, in 1971 the supporters of the mainstream press had achieved one of their most dramatic successes in *New York Times Co. v. United States*.[3] There, emphasizing their distaste for prior restraints on speech, a majority of the justices concluded that the First Amendment barred the issuance of an injunction against the publication of classified documents dealing with the background and prosecution of the Vietnam War leaked to the *Washington Post* and the *New York Times*. However, the following year, in *Branzburg v. Hayes*, the newly appointed Justices Lewis Powell and William Rehnquist joined Chief Justice Warren Burger and Justices Harry Blackmun and Byron White to reject claims that newspaper reporters had a First Amendment right to refuse to divulge their sources in a grand jury proceeding.[4] In addition, in *Lloyd v. Tanner*, the same majority concluded that the First Amendment did not require owners of shopping centers to allow the distribution of handbills unrelated to the shopping center's operations.[5]

The 1972 term itself brought a continuation of the same trend. During the term, the Court addressed speech and press issues in a variety of different contexts. For example, in *Broadrick v. Oklahoma* and *United States Civil Service Commission v. National Association of Letter Carriers*, Justice Potter Stewart joined the members of the *Branzburg* majority in holding that civil service employees could be barred from participating in political activity.[6] However, it was the Court's approach to the politically explosive issue of obscenity that generated the greatest public interest.

Although Richard Nixon focused primarily on the Supreme Court's decisions on criminal procedure during the 1968 presidential campaign, the question of the impact of the First Amendment on government authority to regulate the distribution of sexually explicit material was also a political flashpoint in the late 1960s and early 1970s. The Court's consideration of this issue took place against the backdrop of the culture wars that wracked US society during this period. Among the traditional beliefs coming under fire was the idea that widespread dissemination of graphic descriptions and portrayals of sexual activity was inappropriate and damaging to the underlying fabric of society. The assaults on these beliefs were met with vehement responses from those who continued to embrace the traditional perspective. The analogous conflict over the First Amendment principles governing the regulation of sexually explicit materials reached its peak during the 1972 term with the decisions in *Miller v. California* and *Paris Adult Theater No. 1 v. Slaton*.[7]

Like many of the controversial issues decided during the 1972 term, the consideration of the obscenity cases took place against the background of a series of Warren Court decisions that had broken new ground and expanded the scope of the limitations imposed on the state and federal governments by the Constitution. Prior to the late 1950s, the First Amendment had not been held to impose significant restraints on the ability of government to control access to sexually explicit materials. Thus, for example, in 1942, in *Chaplinsky v. New Hampshire*, the Court declared in dictum:

> There are certain well-defined and narrowly limited classes of speech, the prevention and punishment of which have never been thought to raise any Constitutional problem. These include the lewd and obscene. . . . It has been well observed that such utterances are no essential part of any exposition of ideas, and are of such slight social value as a step

> to truth that any benefit that may be derived from them is clearly outweighed by the social interest in order and morality.[8]

However, cases such as *Chaplinsky* did not discuss the question of whether the First Amendment imposed *any* limitations on the government's power to limit the dissemination of sexually explicit material and, if so, what those limits might be.

The Warren Court first addressed this issue in 1957, in *Roth v. United States* and its companion case, *Alberts v. California*.[9] In *Roth*, the defendant was found guilty of violating a federal law that banned the mailing of obscene materials, whereas in *Alberts*, the defendant ran afoul of a California statute that prohibited the sale of such material. Neither case presented the question of whether the particular material on which the defendant's conviction had been based was in fact obscene. Instead, both appeals raised facial challenges to the relevant statutes. The Court found that neither of these challenges had merit and affirmed the convictions.

Justice William Brennan spoke for the majority of the justices in both cases. Although declaring that "all ideas having even the slightest redeeming social importance—unorthodox ideas, controversial ideas, even ideas hateful to the prevailing climate of opinion—have the full protection of the [First Amendment], unless excludable because they encroach upon the limited area of more important interests," Brennan also insisted that, in light of the historical context in which it was adopted, "it is apparent that the unconditional phrasing of the First Amendment was not intended to protect every utterance" and that obscenity in particular was unprotected because it was universally viewed as "utterly without redeeming social importance." In addition, he suggested that the appropriate test for determining whether material was obscene for constitutional purposes was reflected in the most recent tentative draft of the Model Penal Code, which provided that "a thing is obscene if, considered as a whole, its predominant appeal is to prurient interest, i.e., a shameful or morbid interest in nudity, sex, or excretion, and if it goes substantially beyond customary limits of candor in description or representation of such matters."[10]

Three other justices also delivered opinions in *Roth*. Dissenting on behalf of himself and Justice Hugo Black, William O. Douglas argued that the First Amendment provided absolute protection for all speech. By contrast, both Chief Justice Earl Warren and Justice John Marshall Harlan agreed that sexually explicit material could be regulated under some circumstances but expressed reservations about Justice Brennan's analysis.[11]

Warren would have eschewed any discussion of the broad constitutional issues raised by the regulation of sexually explicit material. Instead, he would have focused specifically on the conduct for which the defendants in *Roth* and *Alberts* were convicted. Viewing the cases from this perspective, Warren would have affirmed the convictions because the defendants "were plainly engaged in the commercial exploitation of the morbid and shameful craving for materials with prurient effect."[12]

Harlan's differences with the majority were of a quite different nature. He had two fundamental objections to Brennan's approach. First, Harlan rejected the idea that a conviction could stand simply because a jury or a trial judge had determined as a matter of fact that a book was "obscene" under standards that themselves were consistent with the First Amendment. Instead, he argued that the Supreme Court must conduct an independent review of each book and satisfy itself that the book was in fact obscene for constitutional purposes. Second, unlike most of the other members of the Warren Court, Harlan believed that because the First Amendment by its terms applied only to the federal government, the states had broader authority to regulate speech. Thus, he took the view that the federal government could ban only "hard-core pornography" from the mails but that the states were free to impose criminal liability for the sale of material "whose dominant tendency might be to 'deprave or corrupt' a reader." Against this background, although agreeing that the conviction in *Alberts* should be upheld, Harlan would have reversed the conviction in *Roth*.[13]

In the years that followed the decision in *Roth*, the Court dealt with a variety of obscenity-related questions involving both procedural and substantive problems. However, the justices' next full-scale confrontation with the issue of obscenity came seven years later in *Jacobellis v. Ohio*.[14] Unlike the defendants in *Roth* and *Alberts*, both of whom had been convicted for distributing obscene books, the defendant in *Jacobellis* had been found criminally liable for exhibiting an obscene film. Moreover, the specific film at issue in *Jacobellis* was not primarily about sexual activity. Instead, the conviction was based on a single scene that Justice Arthur Goldberg described as "so fragmentary and fleeting that only a censor's alert would make an audience conscious that something 'questionable' is being portrayed." Moreover, as Justice Brennan observed, the movie as a whole had elicited many favorable reviews and had been characterized by two prominent critics as among the best of the year.[15]

Against this background, the Court reversed the conviction on a six-to-three vote. All of the justices apparently agreed that motion pictures were to be judged by the same general standard as books under the First Amendment. However, they disagreed sharply on virtually every other aspect of the case. Indeed, no single opinion attracted the support of more than two justices.

Justices Black and Douglas reiterated their view that allegedly obscene speech was entitled to the full protection of the First Amendment, whereas Justice Harlan once again asserted that, in his view, states had far broader authority than the federal government to proscribe sexually explicit material. By contrast, Justice White concurred in the result without opinion, and Justice Stewart delivered a brief opinion contending that criminal laws relating to obscenity could only reach "hard-core" pornography and declaring famously that, although he could not define the term with precision, "I know it when I see it."[16]

Speaking for himself and Justice Goldberg, Justice Brennan once again elaborated his position at some length. However, unlike his majority opinion in *Roth*, Brennan's opinion in *Jacobellis* displayed distinct hostility to state regulation of sexually explicit material. The *Jacobellis* opinion explicitly adopted Harlan's view that the Supreme Court must essay an independent analysis of the question of whether a particular book or movie was obscene.[17] In addition, Brennan restated his view of the proper relationship between "redeeming social importance" and "appeal to prurient interest" in a manner that suggested a substantial tightening of First Amendment standards.

In *Roth*, Brennan had asserted that the *reason* obscenity was not protected by the First Amendment was that obscene material was "utterly without redeeming social importance." However, in *defining* obscenity, he had alluded to the tentative proposal of the Model Penal Code, which made no direct reference at all to redeeming social importance but instead focused on the idea that the work predominantly appealed to "prurient interest." Thus, at the time *Roth* was decided, the most plausible reading of the majority opinion was that what lacked redeeming social importance was the decision to produce work that appealed primarily to prurient interest and that any ideas conveyed by the work could be expressed in some other way.

However, Brennan's opinion in *Jacobellis* clearly rejected this view. Instead, he described the lack of redeeming social importance as an independent requirement for the regulation of sexually explicit material, even if that material appealed primarily to prurient interest. He declared:

> Material dealing with sex in a manner that advocates ideas or that has literary or scientific or artistic value or any other form of social

importance may not be branded as obscenity and denied the constitutional protection. Nor may the constitutional status of the material be made to turn on a "weighing" of its social importance against its prurient appeal, for a work cannot be proscribed unless it is "utterly" without social importance.[18]

Finally, Brennan firmly rejected any suggestion that communities could apply local standards in determining whether sexually explicit material was presented in a manner that "goes substantially beyond customary limits of candor." Instead, he declared that "we do not see how any 'local' definition of the 'community' could properly be employed in delineating the area of expression that is protected by the Federal Constitution" because any such regime would have "'the intolerable consequence of denying some sections of the country access to material, there deemed acceptable, which in others might be considered offensive to prevailing community standards of decency.'"[19] Therefore, Brennan concluded that national standards should apply in all obscenity cases. Given the makeup of the Court and Brennan's insistence that judgments on obscenity be reviewed de novo, such standards would almost inevitably be those prevalent among the more tolerant intelligentsia rather than those common in more socially conservative elements of the populace.

Chief Justice Warren dissented in an opinion joined by Justice Tom C. Clark. Warren's opinion was marked by an almost palpable distaste for purveyors of sexually explicit material. Thus, Warren complained that the adoption of Stewart's approach would require further refinement and that in the interim "those who profit from the commercial exploitation of obscenity would continue to ply their trade unmolested." In addition, Warren asserted that "no government—be it federal, state, or local—should be forced to choose between repressing all material, including that within the realm of decency, and allowing unrestrained license to publish any material, no matter how vile."[20]

These observations formed the backdrop for Warren's sharp disagreements with Brennan on doctrinal issues. Like Brennan, Warren declared his allegiance to the test announced in *Roth*. However, the dissent made no mention of the concept of redeeming social importance in discussing its conception of the *Roth* analysis. In addition, Warren argued that local rather than national standards should be used to determine whether the material offended "community standards," observing that "communities throughout the Nation are, in fact, diverse, and it must be remembered that, in cases such as this one, the Court is confronted with the task of reconciling conflicting rights of the diverse communities within our society and of individuals." Finally, Warren contended that the Court should not make an independent determination of whether material that came before it was "obscene" for First Amendment purposes but instead should simply ask whether the record contained "sufficient evidence" to support the conclusion that the material was in fact obscene under the standards enunciated by the Court. Warren insisted that "this is the only reasonable way I can see to obviate the necessity of this Court's sitting as the Super Censor of all the obscenity purveyed throughout the Nation."[21]

In 1966, the Court revisited the obscenity issue in three cases that once again produced a welter of opinions reflecting a wide variety of diverse viewpoints. *Ginzburg v. United States* was an appeal from a conviction for violating a federal statute that prohibited the use of the mail to send "obscene, lewd, lascivious, indecent, filthy, or vile" materials, whereas in *Mishkin v. New York* the defendant had run afoul of a state statute that prohibited hiring people to produce such material.[22] By contrast, *A Book Named "John Cleland's Memoirs of a Woman of Pleasure" v. Attorney General of Massachusetts* arose from a state civil action that had resulted in a book being declared obscene, which in turn subjected those who distributed the book to potential criminal penalties.[23] Although the convictions in *Ginzburg* and *Mishkin* were upheld, the Court reversed the judgment of the lower court in *Memoirs*.

A number of the opinions simply reiterated views expressed in earlier decisions. Dissenting in both *Ginzburg* and *Mishkin*, Justices Black and Douglas continued to assert that sexually explicit materials warranted full First Amendment protection. Justice Stewart voted with Black and Douglas, declaring that "censorship reflects a society's lack of confidence in itself. It is a hallmark of an authoritarian regime." Although reluctantly conceding in the face of what he described as the "almost universal judgment of our society" that hard-core pornography can constitutionally be proscribed, Stewart provided a definition of that concept in a footnote and insisted that none of the material that gave rise to the cases before the Court fell into that category. Conversely, restating his view that states should be allowed more leeway than the federal government to regulate such material, Justice Harlan voted to affirm the lower court judgments in *Mishkin* and *Memoirs* but to reverse the conviction in *Ginzburg*.[24]

Chief Justice Warren, Justice Brennan, and the newly appointed Justice Abe Fortas were in the majority in all three cases. In each case, Justice

Brennan wrote on behalf of this group. In both *Ginzburg* and *Mishkin*, he emphasized that the materials at issue in both cases had been produced, advertised, and distributed with the basic purpose of appealing to prurient interest rather than creating works of artistic merit or advancing the discussion of political issues. The *Mishkin* opinion was perhaps most notable for its reference to the appellant's claim that "some of the books involved in this prosecution, those depicting various deviant sexual practices . . . do not satisfy the prurient appeal requirement because they do not appeal to a prurient interest of the 'average person' in sex, that, 'instead of stimulating the erotic, they disgust and sicken'"—a contention that, not surprisingly, Brennan dismissed out of hand.

By contrast, in *Ginzburg*, Brennan discussed the significance of the defendant's motivation in considerably greater detail. Noting that the "leer of the sensualist" permeated the advertising of the books at issue in the case, Brennan observed:

> The deliberate representation of petitioners' publications as erotically arousing, for example, stimulated the reader to accept them as prurient; he looks for titillation, not for saving intellectual content. Similarly, such representation would tend to force public confrontation with the potentially offensive aspects of the work; the brazenness of such an appeal heightens the offensiveness of the publications to those who are offended by such material. And the circumstances of presentation and dissemination of material are equally relevant to determining whether social importance claimed for material in the courtroom was, in the circumstances, pretense or reality—whether it was the basis upon which it was traded in the marketplace or a spurious claim for litigation purposes. [Thus,] where the purveyor's sole emphasis is on the sexually provocative aspects of his publications, that fact may be decisive in the determination of obscenity.

He also contended that

> a conviction for mailing obscene publications, but explained in part by [evidence of pandering to sexual urges], does not necessarily suppress the materials in question, nor chill their proper distribution for a proper use. Nor should it inhibit the enterprise of others seeking, through serious endeavor, to advance human knowledge or understanding in science, literature, or art. All that will have been determined is that

> questionable publications are obscene in a context which brands them as obscene as that term is defined in *Roth*—a use inconsistent with any claim to the shelter of the First Amendment.[25]

Unlike in *Mishkin* and *Ginzburg*, Brennan spoke only for himself, Warren, and Fortas in *Memoirs*. His brief opinion in the latter basically recapitulated the views he had expressed in *Jacobellis*, once again declaring that, in order for material to be considered obscene for First Amendment purposes, "three elements must coalesce: it must be established that (a) the dominant theme of the material taken as a whole appeals to a prurient interest in sex, (b) the material is patently offensive because it affronts contemporary community standards relating to the description or representation of sexual matters, and (c) the material is utterly without redeeming social value" and emphasizing in particular that the material was entitled to First Amendment protection even if it had only a "modicum of social value." He argued that *Ginzburg* (and, by implication, *Mishkin*) was distinguishable because, in that case, the sellers of the material itself had focused solely on its sexual content, and "where the purveyor's sole emphasis is on the sexually provocative aspects of his publications, a court could accept his evaluation at its face value."[26]

Justice Brennan's opinion in *Memoirs* did not break any new ground. The only surprise was that Chief Justice Warren joined the opinion after having sharply criticized the same approach only two years before in *Jacobellis*. By contrast, the dissenting opinions of Justice White and Justice Clark were notable for different reasons.

Because White came to the Court after *Roth* had been decided and had concurred in the result without opinion in *Jacobellis*, *Memoirs* was the first case in which he expressed his views on the obscenity issue. White purported to embrace the views that had been expressed by the majority opinion in *Roth*, but at the same time he rejected the notion that social importance should be an independent consideration in obscenity analysis. He observed wryly that if otherwise obscene material deserved First Amendment protection solely because it did not utterly lack social importance, then "well-written, especially effective obscenity is protected [whereas] the poorly written is vulnerable." White also contended that "if books like *Fanny Hill* are unprotected, their nonprurient appeal is [not] necessarily lost to the world. Literary style, history, teachings about sex, character description (even of a prostitute), or moral lessons need not come wrapped in such packages."[27]

Clark joined White in rejecting the claim that *Roth* had established the proposition that sexually explicit material could only be suppressed if it was utterly without social importance and concluding that the Constitution allowed the state of Massachusetts to suppress the book at issue in *Memoirs*. In addition, just as he had in *Jacobellis*, Clark took the position that the Court should not determine the question of obscenity de novo but instead should only ask if the lower court's finding was supported by sufficient evidence. However, the most striking feature of Clark's opinion was its tone. Unlike White, Clark made no effort to conceal his personal outrage at the majority's decision.

After asserting that the "public should know of the continuous flow of pornographic material reaching this Court and the increasing problem States have in controlling it," Clark averred that "I have 'stomached' past cases for almost 10 years without much outcry. Though I am not known to be a purist—or a shrinking violet—[*Fanny Hill*] is too much even for me." He also asserted that the plurality opinion in *Memoirs* "rejects the basic holding of *Roth* and gives the smut artist free rein to carry on his dirty business." He characterized the book as composed almost entirely of an "uninterrupted succession of descriptions by [the central character], either as an observer or participant, of sexual adventures so vile that one of the male expert witnesses in the case was hesitant to repeat any one of them in the courtroom." Clark conceded that "there are some short transitory passages between the various sexual episodes" but also asserted that "for the most part, they only set the scene and identify the participants for the next orgy, or make smutty reference and comparison to past episodes." In addition, Clark lampooned the testimony of the experts whom the defense had called at trial to demonstrate that *Fanny Hill* in fact was a work of literary and social significance and cited a variety of different sources he viewed as refuting the claim that there was no real evidence that the distribution of obscene material in fact caused social harm.[28]

The immediate popular commentary on the trio of decisions focused largely on *Ginzburg*, which was viewed as a major victory for those seeking to limit access to sexually explicit books. Thus, for example, the *New York Times* declared that the decision "has revived the near-moribund state and Federal anti-pornography laws" and "was likely to result in mass prosecutions across the country against book publishers, book sellers, and the movie industry."[29] However, in many respects, the exchange between the justices in *Memoirs* was a more apt reflection of the divisions in US society on the issue of pornography.

Clark's opinion reflected the views of a segment of society whose assessment of the stakes in the battle over obscenity was quite different from that of the majority of the justices. For Douglas and Black, and to only a slightly lesser extent Stewart and the members of the Brennan group, the primary danger to be avoided was that of censorship. As two noted scholars who subscribed to that position put it, "The danger of influencing a change in the current moral standards of the community, or of shocking or offending readers, or of stimulating sex thoughts or desires apart from objective conduct, can never justify the losses to society that result from interference with literary freedom."[30] Clark, by contrast, spoke for those whose paramount concern was the maintenance of public morality and who saw the proliferation of sexually explicit material as a threat to the values undergirding the basic fabric of society itself.

This group was often on the political offensive in the late 1960s. In 1967, declaring that "traffic in obscene matters and materials is a matter of grave national concern," Congress passed a statute establishing a presidential commission to study the issue and recommend "advisable, appropriate, effective, and constitutional means to deal effectively with such traffic in pornography and obscenity."[31] The following year, opponents of the Fortas nomination focused in part on his position in *Memoirs,* with Republican senator Strom Thurmond of South Carolina reading sexually explicit materials aloud during the hearings and screening such films to the press in order to dramatize the nominee's views on this issue.[32]

The release of the Presidential Commission on Obscenity and Pornography report on October 1, 1970, brought the divisions over government regulation of sexually explicit materials even more clearly to the fore. Chaired by Dean Charles C. Lockhart of the University of Minnesota Law School, the eighteen-person commission—all but one of whose members was appointed by Lyndon Johnson—included representatives from a variety of interest groups with very different perspectives on the issue. These differences were clearly reflected in the majority and dissenting opinions made public on October 1.

Twelve members of the commission argued for the repeal of all legislation that "seek[s] to interfere with the right of adults who wish to do so to read, obtain, or view sexually explicit materials." They contended that there was "no [empirical] evidence that exposure to or use of explicit sexual materials play a significant role in the causation of social or individual harms such as crime, delinquency, sexual or nonsexual deviancy, or severe emotional disturbances." The majority also averred that "much of the 'problem' regarding materials which depict explicit sexual activity stems from the inability or reluctance of people in our society to be open and direct in dealing with sexual matters" and that "it is exceedingly unwise for government to attempt to legislate individual moral values and standards independent of behavior, especially by restrictions on consensual communications."[33]

The majority report elicited impassioned dissents from three of the commissioners. They attacked the objectivity of the majority, with one dissent asserting that the "commission majority report can only be described as a travesty, preordained by the bias and prejudice of its chairman" and the other describing the majority report as "slanted and biased in favor of protecting the business of obscenity and pornography" and declaring that the "scanty and manipulated evidence contained within [the] report is wholly inadequate to support its conclusions." The dissenters were no less emphatic in opposing the substantive recommendations of the majority, contending that the recommendations "deserve . . . condemnation as inimical to the welfare of the United States, its citizens, and its children" and declaring that

> at a time when the spread of pornography has reached epidemic proportions and when the moral fiber of our country seems to be rapidly unraveling, the desperate need is for enlightened and intelligent control of the poison which threatens us—not the declaration of moral bankruptcy inherent in the repeal of the laws which have been the defense of decent people against the pornographer for profit.[34]

The majority report confidently asserted that most Americans supported its basic principles. However, the reaction of elected officials to the report was overwhelmingly negative. Declaring that the "Commission on Obscenity and Pornography has performed a disservice, and I totally reject its report," Richard Nixon asserted that "pornography can corrupt a society and a civilization. The people's representatives have the right and obligation to prevent that corruption." Similarly, Democratic senator Robert C. Byrd of West Virginia labeled the majority report "shameful" and complained that "this outrageously permissive commission shows how far this nation has traveled down the road of moral decadence." Most of Byrd's colleagues apparently shared his disdain for the majority report. On October 13, with only five dissenters, the Senate passed a nonbinding resolution denouncing the report and rejecting its conclusions.[35]

The proregulation forces lost an important spokesperson on the Court when Clark retired and was replaced by Thurgood Marshall. Nonetheless, the Court's obscenity decisions between 1968 and 1971 were anything but one-sided. On one hand, over the objections of Justices Black, Douglas, and Fortas, in 1968 the Court held in *Ginsberg v. New York* that the government had broad authority to prevent the sale of sexually explicit material to children.[36] On the other, opponents of obscenity regulations won a signal victory in the 1969 decision in *Stanley v. Georgia*, in which the Court unanimously reversed the conviction of a man prosecuted for possessing obscene material in his own home.[37]

Two years later, however, it became clear that in the minds of most of the justices, *Stanley* had not altered the basic structure of the *Roth/Memoirs* analysis. In *United States v. Reidel*—the first major obscenity case in which Chief Justice Burger and Justice Blackmun participated—seven justices voted to uphold a conviction for sending obscene materials through the mail, expressly rejecting the argument that *Stanley* had undermined the vitality of the earlier case law.[38] Speaking for the majority, Justice White relied heavily on *Roth* and declared:

> It is urged that there is developing sentiment that adults should have complete freedom to produce, deal in, possess, and consume whatever communicative materials may appeal to them, and that the law's involvement with obscenity should be limited to those situations where children are involved or where it is necessary to prevent imposition on unwilling recipients of whatever age. The concepts involved are said to be so elusive, and the laws so inherently unenforceable without extravagant expenditures of time and effort by enforcement officers and the courts, that basic reassessment is not only wise, but essential. This may prove to be the desirable and eventual legislative course. But if it is, the task of restructuring the obscenity laws lies with those who pass, repeal, and amend statutes and ordinances [rather than the Supreme Court].[39]

However, despite the conservative victories in *Ginsberg* and *Reidel*, it was clear that as late as 1971, the views of the *Memoirs* plurality continued to control the outcome of most of the obscenity cases that came before the Court and that a majority of the justices were generally suspicious of efforts to suppress the distribution of sexually explicit materials. Leaving *Stanley* aside, between 1967 and 1971, the Court reversed no less than thirty-four state and federal convictions for the sale or distribution of such materials. None of these reversals brought with them a detailed discussion of the reasoning that underlay the decisions. Instead, the 1967 judgment in *Redrup v. New York* was accompanied by a per curiam opinion that outlined the views of all of the justices on obscenity and declared that "whichever of these constitutional views is brought to bear upon the cases before us, it is clear that the [convictions] cannot stand."[40] Subsequent reversals were accompanied by unsigned statements that did nothing more than cite *Redrup*. But rather plainly, the majorities in favor of reversal must have included Brennan, who authored the *Memoirs* plurality opinion; Douglas, Black, and Stewart, all of whom had formally taken the position that the *Memoirs* opinion did not provide sufficient protection for sexually explicit material; and Marshall, whose opinion for the Court in *Stanley* had suggested that he harbored a deep suspicion of government efforts to control the flow of sexually explicit materials to adults.

Although enabling the Court to dispose of large numbers of obscenity cases quickly without requiring any of the justices to engage in the arduous task of preparing formal opinions, this practice masked the formidable institutional problems inherent in the regime of the late 1960s and early 1970s. Both the approach of the *Memoirs* plurality and Stewart's hard-core pornography analysis required the justices to examine each piece of sexually explicit material in detail to determine if it was entitled to the protection of the First Amendment—a task they found increasingly onerous because it wore on their sensibilities. Moreover, because each determination was based on the specific characteristics of the particular material being reviewed, the summary dispositions provided little guidance to lower courts faced with different material.

These concerns provided the backdrop to a full-scale reconsideration of the First Amendment issues raised by sexually explicit material that began during the 1971 term. When *Miller* was first argued in January 1972, the case seemed an unlikely vehicle for a major pronouncement on obscenity law. Only Justice Douglas initially voted to reverse the conviction, with Thurgood Marshall observing that the material at issue was obscene by any standard.[41] By contrast, the justices were far more deeply divided over the proper disposition of *United States v. 12,200-ft. Reels of Film* and *United States v. Orito*, both of which were challenges to the constitutionality of federal laws that had been invoked in an effort to prevent the importation and interstate transportation of sexually explicit material for purely private use.[42]

The initial conference votes in both *12,200-ft. Reels* and *Orito* in January 1972 found the Court split along lines that defied standard ideological characterizations. Arguing that importation of sexually explicit materials for private use was constitutionally protected under *Stanley*, Potter Stewart and Lewis Powell joined William O. Douglas and Thurgood Marshall in asserting that the First Amendment barred the enforcement of the relevant federal statute in both cases. By contrast, William Brennan agreed with Byron White, Harry Blackmun, and William Rehnquist in taking the opposing view. Although Chief Justice Burger passed at the conference, he indicated that he tentatively agreed with the Powell group's view that the United States was powerless under *Stanley* to regulate the noncommercial use of obscene materials. Assigning the opinions to himself, Burger also indicated that he ultimately planned to situate the opinions in both cases in the context of a broader reconsideration of the entire obscenity problem.[43]

On February 29, Burger produced a draft opinion in *12,200-ft. Reels* that concluded that the importation of obscene materials for private use was constitutionally protected under *Stanley*. Three days later, White circulated the draft of a dissent, soon joined by Blackmun. Conversely, on March 13, Douglas circulated an opinion that reiterated his contention that the First Amendment protected all sexually explicit speech from government regulation.[44]

The following day, the chief justice generated a memorandum with a perspective quite different from that reflected in his *12,200-ft. Reels* opinion. Characterizing the earlier draft opinion as "in a sense merely . . . a 'trial balloon,'" dealing with a case that was simply a part of the "whole fabric of the obscenity [issue]," the new memorandum expressed the view that "this whole area ought to be primarily a state problem, with this Court reviewing only egregious departures." He concluded by stating that "I hope to have something on the *Miller* case before long, and then we can see how 'alone' I am."[45]

The promised global treatment of the obscenity question appeared on May 14. The basic theme of the memorandum was that "in the long run, this Court cannot act as an efficient Super Censor, and the sooner we leave the problem [of obscenity] to the States the better off we and the public will be."[46] Against this background, the memorandum focused on three major substantive points.

First, Burger categorically rejected the view that sexually explicit material could be suppressed only if it was "utterly without redeeming social value." He observed that the effect of the application of this standard had been to "permit those who would commercially exploit the market for materials portraying sexual activities in a fundamentally offensive and indecent way to insulate themselves from liability by the formalistic inclusion of some material that might be thought to have some 'value,' but is usually at best only tangentially related to the real matter of interest."[47]

The chief justice was also opposed to the use of a national standard to determine whether material was "patently offensive." Burger asserted that "in a society as diverse as ours, the notion of a homogeneous 'national' consensus of what is or is not tolerable in the commercial exploitation of human interest in sexual matters is completely divorced from reality." Moreover, he asserted that "there is no rational basis whatever in law, logic, or human experience to tell us that the people of every State and community must adjust their ideas of what is decent in the portrayal of sexual activities to what is tolerable in some other and perhaps distant place" and that "in a society that prides itself . . . in supporting pluralism and diversity, there is no sound reason for the law to say that what is found tolerable in the portrayal of sexual activities in Los Angeles or Las Vegas must be accepted in Maine and Vermont."[48]

Finally, Burger emphasized the importance of the jury in determining whether material should be considered obscene for First Amendment purposes. He observed that "for every other purpose within the fact-finding function of jurors, we treat them as in a collective sense 'the conscience of the community.' That this is fraught with hazards and difficulties in the First Amendment area there is no doubt, but that is the essence of our system of justice up to now, and few would be so bold as to say the jury system is any less perfect than other human institutions." Reiterating this point, he later insisted that the "local jury, representing the conscience of the community in which the activities occurred, is peculiarly qualified to apply the standards of that community to the materials and activities involved in the case before it to determine if they fall below what is acceptable. If we do not accept that we condemn the jury system."[49]

Taken as a whole, the approach Burger outlined in his memorandum was plainly designed to leave the states broad discretion in dealing with sexually explicit material. However, the chief justice was not the only member of the Court to be engaged in a fundamental reassessment of the proper relationship between the First Amendment and the regulation of obscenity during the 1972 term. Justice Brennan, who had been the author of both the majority opinion in *Roth* and the plurality opinion in *Jacobellis,* was also rethinking his position on the issue.

Like the chief justice, by 1972 Brennan had come to the conclusion that the doctrinal structure erected in *Roth* and *Jacobellis* did not provide an appropriate framework for resolving the issues presented by the obscenity cases. Brennan's concerns were twofold. First, he had become convinced that experience had shown it was impossible to apply existing doctrine without impairment of the sound administration of justice. In addition, he believed that, in operation, the *Roth/Jacobellis* approach had unduly impaired the free traffic in sexually explicit material that in fact merited constitutional protection.[50] The latter concern was clearly the dominant influence in Brennan's response to Burger's proposed changes in the existing law of obscenity.

Justice Brennan first responded to Burger's missive in a brief memorandum circulated on May 22. Asserting that the "Chief Justice's proposed solution to the obscenity quagmire would, in my view, worsen an already intolerable mess," Brennan sketched the outlines of a quite different approach. Promising that a more detailed exposition of his view would be forthcoming, Brennan suggested abandoning the effort to treat sexually explicit material differently from other forms of speech and instead applying ordinary First Amendment principles to obscenity cases and allowing regulation only to protect the interests of adults who might wish to avoid being unwillingly exposed to such material and to prevent the material from being disseminated to minors.[51]

On June 14, Brennan delivered the promised elaboration of his view. After reviewing the Court's efforts to deal with obscenity in detail, Brennan began his analysis by declaring categorically that "neither the *Redrup* approach [of proceeding through a series of per curiam opinions] nor the underlying effort in *Roth* can be allowed to continue further, for experience has shown that both are flatly inconsistent with abiding principles marked out by our obscenity decisions themselves."[52] Unlike Burger, Brennan paid little attention to any perceived interest of the citizenry at large in preserving the moral tone of society. Instead, the memorandum focused almost entirely on what he perceived as the cardinal principles underlying free speech law more generally.

In particular, Brennan emphasized the problems of vagueness and overbreadth he believed had been inherent in the Court's approach since *Roth*. He observed:

> The objectionable quality of vagueness and overbreadth . . . [is] the danger of tolerating, in the area of First Amendment freedoms, the

> existence of a penal statute susceptible of sweeping and improper application. These freedoms are delicate and vulnerable, as well as supremely precious in our society. The threat of sanctions may deter almost as potently as the actual application of sanctions. Because First Amendment freedoms need breathing space to survive, government may regulate in the area only with narrow specificity.

Against this background, Brennan noted that none of the tests that had been proposed for distinguishing obscenity from protected speech were free from ambiguity and that the problem had been exacerbated by the failure of a majority of the justices to coalesce around a single formulation. He contended that the "result has been not merely to make 'bookselling a hazardous occupation.' We have also necessarily paid an intolerable price by chilling the free dissemination of ideas in the area of protected expression." Brennan also pointed out that the lack of majority support for any single test and the concomitant decision to dispose of cases through per curiam opinions had only magnified the uncertainty connected with the process and, because lower courts lacked definitive guidance, had made it inevitable that some protected speech would be temporarily censored pending ultimate adjudication by the Supreme Court itself.[53]

In short, the experience of the Court in the post-*Roth* era had convinced Brennan that "words are evidently inadequate to describe [the line between obscenity and protected speech] in advance with sufficient specificity to preclude an abridgement of the free and precious traffic in ideas." Thus, he argued that the Court should abandon the effort to define a class of sexually explicit material denied all First Amendment protection and should instead invalidate all regulations of such speech unless the government could show that the regulation advanced "some subordinating governmental interest."[54] Brennan found no such interest in restricting the distribution of sexually explicit material to consenting adults. He did, however, once again concede that government could impose restrictions designed to protect unwilling adults from being exposed to obscene material and to limit the distribution of such materials to minors.

With the battle lines between the chief justice and Justice Brennan clearly drawn, *Miller* was put over for reargument in the 1972 term and scheduled for argument on November 7, 1972. In the interim, the grant of certiorari in *Paris Adult Theater No. 1 v. Slaton* added a new element to the controversy. Unlike *Miller,* which involved the sale of sexually explicit books, *Paris Adult Theater* arose from an action to enjoin the showing of an allegedly obscene movie in a commercial theater that barred minors from entering. Thus, there was no chance that the films at issue would be seen by nonconsenting adults and, in theory at least, minors would have no opportunity to enter the theater to view the films, and one could plausibly argue that the principles underlying *Stanley* should govern *Paris Adult Theater.*

Paris Adult Theater was argued on October 17. At the conference that followed, Justice Brennan restated the views expressed in his previous memorandum and immediately received the support of Justices Marshall and Stewart. By contrast, like Chief Justice Burger, Justice White declared in general terms that he would reaffirm *Roth,* whereas Justice Rehnquist suggested he might prefer Justice Harlan's approach. Justice Blackmun, by contrast, initially refused to definitively commit himself. Although pronouncing himself "closer to White and [the] Chief than Brennan," Blackmun also stated he was "intrigued by Brennan's 'privacy' rationale" in *Paris Adult Theater.*[55]

On October 31, before the reargument in *Miller,* Burger—clearly distressed by Brennan's contention that the Court should prevent the states from taking any action against the distribution of sexually explicit material to consenting adults—circulated another long memorandum dealing with the obscenity cases. In purely doctrinal terms, the memorandum recapitulated many of the same themes as the May submission. Burger argued that the "answer [to the problems created by the existing case law] is more flexibility for the triers [of fact], not less." Implicitly referencing Justice Louis Brandeis's characterization of the states as "laboratories of democracy," Burger observed that a number of distinguished modern justices had "perceived the danger to orderly social progress which results from enforcing a single rigid standard on the fifty states, choking off sources of valuable experimentation and flexibility in overcoming our national problems" and argued that the Court should be willing to countenance a variety of state laws regulating sexually explicit material as long as the laws were "clearly focused on materials that portray sexual activities in a fundamentally offensive way, as distinguished from communication of ideas in works having literary, artistic, political, or social value."[56]

However, the tone of the October 31 memorandum was far different from that of Burger's previous memorandum. Unlike the discussion in Burger's earlier missive, the October 31 memorandum brimmed with indignation over what opponents of the distribution of sexually explicit materials viewed as efforts to subvert traditional standards of morality and civility. Beginning with the premise that "for me the First Amendment was made to protect commerce in ideas," Burger declared that the "assumption that restricting obscenity and pornography will throttle the free flow of such ideas will, in the course of time (if it is not already clear) be seen as one of the greatest frauds ever perpetrated" and that "it demeans the high purposes of the First Amendment and debases the currency of the history of the struggle for free expression to equate robust and free debate with filth that, in turn, debases one of the high values of human existence and demeans human beings to the level of animals." Characterizing the commercial distribution of pornography as an "activity deeply at odds with fundamental sexual morality and with human dignity [that] cannot . . . fail to have a destructive impact on the totality of the environment in which we live," Burger derided the opinion of "'experts' who have written on the subject" and argued that, instead of relying on expert opinion, "our conclusions [should] rest on certain assumptions that have guided civilized people for thousands of years."

Burger conceded that these assumptions were not provable, but noting that "they have centuries of history and experience behind them," he asked, "if good plays, good books, good art, the company of decent people as teachers and exemplars are the determinants of character—as we have always been taught—how can we say that the filth and depravity daily foisted on people of all ages will not have a comparable impact?" Against this background, he concluded, "it simply cannot be that the First Amendment should be read to make us an impotent society in terms of total surrender in dealing with this intangible solution of the national atmosphere."[57]

Byron White added a third voice to the conversation on November 16. Like Burger, White did not accept Brennan's position, which he described as a "rather uncomfortable halfway house," and reaffirmed in general terms his support for the original formulation in *Roth.* In addition, White asserted, "it is time that the Court acknowledged and defined the boundaries of the rather narrow category of materials that the States and the Federal Government are permitted to proscribe." Unlike the chief justice, White argued that the definition of obscenity for First Amendment purposes should be governed by a national standard and outlined the details as akin to hard-core pornography. Although firmly rejecting any suggestion that the Court should reflexively affirm any judgment reached by a properly instructed jury, White also asserted that states should not be required to "structure obscenity proceedings . . . in such cases so as to recognize national standards of prurient appeal, candor, or social value." Four days later, Justice Blackmun wrote that he was in general agreement with

White's position, and on November 27 Justice Rehnquist indicated that he took a similar view.[58]

Although White and Blackmun had significant differences with Burger on the proper standards to be applied in obscenity cases, their views were clearly more closely akin to those of the chief justice than to those of Justice Brennan. After some initial hesitation, Justice Powell ultimately chose to take a similar view. When *Miller* and the other obscenity cases were first argued during the 1971 term, the justices who favored Brennan's position had some hope that Powell could be persuaded to join them. Before taking his seat, Powell had reportedly asked the attorneys at Hunton and Williams to prepare a memorandum dealing with the obscenity issue, and that memorandum was believed to have concluded that government regulation of sexually explicit material should be limited to the prevention of unwilling exposure and distribution of such material to minors. Moreover, during a private conversation with Justices Brennan and Stewart, Powell suggested that he might be willing to join an opinion that took that view, and his initial votes on *12,200-ft. Reels* and *Orito* would have been consistent with such an approach.[59]

However, by the end of the 1971 term, Powell had come to a different conclusion. On June 8, Powell had outlined his views in a private memorandum to his clerks. Powell stated that he had initially been attracted to Brennan's approach because it presented a "way of getting [the] Court out of the censorship business." In addition, although Powell believed that the "quality of a society and of a civilization depends, in a significant degree, upon the presence of some moral standards," he also observed that such standards are not generally determined by law and noted that he favored a "minimum of effort by legislatures and courts to regulate or restrict what may be regarded as 'immoral' conduct."[60]

However, at the same time, Powell also observed that "one of the purposes of law is to afford some protection to the sensibilities and to the values of a majority of the people." In particular, he declared:

> [I am] unpersuaded that those who wish to enrich themselves by producing, selling, and pandering some of the filth that is now available should be accorded a privileged sanctuary by this Court. If we adopt [Brennan's approach,] there will be a flood of material deeply offensive to many—if not most—citizens. Willing purchasers will exist by the tens of thousands. The pornography which they purchase will not be locked in the family wall safe, and viewed or read only in private.

> We know perfectly well that it will be widely disseminated and that in fact it will reach the young through all sorts of channels.

In the same memorandum, Powell indicated he was intrigued by Justice Harlan's approach, which would have imposed stringent limitations on the federal government's authority to suppress sexually explicit material but would have allowed the states far greater leeway to regulate access to such material—a position that once again would have been consistent with Powell's initial positions in *12,200-ft. Reels* and *Orito.*[61]

On September 20, Powell described his convictions in greater detail in another memorandum to his clerks. Powell outlined six principles that, in his view, should govern the Court's approach to the obscenity problem. He asserted that (1) the Court must discontinue its role as a national "super censor"; (2) the quality of life in our society has been degraded, and will continue to be degraded, if the Brennan position were adopted; (3) that the First Amendment was never intended to protect pornographic materials; (4) that in any event minors and nonconsenting adults are entitled to be protected; and (5) that he would prefer a system that reverted to the "original concept of federalism," but that (6) individuals should be free in the privacy of their homes to be as erotic as they "stupidly" wish.[62]

As Powell himself noted in another internal memorandum, in the abstract privacy considerations might also have led him closer to the Brennan position in *Paris Adult Theater.* However, at the same time, Powell also asserted that he and a number of the other members of the Court were more focused on the need to unite a majority of the justices around a single position. Thus, on November 14, Powell informed his colleagues that he supported Burger's "general approach."[63]

Against this background, on November 20 Burger announced that he would take on the task of producing an opinion in which at least five justices could join. On December 11, Powell reiterated his support for this project but also pointedly noted that he would "await further circulations before voting." Blackmun expressed similar sentiments on January 9, 1973.[64]

In large measure, Burger's opinions in *Miller* and *Paris Adult Theater* focused on the themes embodied in his two memoranda on the obscenity issue. The *Miller* opinion explicitly rejected the approach of the *Memoirs* plurality, established the primacy of local standards in determining whether material was patently offensive and appealed to prurient interest, and emphasized the role of juries in making the appropriate factual determinations. By contrast, rejecting the claim that *Paris Adult Theater* should be controlled by the same principles that underlay *Stanley v. Georgia,* the chief justice relied heavily on the theme that states could readily conclude that widespread distribution of pornography can be seen as encouraging antisocial behavior by exerting a "corrupt and debasing impact on society" and that the "development of human personality can be debased and distorted by crass commercial exploitation of sex."[65]

However, at the same time, both of Burger's opinions reflected the influence of other justices as well. In a nod to Justice White, the *Miller* opinion explicitly stated that under the standards adopted by the majority, "no one will be subject to prosecution for the sale or exposure of obscene materials unless these materials depict or describe patently offensive 'hard-core' sexual conduct specifically defined by the regulating state law, as written or construed" and that appellate courts retained the authority to review jury determinations of obscenity de novo. Presumably because he thought this language sufficiently addressed his concerns, White chose not only to join Burger's opinion but also not to publish a concurring opinion he had prepared.[66]

The impact of the views of Justices Powell and Blackmun also emerged clearly in the final forms of the majority opinions in *Miller* and *Paris Adult Theater.* In particular, after Burger sought to change the requirement that the "dominant theme of the work, *taken as a whole,* appeals to the prurient interest" to "the dominant theme of the work, *taken in its setting,* appeals to the prurient interest," Powell and Blackmun—fearing that the new formulation would broaden the potential definition of obscenity for First Amendment purposes—successfully urged Burger to restore the specific language from *Roth.* Similarly, at Powell's behest, the *Paris Adult Theater* opinion specifically endorsed the use of procedures that allowed movie theaters to obtain a judicial resolution of the obscenity question before risking potential criminal liability by actually exhibiting a sexually explicit film.[67]

Ironically, Justice Brennan also had a strong influence on the structure of the majority opinions in *Miller* and *Paris Adult Theater.* Much of the language in *Paris Adult Theater* was drawn almost verbatim from Burger's October 31 memorandum, which, as already noted, was produced in direct response to Brennan's presentation of his views. Moreover, a significant portion of the *Miller* opinion was added late in the process to respond to Brennan's assessment of the institutional costs associated with the regime established by *Roth* and its progeny.

In addition to restating the arguments he had made in his detailed memorandum on the obscenity issue, Brennan's dissent in *Paris Adult*

Theater asserted that "quite apart from the number of cases involved and the need to make a fresh constitutional determination in each case, we are tied to the absurd business of perusing and viewing the miserable stuff that pours into the Court. . . . While the material may have varying degrees of social importance, it is hardly a source of edification to the members of this Court who are compelled to view it before passing on its obscenity."[68] In *Miller*, Burger shot back:

> No amount of "fatigue" should lead us to adopt a convenient "institutional" rationale—an absolutist, "anything goes" view of the First Amendment—because it will lighten our burdens. "Such an abnegation of judicial supervision in this field would be inconsistent with our duty to uphold the constitutional guarantees." Nor should we remedy "tension between state and federal courts" by arbitrarily depriving the States of a power reserved to them under the Constitution, a power which they have enjoyed and exercised continuously from before the adoption of the First Amendment to this day.[69]

Powell in particular was less than pleased by the tenor of Burger's response. Nonetheless, on June 16, Powell notified Burger that he was still willing to join the opinion. Two days later, Blackmun also signaled his concurrence. With White and Rehnquist already firmly committed, Burger's opinions in *Miller* and *Paris Adult Theater* became the official position of the Court on the relationship between sexually explicit material and the First Amendment.[70]

Of all the cases decided during the 1972 term, the immediate furor created by *Miller* and *Paris Adult Theater* was matched only by the reaction to the abortion decisions. Not surprisingly, representatives of the groups that had consistently pressed for stronger regulations of sexually explicit material applauded the Court's decisions. Thus, for example, Governor Ronald Reagan of California described the decisions as "long overdue," and the city prosecutor of Alexandria, Virginia, declared, "I think [the decisions have] been long needed [and are] going to assist prosecutors everywhere."[71]

By contrast, critics of the Court at times characterized the obscenity rulings in apocalyptic terms. Thus, a vice president of Paramount Pictures asserted that the "decision indicates we are headed straight for the Middle Ages," the head of Random House described the Court's actions as a "call to arms for every crazy vigilante group in the country," and a prominent Hollywood director bemoaned a "terrible blow against the basic constitutional rights of every individual." The same groups were also at times openly contemptuous of those who took the view that obscenity should define the regulation of sexually explicit material. For example, one editor of a so-called underground newspaper averred that "all the yahoo D.A.s have been waiting for a chance to jump in [against sexually explicit material.]"[72]

However, the following term, in *Jenkins v. Georgia*, the Court demonstrated that it was unwilling to give a completely free hand to the "yahoos." In *Jenkins*, a theater owner had been convicted for distributing obscene material under the same Georgia statute that underlay *Paris Adult Theater*. However, unlike the movies at issue in *Paris Adult Theater*, characterized by Chief Justice Burger as "'hard-core pornography' leaving 'little to the imagination,'" the criminal prosecution in *Jenkins* was based on the movie *Carnal Knowledge*—a mainstream film widely praised by critics and nominated for a number of academy awards. Moreover, the *Jenkins* Court observed that although the "subject matter of the [film] is, in a broader sense, sex, and there are scenes in which sexual conduct including 'ultimate sexual acts' is to be understood to be taking place, the camera does not focus on the bodies of the actors at such times. There is no exhibition whatever of the actors' genitals, lewd or otherwise, during these scenes."[73]

Speaking for the members of the *Miller* majority, Justice Rehnquist rejected the claim that the Court was required to accept the verdict of the jury on the obscenity issue because it was supported by "some evidence." Instead, he relied on "our own viewing of the film" to conclude that "'Carnal Knowledge' could not be found under the *Miller* standards to depict sexual conduct in a patently offensive way." Concurring in the result, both Justice Douglas and Justice Brennan reiterated the views they had expressed in *Miller* and *Paris Adult Theater*. Further, Brennan asserted that *Jenkins* demonstrated that the approach endorsed by the majority in *Miller* "does not extricate us from the mire of case-by-case determinations of obscenity," thereby suggesting that the Court would continue to be bedeviled by large numbers of cases involving the claim that individual books or movies had been improperly labeled obscene.[74]

In fact, *Jenkins* proved to be something of an anomaly. To be sure, the Court continued to be involved in the dispute over the limits of government power to regulate sexually explicit expression on an irregular basis for the remainder of Burger's tenure as chief justice. However, after 1974, the justices avoided the institutional problems associated with the pre-*Miller* era by the simple expedient of denying certiorari in most of the obscenity cases that came to them from the lower courts—an idea suggested by Justice

Rehnquist in the conference on *Miller*. From the perspective of the members of the *Miller* majority, the advantages of this approach were obvious. Conversely, with five justices firmly committed to the principles outlined in Burger's opinions, the dissenters saw no reason to insist on relitigating the underlying issues.[75] Thus, rather than being perceived to be at the center of the controversy, in the public mind the Court became very much a junior partner in resolving disputes over the proper role of government in the control of "indecent" expression.

The import of the decisions in *Miller* and *Paris Adult Theater* can be viewed from a number of different perspectives. On one level, the obscenity cases were by any standard clearly among the major victories won by conservatives during the 1972 term. Not only did progressives fail to achieve their objective of obtaining additional constitutional protection for sexually explicit material, but the Court also explicitly loosened existing First Amendment constraints on state regulation.

In addition, the outcome of the struggle over obscenity also illustrates the complexity of the forces that generated the pattern of the decisions of the 1972 term more generally. The conservatives prevailed in *Miller* and *Paris Adult Theater* only because Chief Justice Burger was able to craft an opinion that not only allowed greater government regulation of sexually explicit material but also addressed the concerns of three of the four centrist justices—Justice White and, to a lesser extent, Justices Blackmun and Powell. The idiosyncratic views of the centrist justices would determine the direction of the Court's jurisprudence on a variety of other issues as well.

Chapter Five

Criminal Procedure

The 1972 term did not bring any major breakthroughs on the criminal procedure front. Certainly, none of the Court's holdings in this area produced the kind of public reaction generated by the decision in *Furman v. Georgia*. Nonetheless, criminal procedure cases continued to constitute a significant portion of the Court's docket, and the resolution of those cases was determined by much the same dynamic that produced the pattern of decisions on a variety of other issues as well.

The deliberations that ultimately produced the decision in *Almeida-Sanchez v. United States* reflected the complexity of this dynamic.[1] *Almeida-Sanchez* was a challenge to the constitutionality of the warrantless search of an automobile conducted by agents of the US Border Patrol on a state highway in California twenty-six miles north of the border with Mexico. The search had been conducted under the authority of a federal statute that generally authorized searches of automobiles "within a reasonable distance from any external boundary of the United States," together with administrative regulations that defined "a reasonable distance" as 100 miles. Although the search had in fact uncovered a large quantity of illegally imported marijuana, the government conceded that at the time of the search, the agents had had no probable cause to believe that the specific car that had been searched had been engaged in any sort of illegal activity.

In arguing that the trial court had acted properly in admitting the seized marijuana into evidence, the government began with the premise that the resolution of Fourth Amendment issues ultimately turned on the question of whether the search had been "reasonable" under the circumstances. Relying on decisions that had rejected constitutional challenges to areawide warrantless searches related to the administrative enforcement of building codes,[2] firearms regulations, and the regulation of the traffic in alcoholic beverages, the government argued that searches of vehicles near the border were constitutionally permissible as an adjunct to the federal government's plenary authority to prevent the entrance of undocumented aliens.

The conference following the oral argument in *Almeida-Sanchez* found the justices deeply divided over the constitutionality of the search. Justices William O. Douglas, William Brennan, Potter Stewart, and Thurgood Marshall argued that the marijuana should have been excluded from evidence at the trial. Whereas Brennan contended that the statute authorizing the search was unconstitutional on its face, Stewart objected only to the scope of the searches authorized by the regulation. By contrast, although the remaining five justices conceded that some searches authorized by the statute and regulation might violate constitutional norms, they focused only on the specific facts of the case before the Court, concluding that the search in *Almeida-Sanchez* was reasonable and thus did not run afoul of the Fourth Amendment.[3] Against this background, Byron White was assigned the responsibility of writing the majority opinion, and Stewart took on the task of preparing the primary dissent.

Both White and Stewart circulated drafts in early May. Analogizing *Almeida-Sanchez* to the administrative search cases, White argued that random searches near the border were reasonable measures in view of the practical difficulties involved in patrolling the border itself, observing that the "statute represents the considered judgment of Congress that proper enforcement of the immigration laws requires random searches of vehicles without warrant or probable cause within a reasonable distance of the international borders of the country." Stewart, by contrast, initially argued that warrantless searches of automobiles were constitutional only if the searches were the "functional equivalent" of searches at the border itself.[4]

However, in the interim, Lewis Powell had been having second thoughts. Powell was sympathetic to the difficulties the federal government faced in seeking to deal with a constant threat of illegal immigration along a 2,000-mile border and conceded that it would be impossible to maintain the kind of patrols that would prevent undocumented aliens from physically crossing the border. However, at the same time, he was concerned about the "necessity, in our free society, of safeguarding persons against searches and seizures proscribed by the Fourth Amendment."

By May 23, Powell had come to the conclusion that the solution was to require the border patrol to obtain warrants to conduct roving patrols in particular areas near the border. On June 11, he circulated a draft opinion that argued that the "determination of whether a warrant should be issued for an area . . . presents the type of delicate constitutional judgment that ought to be resolved by the Judiciary rather than the Executive." Because no such warrant had been obtained in *Almeida-Sanchez* itself, Powell changed his initial vote and created a majority for the conclusion that the search in the case had run afoul of the Fourth Amendment.[5]

However, Powell's initial draft indicated that he was concurring only in the result. Moreover, the tone of his concurrence differed markedly from that of Stewart's draft. Unlike Stewart, Powell did not condemn roving area searches as unreasonable per se. Instead he explicitly asserted that "under appropriate limiting circumstances, there may exist a constitutionally adequate equivalent of probable cause to conduct roving vehicular searches in border areas."[6]

At this point, White took a different tack. On June 11, he suggested that the remaining members of the original majority might concur in Powell's opinion and also join a draft concurrence that White circulated on the same day. Although acquiescing in the requirement of an area warrant, the draft questioned the effectiveness of such a device in preventing potential abuses of power. However, the following day, when William Rehnquist reaffirmed his allegiance to White's original majority opinion, it became clear that the original majority was irrevocably divided.[7] Conversely, after Stewart removed some of the stronger language from his opinion, Powell agreed to join the opinion rather than simply concurring in the result, thereby creating a majority establishing the proposition that warrantless, areawide searches of automobiles not conducted near the border itself violated the Fourth Amendment.

However, despite his willingness to join Stewart's revised opinion in *Almeida-Sanchez*, Powell felt compelled to write separately as well. Powell's concurring opinion emphasized his conviction that the Fourth Amendment did not bar the border patrol from obtaining search warrants that would allow the use of roving searches in specified areas near the border. Moreover, the opinions ultimately filed made it clear that he had the support of a majority of the Court on this point. To be sure, Stewart's opinion expressly refused to address Powell's argument, instead noting only that the members of the majority were split on the issue. By contrast, in addition to Powell himself, the four dissenters explicitly endorsed the position that immigration-related searches conducted under the aegis of areawide warrants could be constitutional, with Justice White observing, "I would expect that such warrants would be readily issued."[8] In short, although a victory for the progressives in purely formal terms, on balance *Almeida-Sanchez* was something of a split decision.

More often, the ideological orientation of the Court's criminal procedure decisions was less equivocal. For example, in *United States v. Ash*, White and the Nixon appointees continued their campaign to limit the scope of the *Wade/Gilbert* exclusionary rule.[9] *Ash* did not involve a challenge to the admissibility of an identification made at a live lineup. Instead, the case arose from the identification of the defendant from a set of photographs presented to witnesses after the defendant had been indicted and without the presence of the defendant's attorney. Speaking for himself and Justices Douglas and Marshall, Justice Brennan argued that identifications from photo arrays were fraught with the same potential problems as those made in live lineups and that therefore such identifications should not be admissible unless the defendant's attorney was present at the time the identification was made.[10] However, in what Brennan condemned as an "evisceration" of the *Wade/Gilbert* rule,[11] the remainder of the justices disagreed, concluding that the Constitution did not require the presence of the defense attorney during photo arrays.

Speaking for the members of the *Kirby* majority, Harry Blackmun distinguished *Ash* from *Wade* and *Gilbert* on two grounds. First, observing that the Sixth Amendment was designed to ensure criminal defendants would have the assistance necessary to navigate the vagaries of the legal system, he argued that because defendants were not present while photo arrays were being conducted, they could have had no need to consult a person with specialized knowledge at that stage of the process. In addition, Blackmun noted that defense attorneys would have full access to the photos used in the array and would therefore be in a position to effectively challenge the accuracy of the identification at trial. Concurring only in the result, Stewart took a related tack, contending that a "photographic identification is quite different from a lineup, for there are substantially fewer possibilities of impermissible suggestion when photographs are used, and those unfair influences can be readily reconstructed at trial."[12]

The continued erosion of the scope of the *Wade/Gilbert* rule was without question a significant development in the evolution of the law of criminal procedure. However, *Schneckloth v. Bustamonte* was almost certainly the most important criminal procedure decision of the 1972 term.[13] In that case, the justices would address not only the substance of constitutional rules on criminal procedure but also important procedural issues dealing with the circumstances under which such issues could be raised in federal court.

The Warren Court had interpreted the federal habeas corpus statute in a manner that greatly expanded the circumstances in which criminal defendants could raise constitutional challenges to their convictions. For example, in the 1963 decision in *Fay v. Noia,* the Court held that in a habeas corpus proceeding, a person convicted in state court could raise an objection that would have been deemed waived by a procedural default under state law.[14] Similarly, in 1969, in *Kaufman v. United States,* the majority concluded that a person convicted of a crime in federal court could launch a collateral attack on his conviction based on the Fourth Amendment exclusionary rule, notwithstanding the fact that he or she had received a full and fair hearing on the exclusionary rule claim during the initial trial.[15]

Schneckloth itself was a federal habeas corpus proceeding seeking the release of a defendant who had been convicted in state court of possessing a check with intent to defraud. The sequence of events that gave rise to the Supreme Court's consideration of the case began with a warrantless search of a car conducted in the aftermath of what was apparently a routine traffic stop. After the driver of the car had been unable to give the police a driver's license when requested to do so, Joseph Alcala—one of the passengers in the car—produced a license and told the police the car belonged to his brother. Without either explicitly or implicitly threatening to arrest any of the people in the car, the police then asked Alcala if they could search the car. He replied, "Sure, go ahead" and also voluntarily opened the trunk for them. During the course of the search, the police discovered three checks recently stolen from a car wash, and these checks were admitted as evidence at trial after the trial court had rejected the contention that the search had violated the Fourth Amendment. After the defendant was convicted and the conviction was affirmed in the state court, the defendant renewed his Fourth Amendment objection in the federal habeas corpus action.

From a substantive perspective, *Schneckloth* raised the question of the efficacy of Alcala's consent to the search of the car. The US Court of Appeals for the Ninth Circuit had held that consent could only be "voluntary" for Fourth Amendment purposes if the government could demonstrate that the person giving the consent had understood that it could be "freely and effectively withheld." By a vote of six to three, the Supreme Court reversed this judgment.

Justices Douglas, Brennan, and Marshall argued that the judgment should be affirmed. Marshall argued that *Schneckloth* was controlled by the principles established by the Warren Court in *Bumper v. North Carolina,* in which the majority had held that "when a prosecutor seeks to rely upon consent to justify the lawfulness of a search, he has the burden of proving that the consent was, in fact, freely and voluntarily given," whereas Brennan averred that "it wholly escapes me how our citizens can meaningfully be said to have waived something as precious as a constitutional guarantee without ever being aware of its existence." However, speaking through Justice Stewart, a majority of the justices disagreed, concluding instead that "voluntariness is a question of fact to be determined from all the circumstances" and that the state was required to demonstrate only that "consent was in fact, voluntarily given, and not the result of duress or coercion, express or implied."[16]

Although the majority opinion in *Schneckloth* was obviously a defeat for those who sought to use the Constitution to expand the rights of criminal defendants, in many respects the argument of Justice Powell's concurring opinion, joined by Chief Justice Warren Burger and Justice William Rehnquist, would ultimately prove even more significant. Rather than discussing the substantive issue of voluntariness, Powell's opinion argued that *Kaufman v. United States* should be overruled and that federal habeas corpus proceedings should in general not be available as vehicles to relitigate Fourth Amendment challenges to state criminal convictions. Powell observed that at common law, after a person had been convicted of a crime, he or she could only obtain relief through a writ of habeas corpus if he or she could show that the original trial court had lacked jurisdiction over the case. Although conceding that this rule was appropriately relaxed in cases in which a legal error called into question the actual innocence of the petitioner, Powell noted that guilt or innocence was rarely at issue in Fourth Amendment claims. He asserted that in such cases, federal courts should only vacate state criminal convictions if it could be shown that the petitioner had not had a full and fair opportunity to raise the issue and have it litigated in state court.[17]

Because of the majority's disposition of the merits of the Fourth Amendment claim, both Justice Stewart and Justice Blackmun concluded that it was unnecessary to reconsider *Kaufman* in *Schneckloth*.[18] However, Blackmun also averred that he agreed with "nearly all" of what Powell said in his opinion, and Stewart had dissented in *Kaufman* itself. Thus, in 1976 it came as no surprise when both joined Powell's majority opinion in *Stone v. Powell*, which formally overruled *Kaufman*.[19]

Cases such as *Schneckloth* and *Stone* demonstrate that, in at least some cases, the Nixon appointees were willing to vote to explicitly overrule Warren Court decisions they found particularly indefensible. More often, however, the Nixon appointees sought to limit the expansion of principles that had been established by prior case law. The Court's treatment of the school desegregation cases illustrate this point.

Chapter Six

School Desegregation

Of all the politically charged issues that confronted the Court during the 1972 term, none aroused more passion than the ongoing dispute over school desegregation. The Supreme Court had been at the epicenter of the conflict since the Warren Court's signature 1954 decision in *Brown v. Board of Education* (*Brown I*), in which the Court unanimously held that public schools could not be formally segregated on the basis of race.[1] However, the context of the debate changed significantly over time. Prior to the appointments of Justices Lewis Powell and William Rehnquist, almost all of the Court's decisions had dealt with the situation in Southern schools. By contrast, during the 1972 term, the justices began to grapple seriously with the constitutional questions implicated by racial imbalance in Northern, urban school districts. By that time, most Americans at least publicly accepted the basic principle that the Constitution prohibited the government from intentionally segregating schools by law. However, the question of what remedies should be ordered in school desegregation litigation remained highly controversial.

The Burger Court's encounters with the remedial issue took place against the background of a long struggle to implement the promise of *Brown I* in the states that had previously maintained schools that were segregated by law. The year after *Brown I* was decided, the Court first confronted the remedial issue in *Brown II*.[2] In *Brown II*, the plaintiffs argued that the justices should require "desegregation as quickly as prerequisite administrative and mechanical procedures can be completed." However, the Court rejected this formulation, instead instructing district courts to give some weight to practical considerations and to enter "orders and decrees . . . as are necessary and proper [to create desegregated schools] with all deliberate speed."[3]

What followed was a period marked by a great deal of deliberation and very little speed.[4] The governments of most Southern states deployed a variety of formal and informal strategies designed to nullify or minimize the impact of *Brown I* on the actual racial composition of schools, and the federal judges in the South in the 1950s often showed little inclination to press hard for integration. Moreover, for several years, the Supreme Court itself did very little to speed the progress of desegregation. To be sure, in the early 1960s the Court did show considerable sympathy for the campaign against racial segregation in a number of other contexts. However, with the notable exception of the 1957 decision in *Cooper v. Aaron*, in which the Court condemned the open defiance by the state government of Arkansas in the strongest possible terms, between 1955 and 1964 the justices studiously avoided every opportunity to significantly amplify the principles underlying *Brown I* and *Brown II*.[5]

However, in 1964 the justices faced a show of defiance from Prince Edward County, Virginia, that they felt that they could not ignore. A lawsuit challenging the segregation of the Prince Edward County schools had been one of the group of cases decided together with *Brown I* itself. However, in the wake of the *Brown* decisions, the government of the state of Virginia as a whole strongly resisted all efforts to desegregate any of its public schools. Initially, the Virginia legislature passed a statute closing all public schools attended by whites and African Americans together, cutting off all state funding for such schools, providing tuition grants for students to attend newly created private schools, and allowing teachers in these private schools to participate in the retirement system for state employees. After the Virginia courts found that this statute violated the state constitution, in January 1959 the state legislature enacted a new tuition grant program and repealed the state compulsory school attendance law, instead making regulation of school attendance a matter of local option.[6]

The government of Prince Edward County was, if anything, even more militant than the state government as a whole in its opposition to school desegregation.[7] For example, in 1956, the county board of supervisors declared that it would never operate an integrated school system, and subsequent judicial decisions did nothing to weaken the resolve of the county government in this regard. In June 1959, after the US Court of Appeals for the Fourth Circuit decreed that Prince Edward County should take "immediate steps" to desegregate its schools, the board of supervisors instead refused to levy any school taxes, and the public schools did not reopen in the fall of 1959. Prince Edward County thus became the only county in Virginia to close its public schools to avoid segregation. In addition, the county government gave additional financial support for students who attended private schools and provided tax relief for such schools.

In response, finding that the "end result of every action taken by [the board of supervisors] was designed to preserve separation of the races in the schools of Prince Edward County," the local federal district court enjoined the county from paying tuition grants or giving tax credits as long as its public schools remained closed. Soon thereafter, the same court ordered that the county public schools reopen. However, on appeal the Fourth Circuit reversed the judgment of the district court, concluding that the court should have abstained from reaching the merits until the Virginia state courts had passed on the legality of the tuition grant program under state law.

After granting certiorari, in *Griffin v. County School Board of Prince Edward County*, the Supreme Court reinstated the judgment of the district court. Speaking for the Court, Justice Hugo Black first determined that abstention was not appropriate. Black then declared that "Prince Edward's public schools were closed and private schools operated in their place with state and county assistance, for one reason, and one reason only: to ensure, through measures taken by the county and the State, that white and colored children in Prince Edward County would not, under any circumstances, go to the same school." The justices unanimously concluded that "whatever nonracial grounds might support a State's allowing a county to abandon public schools, the object must be a constitutional one, and grounds of race and opposition to desegregation do not qualify as constitutional." In addition, the Court averred that the "time for mere 'deliberate speed' has run out, and that phrase can no longer justify denying [the African American children of] Prince Edward County . . . their constitutional rights to an education equal to that afforded by the public schools in the other parts of Virginia."[8]

Although in many respects the situation in Prince Edward County was unique, the language of the majority opinion suggested that the justices were becoming increasingly impatient with Southern resistance to the implementation of the principles underlying *Brown*. Their frustration was entirely understandable. Despite the Court's unequivocal condemnation of school segregation in *Brown*, at the time *Griffin* was decided a decade later, only 2.3 percent of the African American students in the South attended school with whites.[9] However, beginning in the mid-1960s, nonjudicial forces would dramatically change this reality.

By 1964, pressure against the system of racial apartheid of which school segregation was an important part was building from a variety of different quarters. In the early 1960s, African Americans and their allies increasingly demonstrated in large numbers against segregation, and Northern television viewers were transfixed by the images of the sometimes violent response of state government authorities to these demonstrations. Supporters of the political movement against segregation were further galvanized by the March on Washington, a demonstration that attracted 250,000 people to the grounds of the Lincoln Memorial on August 28, 1963, and culminated in Martin Luther King, Jr.'s famous "I Have a Dream" speech.

Against this background, the administration of President John F. Kennedy began to take an increasingly active role in promoting the antisegregation movement. Lyndon Johnson, who succeeded to the presidency after Kennedy was assassinated in November 1963, moved even more aggressively against racial segregation. Johnson led the successful political campaign that culminated when he signed the Civil Rights Act of 1964 into law on July 2, 1964, less than two months after *Griffin* had been decided.

The passage of the Civil Rights Act proved to be a turning point in the battle over school desegregation. Title VI of the statute prohibits racial discrimination in programs receiving federal funds, and almost immediately after the statute was adopted, the US Justice Department began using this provision to pressure Southern governments to desegregate their schools. The efforts of the Justice Department soon bore fruit. By 1968, 32 percent of African American students in the Southern states were attending school with whites.[10]

At this point the justices decided to actively reenter the struggle over school desegregation in the South. Their vehicle was the 1968 decision in *Green v. County School Board of New Kent County*.[11] In the decade following the decisions in *Brown I* and *Brown II*, New Kent County, a small rural county in Virginia, had continued to operate one school that provided elementary and secondary education for all white students and a different school that provided the analogous services for all African American students. However, in 1965, in response to a newly filed lawsuit and the threat of losing federal funding, the school district adopted a freedom-of-choice plan that essentially allowed students in the district to choose to attend either of the two schools. By 1968, 15 percent of the county's African American students had chosen to attend the formerly all-white school, but no white students had chosen to attend the formerly all African American school. Despite these results, the Department of Health, Education, and Welfare (HEW), the agency responsible for administering the relevant portions of the Civil Rights Act, approved the plan.

However, the Supreme Court unanimously held that the freedom-of-choice plan was not an adequate remedy for past segregation. Justice William Brennan's opinion for the Court clearly reflected the impact Southern intransigence had had on the thinking of the justices. Beginning with the premise that, under *Brown*, "school boards such as [that of New Kent County were] clearly charged with the affirmative duty to take whatever steps might be necessary to convert to a unitary system in which racial discrimination would be eliminated root and branch," Brennan noted the refusal of the New Kent County school board to take any steps toward disestablishment of its dual school in the years immediately following the decision in *Brown*. Observing that "this deliberate perpetuation of the unconstitutional dual system can only have compounded the harm of such a system," Brennan averred that "the time for mere 'deliberate speed' has run out." He declared, "The burden on a school board today is to come forward with a plan that promises realistically to work, and promises realistically to work *now*."[12]

Brennan concluded that, measured against this standard, the New Kent County Board of Education had failed to meet its constitutional obligations. He asserted:

> The New Kent School Board's "freedom of choice" plan cannot be accepted as a sufficient step to "effectuate a transition" to a unitary system. . . . The school system remains a dual system. Rather than further the dismantling of the dual system, the plan has operated simply to burden children and their parents with a responsibility which Brown II placed squarely on the School Board. The Board must be required to formulate a new plan and, in light of other courses which appear open to the Board, such as zoning, fashion steps which promise realistically to convert promptly to a system without a "white" school and a "Negro" school, but just schools.[13]

The difference in tone between *Brown II* and *Green* could hardly have been more stark. The dramatic change in the Court's attitude no doubt reflected the influence of a number of different factors. First, between 1955 and 1968, public opinion outside the South had hardened against segregation, which the educated elite of the remainder of the country had come to view as an unalloyed evil. Moreover, the makeup of the Court itself had changed significantly; the seats that had been occupied in 1955 by Felix Frankfurter, Stanley Reed, and Tom Clark were filled in 1968 by Abe Fortas, Byron White, and Thurgood Marshall, respectively, all of whom were far more committed to an aggressive judicial role than their predecessors. Finally, the justices were almost certainly angered by the concerted efforts of Southern governments to evade the clear import of *Brown*.

But in any event, in 1968, the full significance of the Court's newfound willingness to aggressively confront state-imposed school segregation was not yet clear. In many respects, the issues presented by *Green* were relatively simple. New Kent County was a small, rural school district without clearly demarcated white and African American residential areas. Thus, racial segregation in the school system could only be maintained by transporting both white and African American students considerable distances in order to attend the school that served their respective races. Conversely, if school district officials had not considered race in determining school attendance, they would almost certainly have adopted standard geographically based attendance zones, which in turn would have led to the creation of racially mixed schools. Thus, the judgment in *Green* did nothing more than place county students in the position they would have been in if no constitutional violation had ever occurred.

By contrast, the situation in more populous school districts presented issues of greater complexity. In such districts, students at all levels were of necessity distributed among a substantial number of schools. Moreover, particularly in urban areas, the geographical distribution of students was a by-product of housing patterns that themselves reflected profound and deeply rooted racial segregation. As a result, a simple requirement that the local school district assign students on a geographical basis would almost inevitably create a regime under which racial groups would be distributed unevenly among district schools.

Moreover, this phenomenon was not limited to school systems previously segregated by law. These imbalances were no less prevalent in Northern, urban districts where segregation was prohibited by law. In either case, efforts to change the racial balance of the schools frequently required the reassignment of students away from the schools closest to their homes. Often, such reassignment required students to be transported to more distant schools on school buses.

Busing had been commonly used for a variety of purposes before the decisions of the Supreme Court had elevated the national profile of the dispute over segregated schools. Nonetheless, the idea of transporting students for the purpose of achieving racial balance was controversial even among those who professed allegiance to the principles established in *Brown*. Although progressives typically argued that in many cases busing would be the only device available to effectively combat segregation, a wide swath of the public saw the issue quite differently and aggressively supported the idea of "neighborhood schools." Thus, by 1969, in the words of one columnist, "the school bus [has] come to represent for thousands of people the stupid, stubborn, clumsy, inept attempt by a heavy-handed [government] to force school integration, a problem they believe only time can solve."[14]

Not surprisingly, the debate over school busing also became an issue in national politics. As early as 1964, the Republican platform condemned the "abandonment of neighborhood schools, for reasons of race," and in 1968 the House of Representatives attempted to attach an amendment to the appropriations bill for HEW that would have banned compulsory busing of students.[15] Although the amendment was ultimately removed from the bill, the initial House vote demonstrated the potency of busing as a political issue.

The issue of school busing also played an important role in Richard Nixon's attempt to navigate the complex political crosscurrents generated by the debate over school desegregation. During his 1968 campaign for the presidency, Nixon sought to appeal to white, Southern voters and in particular to convince such voters to support him rather than George Wallace, the openly segregationist ex-governor of Alabama, who was running as a third-party candidate. However, at the same time, Nixon also needed to avoid alienating Northern voters who believed that (at least in theory) state-imposed racial segregation was fundamentally immoral.

Nixon sought to resolve this dilemma by steering a middle course. Although emphatically declaring his allegiance to the principles established in *Brown*, Nixon also attacked the use of school busing to achieve racial balance and criticized HEW for threatening to withhold federal funds from districts that did not take adequate measures to dismantle systems of state-imposed segregation. However, in sharp contrast to Nixon's outspoken attacks on judicial decisions that expanded the rights of criminal defendants, he generally did not single out the federal courts for criticism for their performance in desegregation cases. Indeed, at one point Nixon even seemed to implicitly endorse the decision in *Green*, stating that he could not condone the use of freedom-of-choice plans used as camouflage for continued segregation.[16]

After his victory in the 1968 election, Nixon continued to refine his public posture on school desegregation. On March 24, 1970, he issued a policy statement clearly drafted with an eye toward positioning himself for the 1972 election. On one hand, the statement explicitly endorsed the view that segregation "must be eliminated 'root and branch'—and it must be eliminated now." On the other hand, Nixon emphatically reaffirmed his opposition to busing for purposes of achieving racial balance and emphasized the distinction between de jure segregation—segregation mandated by law—and de facto segregation—segregation that resulted from formally private decisions that had created racially segregated housing patterns. Nixon asserted that if the racial composition of the schools in a system reflected both de jure and de facto segregation, the federal government could move against the former but not the latter.[17]

Nixon's policy statement drew an angry response from civil rights activists. For example, Jack Greenberg, the leader of the NAACP Legal Defense Fund (LDF), declared that the president was "pay[ing] lip service to integrated schools and an integrated society while acquiescing in the continuation of segregation." A spokesperson for the NAACP itself was even blunter, describing Nixon's message as a "clear invitation" to segregationists "to continue their resistance, to multiply their evasions, and to turn the clock back."[18]

The heated political debate over busing provided the backdrop for the Court's 1971 decision in *Swann v. Charlotte-Mecklenburg Board of Education*.[19] In many ways, the structure of the Charlotte-Mecklenburg school district could not have been more different from the rural Virginia district that had been the subject of the *Green* litigation. Formed in 1960 by the merger between the public schools of the city of Charlotte, North Carolina, and those of the adjacent suburbs of Mecklenburg County, the district spanned 550 square miles and in 1969 operated 107 schools serving more than 84,000 students, approximately 29 percent of whom were African American. Moreover, although the schools in North Carolina had been segregated by law prior to 1954, neither the state government in North Carolina nor the local authorities in Charlotte and Mecklenburg County had openly defied the decision in *Brown*.

Nonetheless, in real terms, progress toward integrating the Charlotte-Mecklenburg schools was for the first decade after *Brown* hardly more significant than that of rural Virginia. By 1965, only 2 percent of the African American students in the district were attending schools with white students, and more than 80 percent of those attended a single school with seven white students. In that year, with the avowed purpose of increasing integration, the school board adopted a plan based primarily on geographical considerations with the proviso that all students would be free to transfer to any school in the system as long as that school was not overcrowded. *Swann* was filed as a challenge to this proposal, with the plaintiffs arguing that the plan did not sufficiently integrate the schools. However, District Judge J. Braxton Craven, Jr., rejected this argument, and Craven's judgment was affirmed by the Fourth Circuit and not appealed to the Supreme Court at the time.

The 1965 plan created considerably more racial integration in the Charlotte-Mecklenburg school system. Nonetheless, because the African American population was concentrated in racially segregated areas within the city of Charlotte, the use of geographical attendance zones inevitably left many students racially isolated in the schools as well. Thus, as late as 1969, 14,000 of the 24,000 African American students in the system continued to attend schools that were at least 99 percent African American.

In 1965, the plaintiffs did not appeal the Fourth Circuit decision to the Supreme Court because they feared that the Court would uphold the plan and create an unfavorable precedent for future desegregation litigation. However, after *Green* changed the jurisprudential landscape, the *Swann* plaintiffs moved for further relief that would create more racial balance in the Charlotte-Mecklenburg schools. Judge James B. McMillan, who had been assigned to *Swann* after Judge Craven had been appointed to the court of appeals, sided with the plaintiffs. On December 1, 1969, he declared that "the court will start with the thought . . . that efforts should be made to reach a 71–29 ratio in the various schools so that there will be no basis for contending that one school is racially different from the others" and that "pupils of all grades should be assigned in such a way that as nearly as practicable the various schools at various grade levels have about the same proportion of black and white students."

Against this background, Judge McMillan ordered widespread transportation of students for the purpose of changing the racial composition of the schools. However, in deference to the realities of the population distribution in the Charlotte-Mecklenburg district, both McMillan and the defendant's expert he appointed to produce a desegregation plan showed a willingness to accept substantial deviations from the racial makeup of the district as a whole in individual schools. Thus, for example, under the final order of the district court, the elementary schools in the district were to have student bodies including between 9 percent and 38 percent African Americans, with the vast majority having student bodies that ranged from 20 percent to 38 percent African American. However, a fragmented

US Court of Appeals for the Fourth Circuit took a different view, rejecting Judge McMillan's plan for the elementary schools but ordering a remand that required the school board to take all "reasonable" efforts to integrate the schools.[20] Recognizing that the issues presented by *Swann* had nationwide implications, the justices of the Supreme Court voted to grant a petition for certiorari to review the Fourth Circuit's judgment.

Although no formal tally was taken at the conference that followed the oral argument in *Swann*, the tenor of the discussions clearly revealed that the justices were deeply divided over the propriety of the sweeping order issued by Judge McMillan.[21] Justices William O. Douglas, William Brennan, John Marshall Harlan, and Thurgood Marshall expressed their strong support for McMillan's approach, and Justices Potter Stewart and Byron White also indicated that they generally supported this approach, albeit with some reservations. By contrast, Chief Justice Burger objected to what he saw as McMillan's emphasis on racial balance, and Justice Black (who had concurred only reluctantly in *Green*) vehemently objected to judicially imposed busing orders. Although not expressing firm opposition to the McMillan plan, Justice Harry Blackmun also initially seemed ambivalent.

Despite his clear differences with a majority of the justices, Burger took advantage of the lack of a formal vote to assign to himself the task of writing a majority opinion. The first draft he circulated was almost unremittingly hostile to the order of the district court, excoriating Judge McMillan for what Burger saw as attempting to create "racial balance" in each of the schools in the Charlotte-Mecklenburg system. However, a number of Burger's colleagues reacted strongly against this draft. Indeed, left solely to their own devices, a majority of the justices would almost certainly have voted simply to reinstate the order of the district court.

However, the justices who took this view faced a different problem. Given the escalating political conflict over busing, they believed strongly that any opinion that vindicated the authority of the federal courts to order the widespread transportation of students as a remedy for segregation should command the support of a unanimous Court. In order to gain the support of Chief Justice Burger and Justice Black, they were forced to make a variety of concessions, which in turn led to the creation of an opinion issued under the name of Chief Justice Burger that might appropriately be described as Janus-faced on the key issues presented in *Swann*.

In ordering a remand, the opinion cited *Green* and declared that a "school authority's remedial plan or a district court's remedial decree is to be judged by its effectiveness" and that "awareness of the racial composition of the whole school system is likely to be a useful starting point in shaping a remedy to correct past constitutional violations." In addition, the opinion explicitly approved the use of busing as a significant element in a comprehensive desegregation plan. However, at the same time, the opinion also averred that the "constitutional command to desegregate schools does not mean that every school in every community must always reflect the racial composition of the school system as a whole" and that "if we were to read the holding of the District Court to require, as a matter of substantive constitutional right, any particular degree of racial balance or mixing, that approach would be disapproved."[22]

Despite these reservations, the basic thrust of the *Swann* opinion was clear: district judges in the South would have broad discretion to impose far-reaching changes on school systems that had a history of segregating students on the basis of race. Any lingering doubts on this score were removed the following year by the decision in *Wright v. Council of the City of Emporia*.[23] *Wright* arose from the relationship of the city of Emporia, Virginia, to Greensville County, which surrounds Emporia. In 1967, Emporia was incorporated as a city of the second class under Virginia law and thus for the first time came under an obligation to establish a school system separate from that of Greensville County, which was at the time operating under a freedom-of-choice desegregation plan. Initially, however, Emporia simply contracted with the county to provide educational services for the children of the city, thereby effectively remaining part of the county system.

Two years later, in the wake of the decision in *Green*, the district court imposed a *Swann*-type desegregation plan that treated Emporia and Greensville County as a single entity for desegregation purposes. Almost immediately after the imposition of that order, Emporia sought to end its contractual relationship with Greensville County and establish a truly independent school system that would have had a racial composition that differed from that of the county as a whole. Thus, whereas the student population of the combined city and county schools was 66 percent African American and 34 percent white, the city schools alone would have been 52 percent African American and 48 percent white, and the schools in the remainder of the county would have been 72 percent African American and 28 percent white. Given these circumstances, the district court held that Emporia's operation of its own schools would "impede the dismantling of the dual system" and ordered the city to remain a part of the county school system. However, the US Court of Appeals for the Fourth Circuit reversed the district court, concluding that Emporia should be allowed to establish its own system.[24]

With Lewis Powell and William Rehnquist having joined the Court since the decision in *Swann*, Chief Justice Burger spoke for the four Nixon appointees in arguing that the judgment of the Fourth Circuit should be affirmed in *City of Emporia*. In his opinion, Burger focused on the importance of maintaining local control over issues related to education and asserted that there was no basis for concluding that the effort of the city to establish a separate school system was motivated by racial considerations. Relying on *Swann* for the principle that the Constitution did not guarantee any particular degree of racial balance in the schools, Burger characterized the potential changes in the racial composition of the schools as insignificant and concluded that the "proposed arrangement [of separate city and county schools] would completely eliminate all traces of state-imposed segregation."[25]

However, the remaining five members of the Court took a different view. In his majority opinion, Justice Stewart specifically declined to hold that the change in the racial composition of the schools alone would be sufficient justification for refusing to allow the city to establish a separate system. However, he concluded that the district court had authority to enjoin the creation of the separate system because, in addition to the direct racial impact of the change, (1) the whites who remained in the county system might be more likely to enroll in private, all-white academies, and (2) the creation of a separate school district in Emporia might have an "adverse psychological impact" on the African Americans who remained in the county schools.[26]

Despite Stewart's disclaimer and the language of *Swann*, that case and *Emporia* created a regime in which the pursuit of racial balance would almost inevitably be a key element in remedial orders dealing with the formerly segregated systems of the South. But notwithstanding those decisions, the heated political debate over the desirability of using busing for the purpose of achieving racial balance continued unabated. However, the locus of the struggle over busing turned from the South to the North.

Unlike the South, by the mid-twentieth century, public schools in the North were not formally segregated by law. Indeed, in some states such segregation was explicitly forbidden by the relevant state constitution. In many cases, however, a race-neutral legal regime did not translate into schools that were meaningfully integrated in fact. Thus, ironically, even before *Swann* was decided, the legal assault on segregation in the South had created a situation in which African Americans in the South were actually more likely to attend schools in which whites were a majority than were their counterparts in the North. Indeed, in 1968, almost 60 percent of minority students in the Northern states attended schools that were at least 95 percent African American.[27]

Although the racial imbalance in Northern schools was largely a byproduct of residential segregation, the districting process in the North was sometimes not entirely race blind. Particularly in close cases, school authorities were at times influenced by the desire of white students and their parents to have the students attend predominantly white schools. Given residential patterns, such decisions were not the primary cause of racial imbalance in Northern school districts. Nonetheless, the decisions could have a significant impact on the racial composition of specific schools within the district. In addition, preexisting school district lines had a major impact on the racial composition of Northern schools. African Americans in the North were concentrated within the cities themselves, which in turn were surrounded by suburbs in which few if any racial minorities lived. Thus, unless African American students were transported across district lines to attend suburban schools, those schools would inevitably remain almost entirely white.

Against this background, the question of whether Northern students should be bused for purposes of creating racial balance became one of the hot-button issues in US politics in the early 1970s. Moreover, the complexities involved in dealing with this issue destabilized the political alliances that had shaped the debate over racial segregation during the 1960s. As long as segregation was viewed as fundamentally a Southern problem, Northern politicians could safely press for aggressive measures designed to achieve racial balance in the schools. However, after the focus turned northward, the same politicians were forced to confront the reality that their own white constituents were often no less strongly opposed to busing and similar measures than were whites in the South. Thus, although many Northern progressives remained committed to the idea that the federal government should not distinguish between de jure and de facto segregation for legal purposes, some of their erstwhile allies who had supported both the judicial philosophy underlying *Green* and strong enforcement actions by HEW showed markedly less enthusiasm for the prospect of taking similar action to create racial balance in the face of de facto segregation.

The change in the political dynamic emerged clearly on April 20, 1971—the same day the decision in *Swann* was announced—when Democratic senator Abraham A. Ribicoff of Connecticut introduced an amendment to an education funding bill that would have required all schools in each metropolitan area to have a percentage of minority students at least half that of the percentage of minority students in the metropolitan area as a whole. A bitter debate ensued as Ribicoff challenged Northern progressives who had consistently pressed for aggressive action against segregation in the South to support his proposal, declaring that "we in the North can no longer be hypocritical and tell the South how to achieve desegregation and do nothing about the North." When Republican senator Jacob K. Javits of New York—a progressive who consistently supported civil rights legislation—stated that he would oppose the Ribicoff amendment because it threatened to kill the entire bill, Ribicoff charged Javits with "hypocrisy" and accused him of being "unwilling to accept desegregation for his state, though he is willing to shove it down the throats of . . . Mississippi" and stated, "I don't think you have the guts to face your liberal constituents who have moved to the suburbs to avoid sending their children to school with blacks."[28]

Progressives such as Ribicoff found unlikely allies in conservative Southerners such as Democratic senator John C. Stennis of Mississippi.[29] Like most Southerners who had formerly been avowed segregationists, by the late 1960s Stennis had at least formally changed his position to firm support for the concept of neighborhood schools. However, at the same time, he and other white Southerners were genuinely offended by what they saw as unequal treatment of the South. Moreover, former segregationists understood that if efforts were made to force integration on Northern schools, the political pressure against all such efforts would intensify.

Ultimately, the Senate rejected the Ribicoff proposal and chose instead to adopt a largely symbolic measure declaring that it was the "policy of the United States" to treat segregation that resulted from residential patterns in the same manner as that established by law. Nonetheless, the dispute over busing remained a flashpoint in national politics. Seeking to consolidate his support among both Southern whites and blue-collar whites generally, Richard Nixon continued to loudly proclaim his adamant opposition to busing. On March 14, 1972, he proposed a bill that would have severely limited the authority of federal courts to order the transportation of students away from the nearest school in order to achieve racial balance. Similarly, on June 8, Congress passed a bill with antibusing language but only after the Senate refused to accept an even stronger antibusing measure that had been adopted by the House of Representatives.[30]

By contrast, those seeking the Democratic nomination were deeply divided on the issue. Not surprisingly, George Wallace, the segregationist former governor of Alabama who had run as a third-party candidate in 1968, made opposition to school busing the centerpiece of his campaign for the Democratic nomination in 1972. However, the political potency of the issue was such that even Hubert Humphrey, who throughout his long political career had been a staunch supporter of civil rights legislation, wavered in his support for the idea that students should be bused for the purpose of achieving racial balance.[31]

Ultimately, however, the Democratic nomination went to the progressive Senator George McGovern of South Dakota, a strong supporter of the concept of taking whatever measures were necessary to achieve more racial balance in the public schools. After Nixon delivered his March 14 speech explaining his antibusing proposal, McGovern declared that "what we have just witnessed is a collapse of moral and political leadership by the President" and asserted that the proposal was a "back door, sneak attack on the Constitution of the United States." With the battle lines thus drawn, the platforms adopted by both political parties explicitly endorsed the positions taken by their respective nominees.[32] In the midst of this political conflict, the Court considered *Keyes v. School District No. 1*—the first case in which the justices were called upon to address the constitutional issues presented by racial imbalance in Northern schools.[33]

Keyes arose from a lawsuit brought against the school district that encompassed the city of Denver, Colorado. Although complicated by the fact that the Denver school district had substantial populations of both African Americans and Latino/as, the issues that emerged from the suit were in many ways typical of those raised in desegregation suits involving urban school districts in the North more generally. Unlike Southern school districts, neither the city of Denver nor the state of Colorado had ever formally instituted a policy of segregating students by race. Nonetheless, the racial composition of many of the schools in the district differed radically from that of the school district as a whole.

Much of the imbalance was a by-product of the combination of housing patterns and the school board's general policy of sending students to the schools nearest their homes. However, the district court also found that in some cases, the school board had manipulated the lines of the attendance zones for race-related reasons. Although the school board had assigned only a relatively small number of students to schools based on such reasons, the decisions had had some impact on the racial composition of the schools serving a very significant portion of the school district's African American population.

The situation of the Denver schools was further complicated by other actions that had been taken by the Denver Board of Education. In 1968, the board had passed three resolutions that had explicitly proposed to change attendance zones in order to spread the African American student population more evenly among the city schools. But before these resolutions could be fully implemented, two new school board members had been chosen in an intervening election where they had campaigned specifically on the promise to revoke the racial-balance resolution. After the election of these two members, the reconstituted board rescinded the resolutions.

The district judge explicitly found that most of the racial imbalance in the Denver schools, including the composition of what he described as the "core" African American schools, was not attributable to the actions of the school board. Nonetheless, based largely on his conclusion that the students in the predominantly African American schools consistently received an inferior education, the district judge issued a wide-ranging remedial decree that, among other things, sought to distribute African American students more equally among the Denver schools. The Tenth Circuit Court of Appeals, however, took a different view, concluding that such a sweeping remedy was not justified in the Denver case.[34] In *Keyes*, the Supreme Court was called upon to choose between these two perspectives.

Although the Supreme Court heard arguments in *Keyes* only a month before Nixon's landslide victory over McGovern in the general election, the justices had in fact had two previous encounters with issues related to the dispute over the Denver schools. After the district court had issued its first preliminary injunction in 1969, the court of appeals had vacated the injunction. However, on August 29 of that year, Justice Brennan, acting as circuit justice because Justice White had recused himself, reinstated the injunction, issuing a brief opinion relying on the principles established in *Green*.[35]

Almost two years later, the full Court had also considered an appeal from a Tenth Circuit decision staying the implementation of the lower court judgment pending appeal. Initially, the appeal generated sharp disagreement among the justices, with Justices Douglas, Brennan, Stewart, and Marshall arguing that the lower court should be allowed to order the transportation of students to remedy de facto segregation. However, the case was ultimately remanded to the Tenth Circuit to be reconsidered in light of the decision in *Swann*.[36]

For obvious reasons, none of the justices showed any inclination to pursue an analogous course of action as they proceeded to a full-blown consideration of the merits of *Keyes* in late 1972. At the conference that followed the argument, the justices were tentatively divided five to three in favor of reversing the judgment of the court of appeals, with Chief Justice Burger and Justices Powell and Rehnquist in dissent. Among the members of the majority, Justices Douglas, Brennan, and Marshall all seemed to express some willingness to jettison the distinction between de jure and de facto segregation. By contrast, Justice Stewart took the view that the district court had applied the incorrect legal standard in determining that the racial composition of the core schools was not the product of de jure segregation and that the case should be remanded for a reconsideration of that issue based on the appropriate standard—a view with which Brennan also agreed. Although Justice Blackmun also stated that he would "go along" with a remand, he seemed less certain about the proper disposition of *Keyes*, expressing the views that the district court decision was wrong and that there was "merit" in the concept of neighborhood schools.[37]

Against this background, Justice Brennan took on the task of writing the majority opinion. The draft opinion he circulated on November 30 made almost no mention of the idea of de facto segregation or of a right to equal education. Instead, the draft focused only on the question of "whether the [lower court] applied an incorrect legal standard in addressing [the] contention that [the Denver school board] engaged in an unconstitutional policy of deliberate segregation in the core city schools." In discussing this issue, Brennan averred that a "finding of intentionally segregative school board actions in a meaningful portion of a school system, as in this case, creates a presumption that other segregated schooling within the system is not adventitious." Moreover, Brennan made it clear that the invocation of a consistently maintained policy of preserving neighborhood schools would not suffice to satisfy this burden, declaring that "it is not enough . . . that the school authorities rely upon some allegedly logical, racially neutral explanation for their actions. Their burden is to adduce proof sufficient to support a finding that segregative intent was not among the factors that motivated their actions."[38]

Justices Douglas and Marshall quickly signaled their concurrence in Brennan's opinion. One week later, Justice Stewart also indicated that he was in "basic agreement" with Brennan's analysis.[39] However, although the opinion had plainly been drafted with a view toward retaining the support of Justice Blackmun, whose vote was indispensable to the majority, Blackmun did not immediately commit himself.

By contrast, Justices Rehnquist and Powell voiced separate objections to Brennan's approach. On one hand, Rehnquist argued simply that the courts should not infer discriminatory intent from de facto imbalance in urban school districts such as Denver and accused Justice Brennan of adopting the presumption by "judicial fiat."[40] Powell's argument, on the other hand, reflected the distinctive perspective of a pillar of the Southern white establishment who had been intimately involved in the political and legal conflicts over desegregation that followed the decision in *Brown*.

Powell had served on the Richmond school board from 1955 to 1961 and on the Virginia Board of Education from 1961 through 1968. During this period he had earned a reputation as a moderate on racial issues, at least as that term was defined in the South. Powell had been willing to accept the formal verdict of *Brown I* and had vigorously opposed the policy of massive resistance. However, at the same time, he had shown no particular interest in making affirmative efforts to achieve greater racial balance in the Richmond schools.[41]

Powell remained actively involved in the struggle over desegregation even after he left the state board of education. In 1970, he was one of the primary architects of an amicus brief filed by the state of Virginia in *Swann* that urged the Supreme Court to reject the idea that racial balance should be the sina qua non for remedial orders in desegregation cases in favor of a greater emphasis on educational quality for all students. In particular, the brief was harshly critical of the idea of requiring extensive transportation of students for purposes of achieving racial balance. The brief noted the financial cost of busing and the likelihood that "white flight" would accelerate from cities placed under such orders.[42]

However, the core of Powell's argument in *Swann* was a paean to the virtues of the neighborhood school. He asserted that "educational effectiveness is . . . dependent on the attitude of parents toward their children's education, and rationally configured systems of neighborhood schools play a vital role" and also declared that "community schools, when designed in such a way as to avoid the feelings of disaffection which attend systematic ghettoization . . . foster such an active parental role because of their very accessibility."[43]

The same aversion to busing was reflected in Powell's intraoffice communications specifically related to the consideration of *Keyes*. For example, he asserted that, in Southern cities, "present and future generations of children are being penalized—in terms of being bused away from their neighborhoods—in a highly punitive manner for the 'sins' of their forefathers, even though there is no causal relationship . . . between such 'sins' and the condition of segregation which exists." He later declared, "There is not the slightest justification in the Constitution or any rational basis for such a travesty."[44]

In addition, like Senators Ribicoff and Stennis, Powell felt strongly that white Southerners were being unfairly singled out for criticism by hypocritical residents of the North, where segregation might not have been mandated by law but where society was in fact hardly less divided on the basis of race than that of the South itself. This point also emerged in his internal memoranda. Powell insisted that "since *Brown v. Board of Education* . . . the segregation of schools in the larger cities [in both the North and the South] has resulted primarily from social and economic causes and has been influenced very little by any intention on the part of government at any level to impose and continue segregation" and averred that "putting constitutional principles aside . . . it seems immoral to hold this generation of Southerners responsible for the 'sins' of their fathers with respect to segregated schools because there was 'state action,' and to impose no comparable responsibility on the same generation of other sections of the country even though the schools are just as segregated."[45]

Against this background, Powell produced an opinion in *Keyes* that attacked the legal distinction between de facto and de jure segregation and at the same time advocated stringent limitations on the authority of the federal courts to require large-scale transportation of students as a means to achieve racial balance. As a prelude to his detailed legal analysis, Powell vented his disdain for what he viewed as the self-righteous attitude of many Northerners toward the South:

> Unwilling and foot-dragging as the process was in most places, substantial progress toward achieving integration has been made in Southern States. No comparable progress has been made in many non-Southern cities with large minority populations, primarily because of the de facto/de jure distinction nurtured by the courts and accepted complacently by many of the same voices which denounced the evils of segregated schools in the South. But if our national concern is for those who attend such schools, rather than for perpetuating a legalism rooted in history rather than present reality, we must recognize that the evil of operating separate schools is no less in Denver than in Atlanta.

Later in the opinion, Powell maintained that the emphasis on finding de jure discrimination had created a "distinction whose duality operates unfairly on local communities in one section of the country and on minority children in the others" and contended that "rather than straining to perpetuate any such dual standard, we should hold forthrightly that significant segregated school conditions in any section of the country are a *prima facie* violation of constitutional rights."[46]

After reviewing the evolution of the Court's desegregation jurisprudence from *Brown I* through *Swann* and asserting that the "rationale of *Swann* points inevitably toward a uniform, constitutional approach to our national problem of school segregation," Powell then outlined his own version of the obligations of urban school systems faced with racially unbalanced schools. Although Powell observed that "where school authorities decide to undertake the transportation of students, this [transportation] must be with integrative opportunities in mind," any suggestion that busing was mandated by the Constitution was conspicuously absent from his description of those obligations. Instead, Powell contended that

> a system [should be considered] integrated in accord with constitutional standards if the responsible authorities had taken appropriate steps to (i) integrate faculties and administration; (ii) scrupulously assure equality of facilities, instruction, and curriculum opportunities throughout the district; (iii) utilize their authority to draw attendance zones to promote integration; and (iv) locate new schools, close old ones, and determine the size and grade categories with this same objective in mind.

Powell also made it clear that these were the same tools he thought should be used by the federal courts to remedy violations in cases in which local authorities had defaulted on their obligation to maintain desegregated systems.[47]

Although stopping short of advocating an outright ban on requiring the transportation of students for the purpose of achieving racial balance, Powell also made it clear that, in his view, the kind of widespread busing plans that had been routinely imposed on Southern cities in the aftermath of *Swann* were rarely justified under the rule of reason he insisted had been established by *Swann* itself. He declared, "The single most disruptive element in education today is the widespread use of compulsory transportation, especially at elementary grade levels [, which] has risked distracting and diverting attention from basic educational ends, dividing and embittering communities, and exacerbating, rather than ameliorating, interracial friction and misunderstanding."[48]

Powell also deployed a number of specific arguments in defense of his view. Contending that racial imbalance in most cities both North and South was primarily the result of demographic factors beyond the control of the school boards, he asserted that orders that focused on achieving racial balance went beyond the scope of the constitutional violation. In addition, noting that the parents and children of the students being transported had no responsibility for whatever constitutional violations had occurred, Powell insisted that busing orders violated equitable principles by imposing the burden of the remedy on innocent parties. He also noted the costs associated with busing programs, observing that they would inevitably fall disproportionately on school districts with racially diverse populations.

The distribution of Powell's opinion on April 2 generated a brief flurry of activity. The next day, Brennan produced a response that stated that he also supported the idea of jettisoning the distinction between de jure and de facto discrimination but initially thought this view would not have commanded the support of a majority of the justices. Although asserting that Powell's suggested approach would work a "substantial retreat from our commitment of the past twenty years to eliminate all vestiges of state-imposed segregation from the public schools," Brennan also declared that "if we can eliminate the distinction without cutting back on our commitment, I would gladly do so."[49]

Replying the following day, Powell sought to take the moral high ground by adverting to his long experience with public education and declaring, "I am convinced that the ultimate goal must be the best possible education for all children." He argued that in view of the "pluralistic nature of our population," the pursuit of this goal required that the courts consider other factors in addition to the racial composition of the schools. Instead, he contended that "it must mean less drastic overseeing of federal courts of the operation of the schools by the duly constituted local authorities; and, unless we wish to risk ultimately the grave impairment of public school education, it means a rule of reason with which school board[s] and widely varying communities can live."[50]

Powell also asserted that his opinion in no way retreated from the principles established in *Swann* itself but only from what he viewed as the unduly broad reading of the Court's opinion by the lower courts. The problem, as he saw it, was that although the principles enunciated in *Green* might have been appropriate for a small, rural school district, applying those principles to the problem of racial imbalance in large, urban school systems undermined the effectiveness of the educational process for *all* students in those districts, essentially placing the Court itself "in the unenviable position of enunciating a formula that cannot be complied with in many school districts without the most serious disruption."[51]

The tenor of the two memoranda made it clear that Brennan and Powell were divided by an unbridgeable gap in *Keyes*. With White not participating, Rehnquist committed to dissenting, and Burger also expressing grave reservations, only Justice Blackmun could provide the fifth vote necessary for Brennan to claim a majority. On May 30, Blackmun finally committed himself. Although describing both parts of Powell's opinion as "forceful and persuasive" and continuing to express reservations about the durability of the distinction between de jure and de facto segregation, Blackmun formally announced his willingness to join Brennan's opinion.[52] Faced with this reality, Burger chose to concur in the result without opinion.

The decision in *Keyes* plainly had considerable doctrinal and practical significance. Despite maintaining the formal distinction between de facto and de jure segregation, the majority opinion presaged an era in which Northern cities often became the subject of wide-ranging, *Swann*-type orders designed to reduce racial imbalances in the public schools. Nonetheless, the immediate public response to *Keyes* was somewhat muted. To be sure, the *New York Times* declared that the ruling "should dispel doubts and misconceptions about the future of desegregation which have been fostered by segregationists and exploited by politicians." However, lay commentators often seemed to view the case as a relatively straightforward application of the principles established in *Swann*.[53]

In any event, in a very real sense, *Keyes* was only a prelude to the climactic battle that followed. With the public school population of the cities themselves having become increasingly dominated by minority students, all parties to the controversy understood that if judges were required to respect the jurisdictional lines between school districts in designing those programs, even the most extensive transportation program would often generate only a modicum of racial balance. Thus, in an effort to create more racial diversity in the public schools generally, some district judges began to craft orders that in effect required the merger of urban school districts whose populations were primarily African American with nearby suburban districts that were predominantly white. As a result, even as *Keyes* was being decided, all of the stakeholders recognized that the Court would soon have to pass on the legality of such orders.

The Court first encountered this issue in *Bradley v. School Board of Richmond*, decided almost contemporaneously with *Keyes*.[54] In *Bradley*, the justices confronted an order that would have created a cross-district desegregation plan for the metropolitan area of Richmond, Virginia. Prior to the issuance of the order by Judge Robert R. Mehrige, Jr., the response of the Richmond school board to the decisions in *Brown* and its progeny had been typical of that of the state of Virginia generally. The school board had made no move toward desegregating the city schools until the adoption of a freedom-of-choice plan in 1963. Initially, even that plan was not administered in a race-neutral fashion. Moreover, even after the freedom-of-choice plan was implemented in good faith, its impact on racial imbalance was limited. As late as 1970, in a majority of the schools in the city, the student body was either more than 90 percent white or more than 90 percent African American.

Recognizing that this state of affairs did not meet the standards established in *Green*, the school board requested that the HEW prepare a new plan. However, in May 1970, Judge Mehrige rejected the HEW plan out of hand, largely because it would have left many African American students in overwhelmingly African American schools. Instead, on April 5, 1971, Mehrige approved an interim plan for the 1971–1972 school year that used busing and many of the other techniques approved by the Supreme Court in *Swann* in order to achieve far greater racial balance in the Richmond schools. He noted that this plan would eliminate the "racial identifiability of each facility to the extent feasible within the City of Richmond."[55]

The difficulty was that the "extent feasible within the City of Richmond" was limited by the changing demographics of the city itself. Like many urban centers in the United States, Richmond had become an increasingly African American city in the years following *Brown*. At the time *Brown I* was decided, the school population of Richmond was 56.4 percent white and 43.6 percent African American. By 1970, the same population was 64 percent African American and 36 percent white—a shift that would have been even more dramatic if the city had not annexed an overwhelmingly white area of a neighboring county in 1970. As a result, the plan approved by the district court left a number of schools with an African American population in excess of 70 percent.

Unwilling to accept this state of affairs, Judge Mehrige concluded that more drastic action was necessary to remedy the constitutional violation that had been created by the maintenance of segregated schools in Richmond. On January 10, 1972, he issued an order that required the consolidation of the Richmond schools with those of Henrico and Chesterfield Counties, two neighboring school districts that were overwhelmingly white, in order to create a single district with what he described as a "viable racial mix."[56] He also mandated adoption of a system of pupil assignment under which more than 90 percent of the students in the combined district would have attended schools whose student population was between 20 percent and 40 percent African American, and the remainder would have attended schools whose student population was between 15 percent and 20 percent African American.

In support of this decision, Mehrige argued that requiring students to attend "racially identifiable" schools "has adverse effects not only on black pupils and teachers, but the entire community" and that by virtue of the demographic characteristics of the school-age population of the city of Richmond, the "city's entire school system is . . . identifiably black."[57] He also observed that school authorities had been willing to disregard district boundaries for policy reasons in other contexts and emphasized the fact that state as well as local authorities had been deeply involved in establishing and defending the system of racial segregation that had given rise to the decisions in *Brown* and its progeny. These considerations, he argued, justified the issuance of a judicial mandate creating a metropolitan school district in the Richmond area.

Sitting en banc, a deeply divided US Court of Appeals for the Fourth Circuit reversed Judge Mehrige on June 5, 1972.[58] The majority opinion found no persuasive evidence to support the theory that government action was responsible for the overall racial composition of either the Richmond school district or those of the surrounding counties and emphasized the practical difficulties that would have attended the consolidation of the three school districts. These observations provided the backdrop for the majority's legal arguments.

Speaking for the majority, Judge Craven cited the Tenth Amendment in support of the proposition that the Constitution itself protected the right of the states to structure their internal governments as they saw fit. Craven conceded that this prerogative would have had to give way if that structure itself violated the Fourteenth Amendment. However, he asserted that the "facts of this case do not establish . . . that state establishment and maintenance of school districts coterminous with the political subdivisions of the City of Richmond and the Counties of Chesterfield and Henrico have been intended to circumvent any federally protected right" and relied on *Swann* for the principle that "there is no right to racial balance within even a single school district." Craven thus concluded that "because we are unable to discern any constitutional violation in the establishment and maintenance of these three school districts, nor any unconstitutional consequence of such maintenance, we hold that it was not within the district judge's authority to order the consolidation of these three separate political subdivisions of the Commonwealth of Virginia."[59]

When the judgment of the Fourth Circuit was appealed to the Supreme Court, Justice Powell recused himself because of his long association with the Richmond school board. Arguing that the issues presented by *Bradley* should be decided by a Court with a full complement, some of the eight remaining justices contended that either certiorari should be denied outright in *Bradley* or that the consideration of the case should be delayed and combined with a related case from Detroit in the pipeline. Nonetheless, the justices ultimately decided to consider the appeal of the judgment of the Fourth Circuit.

At the conference after the oral argument, it became clear that Justice Stewart and the three participating Nixon appointees believed the order that had been issued by the district court swept too broadly, whereas the four remaining justices would have preferred to reinstate the order. By rule, an equally divided Court would result in the affirmance of the judgment of the court of appeals and with it, the final rejection of the cross-district integration plan ordered by the district court. Seeking to avoid this eventuality, during the conference Justice White suggested that the Court should focus on the Fourth Circuit's erroneous reliance on the Tenth Amendment argument and remand the case for reconsideration without reference to that argument. On April 25, Justice Blackmun circulated a memorandum declaring that he was "intrigue[d]" by that suggestion and stating that "if [White] were willing to prepare a brief outline in writing along that line, I might well be with him."[60]

Justice Blackmun's memorandum generated a variety of different responses from the other justices. Responding to Blackmun's request for a further elaboration of his position, White outlined an approach that would have allowed the federal court to mandate cross-district transportation in a wide variety of circumstances. Noting that the strictures of the equal protection clause applied to the state as a whole as well as to individual school districts, White also observed that Virginia law explicitly permitted school districts to be merged under some circumstances. Against this background, he contended that district "lines, even if never manipulated by the subject districts in this lawsuit, were never sacrosanct as a matter of state policy when segregation was the goal and should not stand as an insuperable barrier to an effective remedy in any of these three districts, each of which officially maintained dual school systems [prior to *Brown*]."[61]

Also arguing for a remand, Justice Brennan took a different tack. Although conceding that the relevant district lines themselves had not been drawn with the intent of keeping African Americans within the confines of the Richmond school district, Brennan also observed that other decisions taken by the school boards of Henrico and Chesterfield Counties might have prevented or discouraged African Americans from relocating to those districts, thereby contributing to racial imbalance in the schools of both those counties and Richmond itself. For example, he noted that "there is evidence that Henrico and Chesterfield Counties had a practice of building 'white' schools in the most populous areas of the counties contiguous to Richmond and of transporting all black pupils to 'black' schools located in the far reaches of the counties" and suggested that these practices might have discouraged the immigration of African American families who wished to live close to the schools their children would attend. He argued that a district court might appropriately conclude that such practices justified the imposition of a cross-district remedy and that a remand was therefore appropriate in *Bradley*.[62]

Chief Justice Burger and Justice Rehnquist led the opposition to the remand effort. On April 26, Burger wrote privately to Blackmun stating that he would only countenance a cross-district remedy in cases where there was (1) no excessive bus transportation, (2) no objective of racial balance, and (3) "no inconsistency with *Swann* and related cases." He also stated that "if anyone tries to persuade me that [the district judge] did not mean racial balance [in *Bradley*,] that is a lost cause." On the same day, Burger also circulated a memorandum to the Court at large declaring that although he would defer voting pending further explanation of Justice White's position, a "remand that gives implied approval to the District Court action would give me a good deal of trouble." Subsequently, Burger circulated another memorandum that formally rejected the idea of a remand, citing the passage from *Swann* in which the Court had explicitly stated that the federal courts could not require a particular degree of racial balance in a desegregation order and asserting that the district court in *Bradley* had been motivated by just such a purpose.[63]

Rehnquist's position was, if anything, even more hostile than that of the chief justice to the idea of cross-district busing orders. Although agreeing that the imposition of such remedies should not be categorically prohibited, Rehnquist argued that cross-district orders were "hardly ever" appropriate. Rehnquist contended that the question of whether the district court was seeking to achieve racial balance was irrelevant, as was the fact that the state allowed the consolidation of school districts under some circumstances. Instead, he reasoned that the very idea of a unitary school system or a desegregated school system "requires a reference to some governmentally defined system as a beginning point in the analysis."

For Rehnquist, the appropriate reference point was the preexisting school district lines. Against that background, he concluded that cross-district remedies would only be appropriate "where the drawing of the boundary lines or use of the boundary lines were themselves a substantial element in the violation of the right, or where the boundary lines were observed largely in the breach." Because no such showing had been made in *Bradley*, he concluded that no remand was necessary, and the decision of the court of appeals should simply be affirmed. On May 11, Justice Blackmun pronounced himself "generally in accord" with these views, leaving the justices split four to four.[64]

The equal division resolved the dispute in *Bradley* itself by leaving the judgment of the court of appeals undisturbed. However, no opinion was issued by the Supreme Court, and the affirmance was without precedential significance. The ultimate resolution of the dispute over cross-district remedies was thus postponed until the next term, when the Court confronted the issue in *Milliken v. Bradley*.[65]

At the time the lawsuit that ultimately gave rise to *Milliken* was filed in federal district court on August 18, 1970, the situation of the school system of Detroit in 1970 was in many ways similar to that of Denver and other urban systems in the North.[66] The demographics of the system showed an ever-increasing percentage of African American students in the city public schools. In 1961, 45.8 percent of the Detroit public school population was African American. By 1970, that percentage had risen to 63.2 percent, and that figure was projected to rise to more than 80 percent by 1980. Moreover, although the Detroit schools had never been segregated by law, African Americans were not distributed evenly throughout the system. In 1970, there were twenty-two schools in Detroit with no white students and eleven schools with no African American students. The imbalance among the city schools was primarily a result of residential housing patterns. However, the district court found that racial housing divisions in the city were themselves in part a by-product of actions by the state and local governments and that in specific instances the Detroit Board of Education had made decisions that at the very least had the predictable effect of exacerbating the racial disparities in the school populations.

On April 7, 1970—four months before the lawsuit was filed—the board of education had adopted a plan designed to achieve more racial balance in the schools by redistributing 12,000 students over the course of three years among twelve of the most segregated schools in Detroit. Opponents of the April 7 plan reacted with a coordinated effort in the state legislature and within the city of Detroit itself. They initiated a campaign to recall the four members of the board of education who had voted for the plan, and in an election on August 4 were successful in replacing supporters of the plan with avowed opponents. Moreover, in the interim, the state legislature had adopted a statute known as Act 48, which would have effectively prohibited the board of education from implementing the April 7 plan until the new members had taken office and in addition would have mandated that the local board of education adopt a hybrid neighborhood school/freedom-of-choice plan that would have perpetuated racial imbalance. Although Act 48 was ultimately held unconstitutional by the US Court of Appeals for the Sixth Circuit, the political conflict surrounding the April 7 plan led the advocates of strong action to achieve racial balance to file the lawsuit in *Milliken*.[67]

Against this background, District Judge Stephen J. Roth concluded that for Fourteenth Amendment purposes, both the Detroit Board of Education and the government of the state of Michigan itself were responsible for the racial imbalance in the Detroit schools. Moreover, although conceding that his task was simply to end segregation in those schools, Judge Roth's remedial order was not limited to the school district of Detroit itself. Instead, he ordered that the Detroit schools be combined with fifty-three other school districts in surrounding counties to create a "desegregation area" that included almost 800,000 students, of whom approximately one-quarter would be African American, and that students be distributed among the schools in this area in a manner designed to achieve racial balance. On June 12, 1973, the Sixth Circuit affirmed this aspect of Judge Roth's decision.[68]

Even before the Sixth Circuit handed down its opinion, the Supreme Court justices had been well aware that the dispute over the Detroit desegregation plan would ultimately be resolved by the Court. On December 18, 1972, during the consideration of *Keyes*, Chief Justice Burger had circulated a memorandum suggesting that there would be "some common ground" between the Detroit and Denver desegregation cases. Subsequently, on May 30, 1973, clearly believing the Sixth Circuit's decision in *Milliken* was imminent, Burger suggested that the decision in *Keyes* should be deferred until the 1973 term, when the case could be considered together with an expected appeal from *Milliken*. This suggestion brought an immediate, irate response from Brennan, who observed that "if you have canvassed the [*Milliken*] issues as I have, you might agree that none of them is remotely connected with any decided in *Keyes*" and reminding Burger that "I thought we all agreed that [*Bradley*] should come down when it did to be sure we'd have a nine-judge court for [*Milliken*]." Facing these objections, Burger decided to abandon his suggestion.[69]

Not surprisingly, the Court granted certiorari in *Milliken* in November 1973. As Justice Blackmun observed privately, the case for cross-district busing had in fact been considerably stronger in the Richmond school desegregation case. In that case, each of the districts involved had itself been guilty of intentionally maintaining schools that were formally segregated by race, and the state government as a whole had a long history of both participating in intentional segregation and leading the resistance to efforts to comply with the mandate of *Brown*. Moreover, Judge Roth's order in *Milliken* involved many more school districts than Judge Mehrige's decision in *Bradley*, thereby compounding the administrative problems attendant to any cross-district remedy.[70]

However, in any event, after the equal division of the Court in *Bradley*, it was clear that Justice Powell would cast the decisive vote in *Milliken*. Blackmun thought the vote would be a "terribly difficult" one for Powell, whom he believed to be in a "bit of a box" because of the rejection of the de jure/de facto distinction in Powell's opinion in *Keyes*.[71] However, this assessment reflected a misunderstanding of Powell's basic approach to desegregation issues.

Although Powell had indeed argued in *Keyes* that the Court should abandon the distinction between de jure and de facto segregation, the opinion also reflected his unalterable opposition to the entire concept of ordering the transportation of students away from their neighborhood schools for the purpose of achieving racial balance, even if the transportation took place within a single school district. His objections to busing for this purpose could only be magnified in a situation that would require the abandonment of traditional school district lines in pursuit of racial balance. Thus, although the equally divided decision in *Bradley* had not established any binding principles of law, and the popular press treated *Milliken* as presenting an important issue still in doubt, in reality the outcome of the appeal had become virtually a foregone conclusion by the time certiorari was granted.

Powell's notes on *Milliken* clearly reflected his antipathy for Judge Roth's order. Powell asked rhetorically, "If all appropriate steps are taken to desegregate D. system, what in Const. *requires* that a Fed. Ct. reach out and enlarge city boundaries for ed. purposes?" and "*Why stop with the 53 districts?* If the answer is that this provides a ratio of 65 Whites to 35 negro, what in the Const. says that this ratio is required? Why not 60–40 or 50–50 or 90–10?" Powell also focused on what he saw as the myriad administrative problems attendant to merging the metropolitan area school district.[72] Against this background, when the justices met in conference to consider *Milliken* on March 1, 1974, the five-to-four vote in favor of reversal was almost a formality.

Chief Justice Burger assigned himself the task of writing the majority opinion. However, rather than focusing on the interdistrict nature of the remedy designed by the district court, Burger's initial draft instead sought to revisit the principles that had been established in *Swann* and *Keyes*, characterizing *Milliken* primarily in terms of a dispute over racial balancing in school desegregation cases.[73] Not surprisingly, Burger's distribution of the draft to the members of the majority on May 31 generated a barrage of comments. Criticism came not only from Justices Stewart and Blackmun, both of whom had been members of the majority in both *Swann* and *Keyes*, but also Justices Rehnquist and Powell, the two most outspoken critics on the Court of busing. All of the circulated memoranda firmly rejected Burger's approach and pressed for an opinion designed to address the specific issues presented by interdistrict remedies. Thus, for example, Stewart wrote, "I . . . firmly believe that racial balance is not an issue in this case and that a discussion of that issue in the Court opinion will serve only to distract attention from the real issue." Similarly, Powell asserted that "whether the [district court] ordered racial balance or not is essentially immaterial to the basic issue in this case" and that

> this case is . . . the test case to resolve two burning issues of great public concern: (1) what conditions, if any, would justify a federal court in ordering consolidation of two or more school districts . . . for the purpose of achieving racial desegregation, and (2) assuming that conditions do justify such a court order, what are the limitations, if any, upon the power of a federal court to order extensive interdistrict transportation to achieve desegregation?[74]

With the 1973 term rapidly coming to a close, Justice Powell's chambers took on the task of producing language that would be acceptable to all members of the slim majority.[75] His analysis, which in turn drew on the argument of the amicus brief submitted by the solicitor general, was embodied in the majority opinion Chief Justice Burger issued on the last day of the term. Citing *Swann* for the proposition that the "controlling principle consistently expounded in our holdings is that the scope of the remedy is determined by the nature and extent of the constitutional violation," the opinion declared:

> Before the boundaries of separate and autonomous school districts may be set aside by consolidating the separate units for remedial purposes or by imposing a cross-district remedy, it must first be shown that there has been a constitutional violation within one district that produces a significant segregative effect in another district. Specifically, it must be shown that racially discriminatory acts of the state or local school districts or of a single school district have been a substantial cause of interdistrict segregation.[76]

Finding no evidence of acts with the requisite interdistrict segregative effect in *Swann*, the opinion concluded that the district court had erred in imposing an interdistrict remedy.

Three different justices penned dissenting opinions in *Milliken*. Justice Douglas spoke only for himself in reiterating his view that the distinction between de jure and de facto discrimination should be discarded for purposes of constitutional analysis. By contrast, the opinions of Justice White and Justice Marshall each had the support of all four dissenting justices. White asserted:

> The majority's arbitrary limitation on the equitable power of federal district courts, based on the invisible borders of local school districts, is unrelated to the State's responsibility for remedying the constitutional wrongs visited upon the Negro schoolchildren of Detroit. It is oblivious to the potential benefits of metropolitan relief, to the noneducational communities of interest among neighborhoods located in and sometimes bridging different school districts, and to the considerable interdistrict cooperation already existing in various educational areas. Ultimately, it is unresponsive to the goal of attaining the utmost actual desegregation consistent with restraints of practicability, and thus augurs the frequent frustration of the remedial powers of the federal courts.[77]

The tone of Justice Marshall's dissent was markedly different from that of the other two opinions.[78] For most of his adult life prior to his appointment to the federal bench, Marshall had been in the trenches, deeply engaged in the legal struggle to end segregation and to enhance the opportunities available to African Americans generally. He well understood that, given the demographics of the urban United States, the effect of the majority opinion would be to leave many African Americans in schools in essence segregated in fact if not by law. He also no doubt believed that the children in urban school districts would receive an inferior education as a result.

Against this background, Marshall made no effort to hide his anger with the decision of the majority. Describing the decision as "more a reflection of a perceived public mood that we have gone far enough in enforcing the Constitution's guarantee of equal justice than it is the product of neutral principle of law," he declared that the "rights at issue in this case are too fundamental to be abridged on grounds as superficial as those relied on by the majority today. We deal here with the right of all of our children, whatever their race, to an equal start in life and to an equal opportunity to reach their full potential as citizens. Those children who have been denied that right in the past deserve better than to see fences thrown up to deny them that right in the future." Marshall further asserted that the position adopted by the majority "provide[s] no remedy at all for the violation proved in this case, thereby guaranteeing that Negro children in Detroit will receive the same separate and inherently unequal education in the future as they have been unconstitutionally afforded in the past." After recounting the many ways in which he viewed the state of Michigan as a whole as bearing partial responsibility for the racial imbalance in the Detroit system, Marshall concluded bitterly,

> It is a hollow remedy indeed where, 'after supposed "desegregation," the schools remained segregated in fact.' We must do better than '"substitute . . . one segregated school system for another segregated school system."' To suggest, as does the majority, that a Detroit-only plan somehow remedies the effects of de jure segregation of the races is, in my view, to make a solemn mockery of Brown I's holding that separate educational facilities are inherently unequal.[79]

The country at large was no less deeply divided than the justices themselves on the merits of the decision in *Milliken*. Many suburban whites rejoiced. One banner headline read, "Many white parents [in the Detroit suburbs] now see their children as safe." Similarly, Vice President Gerald Ford characterized the decision as a "great step forward to finding another answer to quality education," and Governor William Milliken of Michigan asserted that *Milliken* would be "very well received in the country and in Michigan." By contrast, the *New York Times* opined that the decision was "as wrong as a matter of law as it is unfortunate as a matter of social policy," and the general counsel of the NAACP LDF characterized the holding as a "giant step backward."[80]

Whatever one's view of the merits of the Court's decisions, when considered together, *Swann*, *Keyes*, and *Milliken* at least had the virtue of clearly establishing the rules for dealing with racial imbalance in metropolitan areas throughout the nation. All or almost all urban school districts were guilty of the kinds of practices that gave rise to the *Swann*-type order in *Keyes* and thus were generally required to take aggressive measures to distribute whites and African American students equally throughout their schools. These requirements in turn often fanned the flames of resentment among some whites who lived in the affected cities. Thus, for example, the atmosphere surrounding the effort to desegregate the Boston schools in the mid-1970s was as tumultuous as any that accompanied desegregation orders in the South in the 1950s and 1960s, and both candidates for president took strong stands against school busing during the 1976 campaign.

However, at the same time, advocates for remedies that required transportation of students across school district lines could only rarely prove the kind of interdistrict violations *Milliken* required as a predicate for such remedies. As a result, white families remained free to escape the strictures of desegregation remedies by the simple expedient of moving to the suburbs, and as the school districts of the cities themselves became increasingly dominated by minority students, the degree of racial balance that could be achieved without cross-district remedies became ever more limited. With this option available to the natural opponents of busing, the intensity of the national debate over the issue gradually waned and, by the end of the 1970s, had been displaced by the dispute over affirmative action as the primary focal point for discussion of constitutional doctrines related to race relations.

In any event, school desegregation was not the only context in which the decisions of the late Warren era had created the impression that the Court might deploy the equal protection clause to aggressively advance progressive values. During the late 1960s, progressives had also been given at least some reason to hope that the Fourteenth Amendment might be used to invalidate a wide variety of laws that placed poor people at a disadvantage. However, by the end of the 1972 term, these hopes had been almost completely dashed.

Chapter Seven

Equal Protection and Wealth Discrimination

The mid- to late 1960s was a heady time for those who believed the federal government should play an active role in easing the plight of the poor in the United States. Under the rubric of the "Great Society" and the leadership of President Lyndon Baines Johnson, Congress passed a variety of social welfare statutes unmatched since the early years of the Franklin Delano Roosevelt administration. Notable legislation of this era included not only the Civil Rights Act of 1964 and the Voting Rights Act of 1965, which were aimed specifically at the problem of racial discrimination, but also a number of enactments aimed at improving the lot of the poor more generally, including, for example, the Economic Opportunity Act of 1964, the Food Stamp Act of 1964, the Elementary and Secondary School Act of 1965, and the Social Security Act of 1965, which created both the Medicare and Medicaid programs.

During this period, progressives saw the Supreme Court as a potential ally in what Johnson described as the "war on poverty." Their attitude toward the judiciary was quite different from that of their counterparts of the early 1930s. During Roosevelt's first term, the Court had often invoked the Constitution to invalidate federal laws designed to implement the New Deal.[1] Not surprisingly, progressives reacted by decrying the Court's intervention and urging the justices to defer to the policy judgments of other branches of government.[2] By contrast, during the late 1960s and early 1970s, progressive commentators pressed the justices to actively invoke the Constitution to advance the interests of the groups the Great Society was designed to benefit. Thus, for example, Frank I. Michelman argued that the Warren Court should not only reject all constitutional challenges to federal authority to pass social welfare legislation but should also independently use its own authority to constitutionalize a variety of significant additional protections for poor people.[3] In particular, progressives urged the Court to closely scrutinize rules that required the payment of fees in order to obtain government services and to both require states to equalize spending on public schools and constitutionalize the right of indigents to receive government assistance. The effort to achieve these goals bore some fruit in the late 1960s and early 1970s. However, by the end of the 1972 term, it had become clear that the Burger Court would act to provide special protection for the interests of the poor as a class only in the narrowest of circumstances.

During the 1972 term, the debate over wealth discrimination took place against the backdrop of the two-tiered structure of equal protection analysis that had been developed by the Warren Court. Under this approach, legally established distinctions were divided into two categories. If such a distinction was based on one of a small group of suspect classifications or implicated one of a limited number of fundamental rights, then the distinction was subjected to "strict scrutiny" and would only survive a constitutional attack if the government could demonstrate that the distinction was necessary to serve a compelling governmental interest. In practice, this standard was so stringent that the level of scrutiny was famously described by one commentator as "strict in theory but fatal in fact."[4] By contrast, the constitutionality of all other classifications was determined by a rational basis test as deferential as strict scrutiny was harsh. Thus, the only really significant questions were which particular classifications should be considered suspect and which rights should be viewed as fundamental.

During the Warren era, the Court handed down a number of decisions that seemed to suggest wealth-based classifications should be considered suspect for purposes of two-tiered analysis. The first indications the Court might be moving toward the view that the equal protection clause should be interpreted to require enhanced scrutiny of classifications based on wealth came in a series of cases dealing with criminal procedure issues. The majority opinion in the 1963 decision in *Douglas v. California* provides one particularly striking example of language suggesting that the interests of the poor were entitled to particularly strong solicitude in equal protection analysis. In concluding that the state of California was constitutionally required to provide indigent criminal defendants appointed counsel in appeals as of right, Justice William O. Douglas declared that "there is lacking that equality demanded by the Fourteenth Amendment where the rich man, who appeals as of right, enjoys the benefit of counsel's examination into the record, research of the law, and marshaling of arguments on his behalf, while the indigent, already burdened by a preliminary determination that his case is without merit, is forced to shift for himself."[5]

In 1966, once again speaking for the majority, in *Harper v. Virginia Board of Elections* Justice Douglas focused on discrimination between the rich and the poor in a quite different context.[6] As already noted, *Harper* struck down a state requirement that citizens pay a poll tax in order to be eligible to vote. In holding that this requirement violated the equal protection clause, Douglas asserted that "wealth, like race, creed, or color, is not germane to one's ability to participate intelligently in the electoral process" and that "lines drawn on the basis of wealth or property, like those of race, are traditionally disfavored." Three years later, in dictum, Chief Justice Earl Warren spoke for a unanimous Court in declaring that discrimination based on wealth was a factor that "independently render[s] a classification highly suspect and thereby demand[s] a more exacting judicial scrutiny."[7]

Even after the arrival of Warren Burger and Harry Blackmun, the Court continued to expand the scope of constitutional protections for the rights of indigent people. The 1971 decision in *Boddie v. Connecticut* was the first case in which the Court invoked the Fourteenth Amendment to invalidate the requirement that a fee be paid in order to initiate a civil action.[8] *Boddie* was a challenge to a Connecticut statute that required a person seeking a divorce to pay a fee that averaged $50 in order to have his or her petition adjudicated. With only Justice Hugo Black dissenting, the *Boddie* Court held that the state of Connecticut could not constitutionally require an indigent person seeking a divorce to pay the fee. In reaching this conclusion, Justices Douglas and Brennan would have relied on the same equal protection analysis that had animated the decisions in *Douglas* and *Harper*. However, Justice John Marshall Harlan's majority opinion focused instead on the due process clause of the Fourteenth Amendment.[9]

In concluding that the Connecticut fee requirement ran afoul of the due process clause, Harlan—who had dissented in both *Douglas* and *Harper*—explicitly declined to express any view on the question of whether the Constitution protected the right to pursue civil actions generally. Instead, Harlan focused on two specific characteristics of divorce proceedings. First, he noted that divorce involved the "adjustment of [the] fundamental human relationship" of marriage, which the Court had consistently characterized as an interest "of basic importance in our society." In addition, the majority opinion repeatedly emphasized the fact that the parties were powerless to adjust their marital status without judicial intervention. Against this background, Harlan concluded that the state could not "pre-empt the right to dissolve this legal relationship without affording all citizens access to the means it has prescribed for doing so."[10]

The carefully worded opinion in *Boddie* left the status of other constitutional challenges to laws that required the payment of fees uncertain. However, in 1973 this uncertainty was removed, and the claim that discrimination on the basis of wealth should generally be subject to strict scrutiny was decisively rejected in *United States v. Kras.*[11] *Kras* was a constitutional challenge to a requirement that those seeking a discharge of their debts in bankruptcy pay a fee in order to have their petitions considered by the federal judiciary. Relying heavily on *Boddie,* an indigent petitioner claimed he was unable to pay the fee and raised both due process and equal protection challenges to the requirement. Although four justices concluded that the imposition of the fee was unconstitutional, Byron White joined the four Nixon appointees to form a majority that rejected the constitutional challenge.

The justices in the majority were moved by a variety of different considerations in reaching their conclusions in *Kras.* For example, despite observing privately that "in a way it is hard to distinguish *Boddie* from this case," Justice Blackmun also noted that the fees charged to petitioners financed the operation of the bankruptcy system and that "I cannot escape the feeling that there is some merit in the principle that those utilizing bankruptcy should pay for it." While conceding that "the bankrupt is out [because] he has to produce the fee," Blackmun also believed that any hardship from the requirement that the fee be paid was more than counterbalanced by the benefit the debtor received from the relief of his or her debt and that the "only ones who really suffer by the imposition of fees are the creditors" because the fees reduce the size of the estate from which they could collect. At the conference after oral argument, Blackmun also asserted that Kras himself was "obviously a phony."[12]

Other justices cited different reasons for distinguishing *Boddie.* Lewis Powell saw the interest at stake in *Boddie* as "more fundamental" than that involved in *Kras.* In addition, both Powell and Warren Burger observed that whereas the state had a monopoly on the process of dissolving a marriage, a debtor who was denied access to bankruptcy proceedings retained the option of negotiating privately with his creditors to reduce his financial obligations. In addition, Powell saw the impact of the fee as de minimus, noting that $1.27 per week was the price of three packages of cigarettes. This factor was also apparently critical for White, who asserted at the conference that the constitutional challenge to the fees charged under the bankruptcy statute was "close to frivolous."[13]

The influence of all of these factors was apparent in Justice Blackmun's majority opinion in *Kras*. Not surprisingly, much of the opinion focused specifically on the problem of distinguishing *Kras* from *Boddie*. After noting that in the *Boddie* opinion itself Justice Harlan had specifically noted that his analysis was designed to go "'no further than necessary to dispose of the case before us,'" Blackmun emphasized the fact that the Court had subsequently declined to review lower court decisions that had rejected constitutional challenges to the very fees at issue in *Kras*. Although conceding that a "denial of certiorari normally carries no implication or inference," Blackmun noted that the denial of certiorari in these cases had drawn dissents from Justices Black and Douglas and argued that the "pointed dissents . . . so soon after *Boddie*, and Mr. Justice Harlan's failure to join the dissenters, surely are not without some significance as to their and the Court's attitude about the application of the *Boddie* principle to bankruptcy fees."[14]

Blackmun then turned to a detailed analysis of what he saw as the substantive differences between *Boddie* and *Kras*. Echoing Powell's view that, for constitutional purposes, access to divorce was more important than access to bankruptcy, he asserted that the "*Boddie* appellants' inability to dissolve their marriages seriously impaired their freedom to pursue other protected associational activities. Kras's alleged interest in the elimination of his debt burden, and in obtaining his desired new start in life, although important and so recognized by the enactment of the Bankruptcy Act, does not rise to the same constitutional level" and that "if Kras is not discharged in bankruptcy, his position will not be materially altered in any constitutional sense. Gaining or not gaining a discharge will effect no change with respect to basic necessities." In addition, the majority opinion emphasized the possibility that, unlike those seeking to end their marriages, a debtor might be able to gain significant relief without benefit of judicial intervention by negotiating with his creditors—a point that was also the focus of Chief Justice Burger's concurring opinion.[15]

Finally, once again echoing Powell's comments at the conference on *Kras*, Blackmun emphasized what he characterized as the insignificance of the burden the bankruptcy fees imposed on debtors. Observing that the required weekly payments would be a "sum less than the payments Kras makes on his couch of negligible value in storage, and less than the price of a movie and little more than the cost of a pack or two of cigarettes," he declared that "if [Kras] really needs and desires that discharge, this much available revenue should be within his able-bodied reach when the adjudication in bankruptcy has stayed collection and has brought to a halt whatever harassment, if any, he may have sustained from creditors."[16]

Justices Douglas, Brennan, Stewart, and Marshall saw no cognizable distinction between *Boddie* and *Kras* and would have invalidated the requirement at issue in the latter. Whereas Stewart asserted that "in the unique situation of the indigent bankrupt, the Government provides the only effective means of his ever being free of these Government-imposed obligations," and Douglas contended that the "discrimination in [*Kras*] denies equal protection within our decisions which make particularly 'invidious' discrimination based on wealth or race," Marshall's condemnation of the majority opinion was particularly impassioned.

Marshall decried Blackmun's reliance on Harlan's vote to deny certiorari in the earlier bankruptcy cases, noting that the vote could have been based on any number of considerations that were independent of Harlan's views on the merits. Marshall observed:

> The point of our use of a discretionary writ is precisely to prohibit that kind of speculation. When we deny certiorari, no one, not even ourselves, should think that the denial indicates a view on the merits of the case. It ill serves judges of the courts throughout the country to tell them, as the majority does today, that in attempting to determine what the law is, they must read not only the opinions of this Court but also the thousands of cases in which we annually deny certiorari.[17]

Marshall was even more irate about Blackmun's suggestion that the payment of the required fee would not create serious hardships for those seeking bankruptcy protection. He complained,

> It may be easy for some people to think that weekly savings of less than $2 are no burden. But no one who has had close contact with poor people can fail to understand how close to the margin of survival many of them are. A sudden illness, for example, may destroy whatever savings they may have accumulated, and by eliminating a sense of security may destroy the incentive to save in the future. A pack or two of cigarettes may be, for them, not a routine purchase but a luxury indulged in only rarely. The desperately poor almost never go to see a movie, which the majority seems to believe is an almost weekly activity. They have more important things to do with what little money they have—like attempting to provide some comforts for a gravely ill child, as Kras must do.
>
> It is perfectly proper for judges to disagree about what the Constitution requires. But it is disgraceful for an interpretation of the

> Constitution to be premised upon unfounded assumptions about how people live.[18]

Ironically, the tone of Marshall's dissent might ultimately have contributed to Blackmun's ability to assemble a majority in support of his opinion. Although agreeing that the statute challenged in *Kras* should not be struck down, Byron White believed the decision in *Boddie* had had the salutary effect of encouraging states to reexamine the fees attendant to filing civil suits more generally. Thus, expressing concern about Blackmun's treatment of *Boddie*, on December 7, 1972, White circulated what he privately described as a "chicken narrow" opinion concurring only in the result and focusing on what he characterized as the insignificance of the burden the fee requirement imposed on debtors.[19]

If White had remained steadfast in his decision not to join Blackmun's opinion, Blackmun would have been left one vote short of the majority necessary to create a binding precedent. However, on December 14, White sent Blackmun a brief note stating he had decided not to publish a separate opinion and instead would join Blackmun's opinion "just to settle the dust, at least temporarily." Blackmun noted privately, "I suspect [Marshall's] opinion pushed [White] this way."[20] But whatever the reason for White's decision, Blackmun had his majority, and the principle that states could charge fees for access to the civil court system became firmly ensconced in constitutional doctrine.

Not surprisingly, progressives were disappointed with the result and majority opinion in *Kras*. The decision was clearly a major setback for those who sought to use the Fifth and Fourteenth Amendments as vehicles to create significant constitutional protection for poor people as a class. However, many advocates for the poor were even more dismayed by the Court's disposition of *San Antonio Independent School District v. Rodriguez*.[21]

In *Rodriguez*, the justices were called upon to enter a dispute some progressives analogized to the struggle to end racial segregation in US schools. The problem arose from the system by which public schools were financed in the United States. Although in most cases the state governments provided a significant portion of school funding through statewide taxes, in almost every state each school district was also charged with the obligation of raising a great deal of the necessary funds through the imposition of taxes levied on real property within the district. As a result, the amount of money available to spend on schools often varied widely between districts depending not only on the rate at which property was taxed but also the value of the property upon which taxes could be imposed.

For many years, this regime went largely unchallenged. However, in the late 1960s, progressives filed a series of lawsuits based on the theory that dramatic differences in spending on education inevitably created differences in educational opportunity between students in rich districts and students in poor districts and that the resulting inequality ran afoul of constitutional norms. In 1971, progressives won a signal victory in *Serrano v. Priest* when the California Supreme Court embraced their position and paved the way for dramatic reform in the manner in which the public schools in the state were financed.[22] The proponents of radical change in the school financing system gained further support when a presidential commission that was formed to study the problem issued a report supporting their position.[23]

The case that ultimately brought the issue to the Supreme Court arose from a challenge to the manner in which the state of Texas financed its public schools. Although the Texas system was complicated, one point was clear—the amount of money available to each school district was determined in large measure by the property taxes raised in the district, leading to a substantial disparity of resources between property-poor and property-rich districts. The way in which the system operated was illustrated by a comparison between two different school districts in the metropolitan area of San Antonio, Texas.

The Englewood Independent School District, whose population was composed primarily of minority students, was located in the core city of San Antonio. The median family income in the district was $4,681 per year, and because little commercial and industrial property was located there, the assessed property value per pupil was $5,690. As a result, with a tax rate of $1.05 per $100 of value, the total amount of money available to the Englewood district was $356 per pupil. By contrast, families of students in the predominantly Anglo Alamo Heights Independent School District had a median income of $8,001 per year, and the average assessed value of the real property located in the district was $49,000 per pupil. Thus, with a property tax rate of $0.85 per $100 of assessed value, the Alamo Heights district could spend $594 per student.

Those challenging the constitutionality of the Texas system argued that the heavy emphasis on local property taxes violated the equal protection clause. The plaintiffs contended that the constitutionality of the system should be judged by a more stringent standard than the traditional rational basis test for two separate reasons. First, they asserted that the use of the system discriminated against poor residents of Texas on the basis of wealth. Second, they argued that disparities in access to resources inevitably led to inequality in educational opportunity and that because education should be considered a fundamental right, such disparities should be subject to strict scrutiny. In addition they claimed that, in any event, the Texas system failed to pass even the rational basis test.

Not surprisingly, the justices were deeply divided over the merits of these arguments. Justice Powell in particular was extremely hostile to the claim that discrimination on the basis of wealth should be considered constitutionally suspect. When dealing with the issue of capital punishment in 1972, he had noted "social and economic factors . . . have plagued humanity since the beginning of recorded history, frustrating all efforts to create in any country at any time the perfect society in which there are no 'poor,' no 'minorities,' and no 'underprivileged.'" Moreover, in his notes on *Rodriguez* itself, he described the theory as a "communist" doctrine that had no place in a society based on the principle of free enterprise.[24]

However, even if one accepted the general proposition that wealth should be considered a suspect classification, it was far from clear that the reliance on local property taxes to finance public education qualified as wealth discrimination. As Justice Blackmun observed privately, "The poorness of property evaluations in a given district does not necessarily equate with family wealth or family income." Moreover, even prior to the Court's consideration of *Rodriguez*, a number of studies had demonstrated that converting to a statewide funding scheme might well put poor students in the inner city at a disadvantage because they often lived close to the kind of high-value commercial and industrial property that was a prolific source of revenue from property taxes.[25]

In any event, the basic idea that wealth should be considered a suspect classification was rejected in *Kras*, which, although argued after *Rodriguez*, was decided before the school finance decision was announced. By contrast, the argument that education should be considered a fundamental right could claim a more plausible constitutional pedigree. For example, in *Brown v. Board of Education*, Chief Justice Warren had relied in part on the observation that "education . . . is the most important function of state and local governments" to justify his conclusion that the maintenance of racially segregated schools violated the equal protection clause. Against this background the progressive justices, who would have found the Texas plan unconstitutional, focused their attention largely on the impact of lack of resources on educational opportunity. Thus, although conceding that financial considerations were not the only factor determining the quality of education, at the conference on *Rodriguez* both Justice Douglas and Justice Brennan insisted that the availability of money was an important element in the equation. Byron White, by contrast, based his vote on a somewhat narrower ground. Although observing, "I wouldn't think that inequality of input of dollars alone would make a case," he also noted that, in *Rodriguez* itself, the Englewood district was "locked-in"; that is, under the Texas system, the district had no real opportunity to raise the funds it might deem necessary to improve the quality of education for its students.[26]

By contrast, from the beginning of the consideration of *Rodriguez*, the four Nixon appointees were arrayed against the constitutional challenge. Although his personal belief in the importance of educational opportunity to US society was no less strong than that of the progressive justices, Lewis Powell led the opposition to the constitutional challenge in *Rodriguez*. Drawing on his own experience in Virginia, Powell questioned the relationship between expenditures and quality in public education.[27] However, he was even more concerned by the institutional issues raised by federal lawsuits seeking to reform the mechanism for the funding of public schools.

Even before the oral argument, Powell observed that, in cases such as *Rodriguez*, "I remind myself . . . that we are not a super-legislature [and] that judicial restraint is a cardinal virtue when approaching an issue of constitutionality." Similarly, although acknowledging the imperfections inherent in the system of financing public education through local property taxes in his conference notes on *Rodriguez*, he also declared that the "answer to [problems in the public schools] is not for the Federal Judiciary to enter another field—with vast problems and infinite diversity—which has been occupied for more nearly two centuries . . . by the Legislative & Executive branches."

At the conference on *Rodriguez*, other justices also expressed similar concerns. For example, Justice Blackmun observed that the challengers were in essence calling upon the federal courts to "enter the educational thicket [, which] would be far worse than the reapportionment area." Similarly, Chief Justice Burger complained that the challengers "would overhaul the school systems and the fiscal and taxation structures across the land."[28]

Moreover, for Powell in particular, belief in the importance of public education went hand in hand with a strong preference for local control. He feared that Supreme Court intervention in school financing issues might be the first step toward full national control of the education system—a regime Powell associated with totalitarian governments. Powell was also opposed to the idea of centralizing control of public education at the state level. In part, this view was based on a general preference for having government functions performed at the local level. Thus, he argued that "local government has played a fundamental role in making our system work, in preventing the bigness of even state government from overwhelming the citizen [by] keeping control of local municipal services . . . largely . . . where the politicians are far more responsive to the needs of the community and the will of the people." In Powell's view, maintaining local control of education was particularly important; he characterized the local school board as a "unique American institution" that "has been the most dynamic force behind the overall effectiveness of our public school system."[29]

Against this background, Powell privately expressed a variety of misgivings about the wisdom of placing the state governments under the obligation of equalizing the funding of local school districts. He observed that "whoever exclusively controls the purse strings in the end will control all programs and policies" and contended that "such a denigration of local school boards would not be in the best interest of education or our country." Once again, Harry Blackmun expressed similar fears, characterizing the effort to require states to fund education on a statewide basis as "just another step leading toward big government and centralized control in another field, to wit, education."[30]

Powell and Blackmun were also concerned with the possibility that placing the states in control of school financing decisions would lead to a decrease in funding for more highly funded districts rather than an increase in spending in those districts where schools were underfunded. Thus, Blackmun worried that, in the event statewide equal spending was required,

> rich districts will give up spending more for schools. Poor districts will receive more, but there will be a limit to what they receive. The result is a disinteresting equality with no one getting anything that is very good. This almost smacks of the type of thing that emerged from the French revolution. Will it also drive those who are interested in quality education into private schools and away from the public schools just when, particularly in the South, public schools need all the support and attendance they can have?[31]

In addition to their misgivings about the potential impact of federal judicial intervention on the operation of the public schools specifically, Powell and Blackmun were deeply concerned about the potential implications of abandoning the rational basis test in *Rodriguez* for the structure of constitutional analysis more generally. Neither showed any inclination to formally abandon two-tiered analysis in *Rodriguez*. For example, after Powell's law clerk urged him to adopt a sliding-scale approach, Powell rejected this argument out of hand, asserting that "this leaves the judgment in the realm of subjectivity, and does not lead to a legal decision."

In addition, for purposes of constitutional analysis, neither Powell nor Blackmun found any principled basis for distinguishing the right to receive a public education from other important governmental services not explicitly mentioned in the Constitution. Thus, in his preliminary analysis of the issues presented by *Rodriguez*, Blackmun asked rhetorically, "If [the Constitution requires] education . . . to be distributed equally throughout the state, why does not the same thesis apply to police protection, hospitals, fire protection, and other such services?" Similarly, in addition to observing wryly that "now that I live in Washington, D.C., and am afraid to walk its streets at night, that public safety seems terribly fundamental," Powell noted that although "I personally would be inclined subjectively to place a higher value on education than on welfare and housing . . . one may doubt that the millions of Americans on welfare, and the other millions who are dependent on government subsidy for housing, would agree."[32]

With his colleagues equally divided, the balance of power in *Rodriguez* rested with Stewart. Although declaring at the conference that he was "not at rest," Stewart tentatively voted to reject the constitutional challenge. Stewart was willing to concede that the amount spent on the schools provided "some index" of educational quality. However, he asserted that the equal protection clause could not appropriately be invoked against the Texas financing system because he could not identify a "discrete class of people invidiously discriminated against."[33]

After the conference vote, with at least a tentative majority in favor of rejecting the constitutional challenge, Powell was assigned the task of preparing the majority opinion in *Rodriguez*. When the first draft of the opinion was circulated, Stewart raised objections to Powell's treatment of the relationship between the equal protection clause and the concept of fundamental rights. In some earlier cases, Stewart had concurred in opinions that had invoked equal protection analysis to apply strict scrutiny on the theory that fundamental rights were being denied to some individuals. In *Rodriguez*, by contrast, he argued that the Court should repudiate the idea that the equal protection clause provides special protection for rights the justices deemed "fundamental," reserving strict scrutiny under equal protection analysis for classifications that discriminated on the basis of race and alienage as well as "perhaps sex, perhaps illegitimacy, and indigency" and specifically excluding relative poverty. Stewart objected to the first draft of Powell's opinion because it reaffirmed the basic structure of the fundamental rights branch of two-tiered analysis. However, after Powell revised the opinion to meet some of his objections, Stewart agreed to concur in the opinion as well as drafting a separate concurrence of his own.[34]

Despite the changes, the majority opinion in *Rodriguez* embraced the basic structure of two-tiered analysis as well as the concerns Powell, Blackmun, and Stewart had expressed during their consideration of the case. After describing the elements of the Texas school financing system, Powell first addressed the contention that the application of strict scrutiny was appropriate because the system discriminated against some students on the basis of wealth. Powell rejected this argument, noting that, unlike the cases in which the Court had relied on wealth discrimination to raise the level of scrutiny, the Texas system discriminated only against a "large, diverse, and amorphous class, unified only by the common factor of residence in districts that happen to have less taxable wealth than other districts" and that this class had none of the traditional "indicia of suspectness." Drawing on the framework developed in the famous *Carolene Products* footnote, he observed that the "class is not saddled with such disabilities, or subjected to such a history of purposeful unequal treatment, or relegated to such a position of political powerlessness as to command extraordinary protection from the majoritarian political process."[35]

The majority opinion then turned to the argument that education should be considered a fundamental right. Referencing earlier decisions in which the Court had declined to give special protection to the rights to receive welfare benefits and have access to adequate housing, Powell emphasized the distinction between the "social importance" of a right and the question of whether that right was "explicitly or implicitly guaranteed by the Constitution." He found no such guarantee with respect to the right to a public education, rejecting the contention that the right should be deemed fundamental because education was necessary to the effective exercise of the right to vote and exercise the First Amendment freedom of speech.[36]

Conversely, Powell argued that the specific nature of the issues presented in *Rodriguez* made the use of strict scrutiny particularly inappropriate. In addition to observing that the Court had consistently emphasized the need to defer to legislative judgments on issues of fiscal policy, he noted the complexity of the issues related to public education and implicitly invoked Benjamin Cardozo's principle of "experimental federalism," averring that the "judiciary is well advised to refrain from imposing on the States inflexible constitutional restraints that could circumscribe or handicap the continued research and experimentation so vital to finding even partial solutions to educational problems and to keeping abreast of ever-changing conditions." Thus, while leaving open the possibility that the Court might take a different view of a case in which public education was *completely* denied to some class of children, Powell concluded that the rational basis test provided the appropriate standard of review in *Rodriguez*. Applying this test, he had no trouble in finding that the Texas system was rationally related to the state interest in ensuring a basic education for each child in the state and at the same time providing for a "large measure of participation in and control of each district's schools at the local level."[37]

Although he joined Powell's opinion, Stewart also filed a separate concurrence, emphasizing his view that, in general, the equal protection clause should not be seen as a vehicle for enforcing fundamental rights. In addition, three separate dissenting opinions were written in *Rodriguez*. Justices Douglas and Brennan joined an opinion by Justice White that concluded that the Texas system lacked a rational basis. White conceded that a financing system would be constitutional if it provided a meaningful opportunity for parents to improve their children's education by increasing per pupil expenditures. However, he argued that no such option was realistically available in property-poor districts such as Englewood. Brennan added a separate opinion contending that education should be considered a fundamental right because, in his view, "there can be no doubt that education is inextricably linked to the right to participate in the electoral process and to the rights of free speech and association."[38]

Douglas also joined an opinion by Marshall that, like Marshall's opinion in *Kras,* differed markedly in tone from the other two dissents. In *Rodriguez*, Marshall emphasized what he viewed as the fundamentality of education for constitutional purposes and criticized the two-tiered approach to equal protection analysis more generally, advocating instead a "sliding scale" approach under which the Court would be called upon to make individualized judgments assessing the significance of the particular right at stake and the importance of the state interest served by the challenged classification. But in addition, he complained bitterly that *Rodriguez* was a "retreat from our historic commitment to equality of educational opportunity and [an] unsupportable acquiescence in a system which deprives children in their earliest years of the chance to reach their full potential as citizens" and complained that, because of the majority's unwillingness to strike down the Texas school financing scheme, "countless children [will] unjustifiably receive inferior educations that 'may affect their hearts and minds in a way unlikely ever to be undone.'"[39]

From a practical perspective, *Rodriguez* was clearly one of the most important decisions of the 1972 term. If the dissenters had prevailed, almost every state in the Union would have been required to dramatically change its system for financing public schools. Thus, opponents of the practice of financing public schools through local property taxes understandably shared Marshall's disappointment with the Court's disposition of the case. Reflecting on the fact that the constitutional challenge had been rejected by the narrowest of margins, one of the architects of the constitutional assault on the Texas system observed, "It hurts when [victory was] so close."[40] In essence, the critics of the existing system of school finance lost the opportunity to triumph nationally with a single stroke.[41]

Of course, *Rodriguez* did not by any means sound the death knell for the movement to drastically alter the system by which public schools were financed in the United States. Proponents of the reform movement continued to press their cause at the state level and won a number of signal victories in state supreme courts that invoked their own constitutions to force the other branches of state governments to adopt major changes in the financing mechanism.[42] Nonetheless, the type of school financing regime challenged in *Rodriguez* remains common in the United States.

From a broader doctrinal perspective, *Rodriguez* was less significant than it might have appeared at first glance. On its face, the majority opinion appeared to be a paean to the idea of judicial deference in general as well as a strong endorsement of the basic principles of two-tiered analysis. However, as already noted, at least some members of the majority were also plainly influenced by an awareness of the magnitude of the task federal judges would have faced if the Court had constitutionalized the debate over school finance. Justice Powell in particular clearly believed that given the complexities of the issues surrounding school finance, the relevant decisions were best left to officials who had a greater familiarity with local conditions. Moreover, during the 1972 term, both Powell himself and a number of the other members of the *Rodriguez* majority demonstrated a clear willingness to deploy the Constitution against specific provisions in social welfare programs they viewed as fundamentally unfair. This point is clearly illustrated by the decisions in *Vlandis v. Kline, United States Department of Agriculture v. Murry,* and *Department of Agriculture v. Moreno.*[43]

In *Vlandis,* the Court was called upon to consider the process by which the state of Connecticut determined the amount of tuition to be paid by certain students who attended the University of Connecticut, the state's flagship public university. Like most public universities, the University of

Connecticut distinguished between Connecticut residents and all other students for purposes of determining tuition rates, with Connecticut residents paying far less for the privilege of attending the state university. The plaintiffs in *Vlandis* conceded that the state could constitutionally make this basic distinction in determining tuition rates. However, at the same time, they challenged the constitutionality of a 1971 Connecticut statute that provided that, for purposes of determining tuition, the resident or nonresident status of a student would be permanently fixed at the time of his application. In other words, under this statute, a student who was not a resident of Connecticut at the time of his application could never qualify for in-state tuition rates during the period of his matriculation at the university.

In general, the class of people adversely affected by the Connecticut statute—students who wished to attend a public university located outside their home state—would hardly qualify as a disadvantaged group or one whose plight was likely to elicit sympathy from the justices. Nonetheless, the impact of the rule on the plaintiff in *Vlandis* itself seemed particularly unfair. In May 1971, the plaintiff, then a California resident attending a public college in that state, became engaged to be married to a Connecticut resident and, because she intended to live with her husband in that state, applied to be admitted to the University of Connecticut as a transfer student. She was duly admitted, and soon after being married on June 26, she and her husband took up residence in Connecticut. Under prior law, the plaintiff would have been eligible for in-state tuition. However, after the new statute took effect on July 1, she was forced to pay the higher rate charged to non-Connecticut residents.

If the constitutional challenge in *Vlandis* had been subjected only to traditional equal protection analysis, this apparent injustice would not have provided a sufficient reason to strike down the Connecticut rule. Under the rational basis test, the mere fact that a rule created an unjust result in one or even a large number of cases was not enough to condemn the rule as unconstitutional. Instead, the only requirement was that the classification have some rational relationship to a permissible state interest. In *Vlandis*, the classification was clearly related to the state interest in limiting access to in-state tuition rates to those whose families were more likely to have made significant contributions in the form of taxes to state revenues, which in turn were used to provide part of the funding for the state's public universities.

Justices Douglas and Rehnquist were persuaded by this analysis and concluded that the challenge to the Connecticut statute should be rejected. After some hesitation, Chief Justice Burger also voted in favor of rejecting the challenge. However, the remainder of the justices disagreed, creating a majority for striking down the statute. At the conference on *Vlandis*, Justices Brennan and Marshall deployed standard two-tiered analysis against the Connecticut statute, analogizing *Vlandis* to *Shapiro v. Thompson* and *Dunn v. Blumstein* and arguing that strict scrutiny should be applied because the tuition differential infringed on the constitutionally protected right to travel by treating longtime residents more favorably than their newly arrived counterparts.[44] In making this argument, they acknowledged the tension between this conclusion and the Court's 1971 decision in *Starns v. Malkerson*, in which the justices had summarily affirmed a lower court judgment rejecting a constitutional challenge to a one-year durational residency requirement for eligibility for in-state tuition rates.[45]

However, when Brennan proposed that the majority opinion adopt this theory, Justice Powell demurred. Although characterizing the statute in *Vlandis* itself as "egregiously irrational," Powell voiced strong objection to any opinion that would have cast doubt on the constitutionality of the type of durational residency requirement that had been at issue in *Starns*. He noted that the imposition of strict scrutiny would be tantamount to a death sentence for such requirements and that, in their absence, out-of-state students could easily produce objective indicia of domicile without in fact having the subjective intention to remain permanently in the state in which they were attending college.

Against this background, no doubt with an eye to the situation of the highly regarded public universities in his home state of Virginia, Powell complained that "if a state is denied the right to impose reasonable limitations on the influx of out-of-state students who immediately claim . . . to be *bona fide* residents . . . a certain amount of fraud would result" and that "if, in the exercise of the right to travel, young people were allowed—in effect—to attend [at reduced cost] merely by saying they are domiciliaries of the state, some of our finest state universities could be overwhelmed with applications." Powell observed that this increase in competition for relatively scarce positions in flagship state universities would work to the detriment of those who were in fact bona fide residents, including lower-income students whose options were limited.[46]

The existing structure of equal protection analysis created a problem for Powell and the other justices who wished to invalidate the Connecticut statute while at the same time preserving the integrity of the preference for bona fide residents generally. Byron White's solution to the problem was to follow the path outlined by Thurgood Marshall in *Rodriguez* and other cases and openly abandon two-tiered analysis altogether in favor of a sliding-scale approach. In *Vlandis*, White argued simply that the statutory classifications lacked sufficient justification in view of the substantiality of the interests involved.[47]

However, Justices Stewart, Blackmun, and Powell remained generally committed to two-tiered analysis and were unwilling to abandon that approach in *Vlandis*. Instead, together with Justices Brennan and Marshall, Blackmun and Powell joined an opinion by Justice Stewart that analyzed the case in procedural due process terms. Stewart argued that the Connecticut statute denied those in the position of the challenger procedural due process by creating an "irrebuttable presumption" that they would never become bona fide residents of Connecticut during their tenure at the University of Connecticut.[48]

Although the genesis of the irrebuttable presumption doctrine can be traced to a number of earlier cases, the doctrine was first clearly articulated in the 1972 decision in *Stanley v. Illinois*.[49] *Stanley* was a challenge to an Illinois statute that provided that children could be declared wards of the state if they had no "surviving parent or guardian" but excluded unwed biological fathers from the definition of "surviving parent." As a result, a child could be removed from the custody of a biological father in that position without a showing that the father was an unfit parent. The constitutionality of the statute was attacked by a man who had fathered three children by a woman with whom he had lived intermittently for seventeen years but had lost custody of the children after her death.

With Chief Justice Burger and Justice Blackmun dissenting and Justices Powell and Rehnquist not participating, the *Stanley* Court concluded that the state must, at the very least, allow unwed fathers the opportunity to prove their fitness before removing children from their custody. Speaking for the majority, Justice White observed that the "interest . . . of a man in the children he has sired and raised undeniably warrants deference and, absent a powerful countervailing interest, protection." White conceded the strength of the state interest in protecting "'the moral, emotional, mental, and physical welfare of the minor and the best interests of the community'" but also noted that the Illinois laws themselves declared that one of the goals of the statutes was to "'strengthen the minor's family ties whenever possible, removing him from the custody of his parents only when his welfare or safety or the protection of the public cannot be adequately safeguarded without removal.'"[50]

In *Stanley*, White appeared to implicitly concede that there might be some rough correlation between the marital status of the biological father and his fitness as a parent. However, at the same time, he also observed that the "State registers no gain towards its declared goals when it separates children from the custody of fit parents" and that "if Stanley is a fit father, the State spites its own articulated goals when it needlessly separates him from his family." Thus, White found the Illinois statute constitutionally infirm, declaring that "procedure by presumption is always cheaper and easier than individualized determination. But when, as here, the procedure forecloses the determinative issues of competence and care, when it explicitly disdains present realities in deference to past formalities, it needlessly risks running roughshod over the important interests of both parent and child. It therefore cannot stand."[51]

Stewart's opinion in *Vlandis* followed much the same pattern. The opinion noted that "Connecticut's statutory scheme . . . makes no distinction on its face between established residents and new residents by statute" but instead "purport[s] to distinguish, for tuition purposes, between residents and nonresidents by granting the lower rates to the former and denying them to the latter." Stewart appeared to concede that the statutory scheme was an inexpensive and reasonably accurate method of preventing out-of-state students from fraudulently claiming they had in fact become bona fide residents of Connecticut. Nonetheless, echoing *Stanley*'s declaration that "'the Constitution recognizes higher values than speed and efficiency,'" he concluded that because "Connecticut purports to be concerned with residency in allocating the rates for tuition and fees in its university system, it is forbidden by the Due Process Clause to deny an individual the resident rates on the basis of a permanent and irrebuttable presumption of nonresidence, when that presumption is not necessarily or universally true, in fact, and when the State has reasonable alternative means of making the crucial determination."[52]

By relying on the irrebuttable presumption doctrine, the majority was able to strike down the specific provision in *Vlandis* without raising the specter of wholesale intervention in social welfare programs that was anathema to justices such as Stewart and Powell. However, the same trait made the doctrine ill suited for use against other statutory provisions that a number of the justices saw as profoundly misguided. In some of those situations, these justices were forced into a choice between temporarily abandoning their allegiance to traditional rational basis analysis and allowing the offending statute to stand. *Murry* and *Moreno* presented the centrist justices just such a dilemma.

Both decisions were part of a broader struggle over the place of constitutional law in determining the allocation of welfare benefits. Until relatively recently, the potential for judicial oversight of the welfare system was limited by the widespread acceptance of the distinction between rights and privileges for constitutional purposes. In simple terms, under this regime, the Constitution was generally seen as protecting only individual "rights." Conversely, the Constitution was viewed as having little to say about access to "privileges." Because under this taxonomy welfare benefits were clearly a privilege rather than a right, constitutional challenges to denials of such benefits had little chance of success. By the late 1960s, however, the right/privilege distinction had fallen out of favor with both the Court and academic commentators. Thus, the doctrinal barriers to constitutional challenges to restrictions on access to welfare benefits were reduced substantially.[53]

The first major constitutional victory for welfare rights activists came with the 1969 decision in *Shapiro v. Thompson*. In that case, over the dissents of Chief Justice Warren and Justice Harlan, the Court held that states could not constitutionally require indigent residents to be present in the state for one year before receiving benefits under the federally funded Aid to Families with Dependent Children (AFDC) program, even if Congress had authorized the imposition of such a durational residency requirement. Justice Brennan's perception of the significance of welfare benefits played an important role in his majority opinion. Brennan repeatedly emphasized the importance of such benefits to indigent families, noting that such families might very well depend on welfare for the "very means to subsist—food, shelter, and other necessities of life" and observing that an "indigent who desires to migrate, resettle, find a new job, and start a new life will doubtless hesitate if he knows that he must risk making the move without the possibility of falling back on state welfare assistance during his first year of residence, when his need may be most acute."[54]

Despite this rhetoric, the majority opinion in *Shapiro* did not ultimately rest on the theory that denials of welfare benefits per se were subject to more than rational basis scrutiny. Instead, Brennan argued that the durational residency requirements were subject to strict scrutiny because they infringed on what he characterized as a fundamental right to travel.[55] Thus, it was not until the following year that two decisions by the Court clearly resolved the question of the place of welfare benefits in modern constitutional jurisprudence.

Goldberg v. Kelly provided another major victory for welfare rights advocates. In that case, welfare recipients argued that the due process clause required the government to provide them formal evidentiary hearings before terminating those benefits.[56] Chief Justice Burger and Justices Black and Stewart would have rejected this argument, with Black asserting that the requirement of a pretermination hearing would "paralyze the government's efforts to protect itself against making payments to people who are not entitled to them."[57] However, with Harry Blackmun having not yet joined the Court, five justices disagreed, concluding that pretermination hearings were in fact required by the Constitution.

The majority once again spoke through Justice Brennan. Distinguishing the fact situation in *Goldberg* from those cases in which pretermination hearings were not constitutionally required, Justice Brennan emphasized the significance of welfare benefits to the recipients even more strongly than he had in *Shapiro*. He observed that "welfare provides the means to obtain essential food, clothing, housing, and medical care [, and therefore] termination of aid pending resolution of a controversy over eligibility may deprive an eligible recipient of the very means by which to live while he waits."[58] In addition, the *Goldberg* opinion sought to portray welfare benefits as an integral part of the US constitutional order. He declared that "from its founding the Nation's basic commitment has been to foster the dignity and well-being of all persons within its borders" and that

> welfare, by meeting the basic demands of subsistence, can help bring within the reach of the poor the same opportunities that are available to others to participate meaningfully in the life of the community. At the same time, welfare guards against the societal malaise that may flow from a widespread sense of unjustified frustration and insecurity. Public assistance, then, is not mere charity, but a means to "promote the general Welfare, and secure the Blessings of Liberty to ourselves and our Posterity."[59]

Thus, Brennan concluded that requiring pretermination hearings served the interests not only of the recipients but also of the government itself.

Welfare rights advocates were understandably heartened by the result in *Goldberg*.[60] Moreover, particularly when considered in conjunction with *Shapiro*, the language of Justice Brennan's opinion might well have been taken to suggest that the justices were prepared to closely scrutinize substantive limitations on welfare benefits as well. However, less than two weeks later, the decision in *Dandridge v. Williams* sounded a very different note.[61]

Dandridge was a challenge to a Maryland regulation that limited the total amount of benefits a family in that state might receive under the AFDC program, no matter how many children might be living in the household. AFDC recipients with large families argued that this limitation not only violated the federal statute that established the program itself but also ran afoul of the equal protection clause. Justices Harlan and White joined the dissenters from *Goldberg* to create a five-justice majority that rejected both challenges.

Although recognizing that the "administration of public welfare assistance . . . involves the most basic economic needs of impoverished human beings," Justice Stewart's opinion for the Court asserted that the resolution of the constitutional challenge in *Dandridge* should be governed by the traditional rational basis test developed in connection with cases involving constitutional attacks on business and economic regulations generally. Against this background, Stewart had no trouble in concluding that the ceiling on benefits was rationally related to the "State's legitimate interest in encouraging employment and in avoiding discrimination between welfare families and the families of the working poor."[62]

Justices Douglas, Brennan, and Marshall dissented in *Dandridge.* Whereas Douglas based his position solely on federal statutory law, Brennan joined Marshall in taking sharp issue with Stewart's constitutional analysis. Foreshadowing the argument that he would later make in *Rodriguez,* Marshall's opinion argued that two-tiered equal protection analysis should be rejected in favor of a sliding-scale approach and contended that, given the importance of welfare benefits to indigent families, the state interest was insufficient to justify the limits on benefits available to poor families.[63] Once again dissenting, he would reiterate this argument the following year in *Jefferson v. Hackney* as the newly appointed Justices Blackmun, Powell, and Rehnquist joined the holdovers from the *Dandridge* majority in applying the rational basis test to reject a constitutional challenge to a Texas plan for calculating the amount of AFDC funds to which indigent families were entitled.[64]

Dandridge and *Jefferson* doomed the efforts of progressives to derive a judicially enforceable constitutional right to basic sustenance from the Constitution. By contrast, during the 1972 term, *Moreno* and *Murry* demonstrated that a majority of the Burger Court justices remained willing to intervene against specific exclusions they viewed as fundamentally unfair. Both cases raised constitutional challenges to amendments to the Food Stamp Act of 1965, which had created a program under which currently needy households whose members complied with a work requirement were entitled to purchase enough food stamps to provide those households with nutritionally adequate diets, with the household paying for the stamps at a reduced rate based upon its size and cumulative income. However, unlike *Dandridge v. Williams* and *Jefferson v. Hackney*, neither case dealt with limitations on benefits to groups or individuals whom Congress considered to be truly worthy of assistance. Instead, both focused on specific aspects of the 1971 amendments to the Food Stamp Act that were designed to address what Congress saw as abuses of the program.

Moreno was a challenge to a 1971 change in the description of the groups eligible to receive food stamps. As originally adopted in 1964, the statute defined a "household" as a group of "related or unrelated" individuals living together as a single economic unit. The 1971 amendment changed the definition to limit access to food stamps to groups of related individuals. The only available legislative history indicated that the change was designed to prevent people who were members of "hippie communes" from qualifying for food stamps.

One of the major problems the justices saw with the statute was that, in attempting to deal with this perceived difficulty, the change in the definition of household had disqualified many individuals living in households with unrelated people for perfectly understandable and even laudable reasons. Thus, the plaintiff in *Moreno* presented a variety of heartrending stories designed to illustrate the hardships that the change in definition created for a substantial number of the very people the food stamp program was designed to help.[65]

Even Justice Rehnquist conceded that "Congress has shot with [a] shotgun rather than [a] rifle." Nonetheless, both he and Chief Justice Burger concluded that the amendment passed constitutional muster under the rational basis test, with Rehnquist observing,

> I do not think it is unreasonable for Congress to conclude that the basic unit which it was willing to support with federal funding through food stamps is some variation on the family as we know it—a household consisting of related individuals. This unit provides a guarantee which is not provided by households containing unrelated individuals that the household exists for some purpose other than to collect federal food stamps.[66]

However, despite its apparent consistency with the traditional approach to rational basis analysis, the remaining seven justices were unpersuaded by Rehnquist's argument. All of these justices joined an opinion by

Justice Brennan that concluded that the new definition failed the rational basis test. Brennan began by rejecting any suggestion that a distaste for "hippie communes" per se provided a constitutionally sufficient justification for the 1971 amendment, asserting that "if the constitutional conception of 'equal protection of the laws' means anything, it must, at the very least, mean that a bare congressional desire to harm a politically unpopular group cannot constitute a *legitimate* governmental interest," although conceding that the prevention of fraud could in theory have provided a constitutionally sufficient justification for the change in the statute. Nonetheless, asserting that those with sufficient means could simply rearrange their living arrangements in order to meet the requirements for eligibility, Brennan insisted that "in practical effect, the challenged classification simply does not operate so as rationally to further the prevention of fraud." He concluded that "in practical operation, the 1971 amendment excludes from participation in the food stamp program *not* those persons who are 'likely to abuse the program' but, rather, *only* those persons who are so desperately in need of aid that they cannot even afford to alter their living arrangements so as to retain their eligibility," and thus it could not stand.[67]

The Court was more deeply divided over the proper disposition of *Murry*. That case arose from a challenge to a provision in the 1971 amendment that denied access to food stamps to any household that included a person over the age of eighteen who had been claimed as a dependent by a member of a different household that was not eligible to participate in the food stamp program. The amendment was designed to combat abuse of the program by college students and other children of wealthy parents, preventing the families of such people from simultaneously benefiting from both the food stamp program and the provisions of the Internal Revenue Code that allowed those families to reduce their tax burden if they were in fact providing support for their adult children, which in turn would reduce the funds available to support those families that were truly in need—a goal that all agreed was legitimate. The difficulty was that, as written, the amendment inevitably had the effect of denying food stamps to a substantial number of truly needy families. Moreover, on its face at least, the amendment could operate to render a family ineligible even where the person claiming the tax deduction had not in fact provided any support for the child being claimed as a dependent.

The situations in which the six plaintiffs in *Murry* found themselves dramatically illustrated the impact of the 1971 amendment on some poor families. The households of each of the plaintiffs were undoubtedly needy but had been denied access to food stamps because one of the members of the household was over eighteen years of age and had been claimed as a dependent on the tax return of a person not eligible to participate in the program. In five of the six cases, no support had ever actually been provided to the alleged dependent. In the remaining case, a small amount of support had in fact been provided to the over-age dependent, but the person receiving the support was one of twelve children and grandchildren living together in a household with a total income of less than 60 dollars per month.[68]

Embracing a suggestion made by the solicitor general, Justice Blackmun argued that the Court should not reach any of the constitutional arguments but should instead remand the case for a construction of the statute by the lower courts. Blackmun reasoned that the constitutional arguments against the application of the 1971 amendment would be weakened considerably if the statute was interpreted to deny eligibility for food stamps only if the attempt to claim the deduction for the dependent was legitimate. Initially, Justice Rehnquist indicated his willingness to accept this disposition of the case, and Justice Powell not only embraced Blackmun's position but also made private efforts to persuade Justice Stewart to join an opinion taking this view. However, Stewart rebuffed Powell on this point, and after it became clear that a majority of the justices were determined to reach the constitutional issue, both Chief Justice Burger and Justice Powell joined an opinion by Justice Rehnquist arguing that the amendment should be upheld against constitutional attack. Rehnquist's argument followed a familiar pattern, arguing that the traditional rational basis test provided the appropriate standard of review and that the 1971 amendment was clearly constitutional under this standard.[69]

However, five justices took a different view, concluding instead that the 1971 amendment violated the due process clause of the Fifth Amendment. Justice Marshall's concurring opinion reiterated his support for a sliding-scale approach, whereas Justice Stewart's concurrence focused solely on the irrebuttable presumption analysis he had deployed in *Vlandis*.[70] By contrast, the analysis of Justice Douglas's majority opinion melded that approach with the kind of enhanced rational basis scrutiny that characterized the opinion for the Court in *Moreno*.

Douglas averred that "we have difficulty in concluding that it is rational to assume that a child is not indigent this year because the parent declared the child as a dependent in his tax return for the prior year [, and in any event] under the [1971 amendment] the issue is not the indigency of the child but the indigency of a different household with which the child happens to be living." He concluded that the "deduction taken for the benefit of the parent in the prior year is not a rational measure of the need of a different household with which the child of the tax-deducting parent lives and rests on an irrebuttable presumption often contrary to fact. It therefore lacks critical ingredients of due process."[71]

The pattern evinced by the welfare cases typified the treatment of the rational basis test by the Court generally during the Burger era. On one hand, in most cases, the decision to apply the rational basis test was tantamount to a holding that a challenged classification would survive an equal protection challenge. On the other, on rare occasions when no other doctrinal formulation was available, a majority of the justices would seize on the requirement of rationality to strike down a classification they found particularly obnoxious.[72]

However, manipulation of the rational basis test was not the only device used by the Burger Court to find that classifications violated the equal protection clause. At times, a majority of the justices seemed to suggest they were willing to formally raise the standard of review on classifications that received rational basis scrutiny during the Warren era. During the 1972 term, the most important example of this phenomenon was the analysis of sex discrimination in *Frontiero v. Richardson*.[73]

Chapter Eight

The Problem of Sex Discrimination

During the 1960s, one of the most significant developments in the social and political life of the United States was the emergence of the modern feminist movement. Although the intellectual origins of modern feminism can be traced to the publication of Simone de Beauvoir's *The Second Sex* in 1949, it was not until after the appearance of Betty Friedan's *The Feminine Mystique* in 1963 that the traditional structure of gender roles in the United States came under serious attack as affluent, well-educated women in particular increasingly demanded the opportunity to have access to better employment opportunities and to take on more active roles in spheres historically dominated by men more generally. Although feminists won signal legislative victories with the passage of the Equal Pay Act of 1963 and the Civil Rights Act of 1964, many laws that discriminated on the basis of sex remained in force at the time Warren Burger ascended to the chief justiceship. Feminists and their allies sought to change these laws through a variety of different mechanisms.[1]

The impact of the feminist movement on the political dynamic was perhaps most clearly reflected in congressional action on the Equal Rights Amendment (ERA). A constitutional amendment that would have prohibited government discrimination on the basis of sex was first proposed by Alice Paul in 1923, and some version of the ERA was introduced in every Congress thereafter. Moreover, every Republican platform beginning in 1940 and every Democratic platform beginning in 1944 voiced support for such an amendment. Nonetheless, supporters never really came close to gaining congressional approval until the early 1970s. However, in 1972, the Senate approved the ERA on a vote of 80–8 after the amendment had passed the House of Representatives by a margin of 354–23.[2] The overwhelming margins in both houses reflected a perception among a wide range of politicians that by the early 1970s, whatever one's actual views about the appropriate roles of women might be, it had become both unfashionable and politically dangerous among the political elites to publicly defend the idea that the government should generally treat men differently than women because of their respective genders.

However, the ratification struggle that followed reflected a more complex political dynamic. To be sure, by early 1973 the legislatures of twenty-five states had ratified the ERA, and five more states would follow by the end of that year. But as the opposition became more organized, it became apparent that obtaining the additional ratifications needed to add the amendment to the Constitution would be far more difficult.

Those who opposed the amendment fell into two camps. Some forthrightly defended the traditional differences between the roles of men and women in society. Thus, for example, anti-ERA leader Phyllis Schlafly rhapsodized about the "Christian age of chivalry" and what she described as the "American way," in which a "man's first significant purchase is a diamond for his bride, and the largest financial investment of his life is a house for her to live in." By contrast, other opponents of the ERA professed to agree that women should in general have equal status in society, but at the same time voiced concerns about both the potential effects of the amendment on single-sex institutions and a variety of privacy-related considerations. Members of this group argued that issues of sex discrimination were best dealt with on an individualized basis by more narrowly tailored federal legislation. Under the weight of such objections, by March 1973, eleven state legislatures had formally rejected efforts to ratify the ERA, and supporters of the amendment had plainly lost momentum, particularly in the Southern and Western states.[3]

However, the effort to have an explicit prohibition on sex discrimination added to the Constitution was only part of a coordinated attack on legally mandated classifications based on gender. At the same time they were pressing hard to have the ERA ratified by the requisite number of state legislatures, feminists were also pursuing a parallel strategy in the federal courts. Through the process of litigation, they sought to have classifications based on gender declared unconstitutional under the Fifth and Fourteenth Amendments, independently of the ERA. The 1973 decision in *Frontiero v. Richardson* grew out of these efforts.[4]

Frontiero was hardly the first case in which the Court had faced the claim that laws that discriminated on the basis of sex violated the Constitution. Indeed, Fourteenth Amendment challenges to such discrimination first came to the Court as early as the 1870s, soon after the amendment was ratified. Although on occasion laws designed specifically to protect women were invalidated during the *Lochner* era, for more than a century the Court showed little sympathy for the claim that sex discrimination per se created significant equal protection problems.[5]

In general, the justices took the view that such discrimination was justified by inherent physical differences between men and women and the different roles played by men and women in society. Thus, in his 1873 opinion in *Bradwell v. Illinois* Justice Joseph P. Bradley rejected the claim that the state of Illinois could not constitutionally exclude women from the practice of law, declaring:

> The civil law, as well as nature herself, has always recognized a wide difference in the respective spheres and destinies of man and woman. Man is, or should be, woman's protector and defender. The natural and proper timidity and delicacy which belongs to the female sex evidently unfits it for many of the occupations of civil life. The Constitution of the family organization, which is founded in the divine ordinance as well as in the nature of things, indicates the domestic sphere as that which properly belongs to the domain and functions of womanhood. The harmony, not to say identity, of interest and views which belong, or should belong, to the family institution is repugnant to the idea of a woman adopting a distinct and independent career from that of her husband.[6]

Against this background, Bradley concluded that "in view of the peculiar characteristics, destiny, and mission of woman, it is within the province of the legislature to ordain what offices, positions, and callings shall be filled and discharged by men, and shall receive the benefit of those energies and responsibilities, and that decision and firmness which are presumed to predominate in the sterner sex."[7]

Although mainstream perceptions of sex roles became less rigid during the first half of the twentieth century, as late as 1961 the Warren Court took a similar view of the constitutionality of gender-based discrimination in *Hoyt v. Florida*. In that case, the justices unanimously rejected an equal protection attack on a Florida statute that provided women an absolute exemption from jury service. The language of Justice John Marshall Harlan's majority opinion evoked echoes of Justice Bradley's opinion in *Bradwell*:

> Despite the enlightened emancipation of women from the restrictions and protections of bygone years, and their entry into many parts of community life formerly considered to be reserved to men, woman is still regarded as the center of home and family life. We cannot say that it is constitutionally impermissible for a State, acting in pursuit of the general welfare, to conclude that a woman should be relieved from the civic duty of jury service unless she herself determines that such service is consistent with her own special responsibilities.[8]

Although Florida's specific treatment of women jurors did not reflect the position taken by a majority of states, Harlan's conception of the place of women in society was an apt reflection of the views shared by the vast majority of Americans in 1961. However, as the feminist critique of these views gained increasing traction, the constitutional analysis embodied in *Hoyt* also came under attack.

Even before the consideration of *Frontiero,* the 1971 decision in *Reed v. Reed* had suggested that the Burger Court would be less deferential than its predecessors in cases involving sex discrimination.[9] *Reed*—argued and decided after Justices Black and Harlan had left the Court but before Lewis Powell and William Rehnquist had been confirmed—was a challenge to an Idaho statute that governed the appointment of administrators of estates when the decedent had died intestate. The statute established a priority ranking for relatives of the decedent in determining who would be selected as the administrator and also provided that in the event two relatives were otherwise of equal priority, the male relative would be preferred over the female. Thus, the widow of the decedent would have priority over all other relatives, but the father of the decedent would automatically have priority over the mother.

The Court unanimously held that the preference for men violated the equal protection clause. Chief Justice Burger's brief opinion for the Court observed that the Idaho Supreme Court had concluded that the purpose of the classification was to "resolve an issue that would otherwise require a hearing as to the relative merits" and conceded "that the objective of reducing the workload on probate courts by eliminating one class of contests is not without some legitimacy." Nonetheless, characterizing the decision as "arbitrary" rather than one having a "fair and substantial relation to the object of the legislation," Burger concluded that "whatever may be said as to the positive values of avoiding intrafamily controversy, the choice in this context may not lawfully be mandated solely on the basis of sex."[10]

Although Burger's opinion sought to characterize *Reed* as a rational basis case, the Idaho statute would clearly have been upheld under the traditional rational basis test. The statutory decision to prefer men to women was not in fact a purely arbitrary choice. Instead, the preference was designed to choose the person who was more likely to be an effective administrator of the estate without having to go through the cost and inconvenience of holding a full-scale hearing on the merits of competing claims to the appointment.

Viewed from this perspective, the preference for men was entirely plausible. The decisions that must be made in connection with the administration of an estate are in many ways akin to those connected with the operation of a small business. For reasons beyond the control of those who drafted the Idaho statute, men were simply more likely than women to have experience in making such decisions. Thus, gender was correlated with the likelihood of being an effective administrator. The standard rational basis test required no more.

Against this background, some commentators initially viewed *Reed* as one of the harbingers of a general tightening of rational basis analysis.[11] After the decision in *Rodriguez*, however, this explanation was clearly implausible. Still, taken alone, *Reed* might simply have been grouped with cases such as *Murry* and *Moreno* as an isolated example of the use of the rational basis test to strike down a classification the justices found particularly offensive—in *Reed*, the idea being that in giving an absolute preference to men, the statute seemed to suggest women were inherently less able to administer estates. However, the 1973 decision in *Frontiero* made it clear that *Reed* had in fact been the first salvo in a much broader constitutional assault on statutory classifications based on gender.

Frontiero was a challenge to the use of gender in the statutory scheme for determining which members of the federal uniformed services would be allowed to claim their spouses as "dependents" for purposes of determining whether the service member was eligible for an increased housing allowance and the spouse was eligible for dental and medical benefits. Under the statute, a husband could automatically claim his wife as a dependent, but a wife could only claim her husband if she could demonstrate that he was in fact dependent on her for more than one-half of his support.

Unlike the Idaho statute overturned in *Reed*, the gender-based classification in *Frontiero* did not make any implicit judgment about the relative abilities of men and women. Instead, the federal statute was best understood as reflecting a reasoned effort to deal with the realities of gender roles and the fact that in general, even as late as the early 1970s, men had far greater earning potential than women, and thus few men were in fact dependent on their wives. Some of the justices clearly understood the potential relevance of the distinction between the two cases. For example, in his argument notes, Lewis Powell characterized *Frontiero* as a close case, observing that the statistical difference in dependency rates "may well constitute a rational basis [for the differential treatment of husbands and wives]." At the conference that followed the argument, Powell also observed that, unlike *Reed*, the statute in *Frontiero* in fact discriminated against men—the members of the military whose pay was being reduced—rather than women.[12]

Nonetheless, at the initial conference that followed the argument in the case, Powell joined Justices Douglas, Brennan, Stewart, and White to form a majority firmly committed to the view that the statutory discrimination was unconstitutional. Justices Marshall and Blackmun also tentatively agreed with this assessment, while the Chief Justice and Justice Rehnquist voted to reject the constitutional challenge.[13] With a majority apparently firmly in hand, Justice Brennan assigned himself the task of preparing an opinion for the Court.

On February 14, 1973, Brennan circulated a draft that explicitly refused to address the question of whether sex should be considered a suspect classification. Instead, the draft simply relied on the standard of review established in *Reed v. Reed* and argued that for constitutional purposes, the "situation [in *Frontiero*] is virtually identical to *Reed*."[14] Noting that the government had justified the statute in terms of administrative convenience, the draft did not dispute the government's assertion that "as an empirical matter, wives in our society frequently are dependent on their husbands, while husbands are rarely dependent on their wives" and observed that approximately 99 percent of all members of the uniformed services were male. Against this background, Brennan also appeared to accept the fact that "Congress might reasonably have concluded that it would be both cheaper and easier simply conclusively to presume that wives of male members [of the uniformed services] are financially dependent on their husbands, while burdening female members with the task of demonstrating dependency in fact." Nonetheless, although conceding that "efficacious administration of government programs is not without some importance," Brennan maintained that this justification was not sufficiently important to justify the statutory discrimination. Declaring that the "Constitution recognizes higher values than speed or efficiency," he concluded that *Reed* established that "any statutory scheme which draws a sharp line between the sexes, solely for the purpose of achieving administrative convenience, necessarily involves 'the very kind of arbitrary choice forbidden by the [Constitution].'"[15]

Even if the February 14 draft had become the opinion of the Court, *Frontiero* would appropriately have been seen as an extremely significant development in the evolution of the constitutional principles governing laws that discriminate on the basis of sex. However, the discussion took a sharply different turn when Brennan simultaneously circulated a memorandum suggesting that *Frontiero* be used as a vehicle to formally declare that sex was a suspect classification. On February 28, he distributed a new draft opinion that defended this view in detail.[16]

Brennan's second draft opinion generated a flurry of responses that reflected a variety of different perspectives. Both William O. Douglas and Thurgood Marshall quickly and fully embraced the notion that sex should be designated a suspect classification. Byron White also agreed in formal terms with this position but at the same time questioned the application of the compelling governmental interest test. As he did in *Vlandis v. Kline*, White embraced the basic theory of equal protection law articulated by Marshall in his *Rodriguez* dissent and opined that the designation of sex as a suspect classification meant that "we will balance or weigh competing interests."[17]

With four justices committed to the position that sex should be considered a suspect classification, Brennan needed one more vote to firmly ensconce that view in constitutional doctrine. Given their stated positions on the merits of *Frontiero* itself, neither Burger nor Rehnquist was a plausible candidate. Rehnquist had already publicly taken the position that only race and national origin should be viewed as suspect classifications, and on March 7, the chief justice observed wryly that the "author of *Reed* never remotely contemplated such a broad concept, but then a lot of people sire offspring unintended!" Having expressed his distaste for the entire concept of two-tiered analysis in his *Rodriguez* concurrence, Stewart was also unlikely to embrace the idea of creating a new suspect classification. Thus, responding two days after Brennan's memorandum of February 14, Stewart not only rejected the notion that the Court should declare sex a suspect classification but also urged Brennan to omit all discussion of the issue from his opinion and instead state simply that the majority found the statutory scheme "invidiously discriminatory."[18]

Lewis Powell and Harry Blackmun also demurred. On March 2, characterizing the question of whether sex should be designated a suspect classification as a "difficult one," Powell circulated a memorandum decrying the idea that men and women should be treated as "fungible" and asserting that the "reasons for different treatment [of men and women] have in no way resembled the purposeful and invidious discrimination against blacks and aliens." In addition, the memorandum observed that "it [may not] be said any longer that, as a class, women are a discrete minority barred from effective participation in the political process."[19]

In addition, while White had relied heavily on the fact that Congress had submitted the ERA to the states in concluding that sex should be considered a suspect classification, Powell and Blackmun drew a quite different lesson from the status of the ERA. They argued that because the ERA was under consideration in 1973, the Court should not be quick to establish sex as a suspect classification under the equal protection analysis. Powell questioned the "desirability of this Court reaching out to anticipate a major political decision which is currently in process of resolution by duly prescribed constitutional process." Three days later, Blackmun indicated that he had similar misgivings.[20]

On March 6, Brennan made a final effort to convince Powell and Blackmun to join an opinion that established sex as a suspect classification. Brennan contended that, despite Burger's protestations, *Reed* could only be understood as having been implicitly based on the theory that sex was a suspect classification. In addition, Brennan noted that the movement to ratify the ERA had lost momentum and described the movement as a "lost cause." At the same time, he observed that Congress and more than half the state legislatures had effectively taken the position that sex-based classifications were suspect by endorsing the ERA.[21]

Powell and Blackmun, however, remained unmoved. On March 8, in an internal memorandum to one of his law clerks, Powell reiterated the view that the course of action advocated by Brennan was both unnecessary and unwise. He asserted that "it is this sort of action which subjects the Court to criticism which even its friends have difficulty in rebutting. I sincerely think that our democratic institutions are weakened—and the ultimate position of the Court in our system also weakened—by unnecessary action of this kind." Conversely, neither Brennan nor any of his allies were willing to accept anything less than an explicit declaration that sex would heretofore be considered a suspect category, whereas Stewart was unwilling to join any opinion that was either implicitly or explicitly based on the two-tiered model of equal protection. Against this background, on March 12, Powell circulated an opinion that expressly declined to reach the question of whether sex should be considered a suspect classification.[22]

Burger and Rehnquist sought to break the impasse on March 16. Seeking to assemble a majority for an opinion that definitively rejected the idea that gender should be treated as a suspect classification, they offered to endorse Powell's opinion if Stewart agreed to join the opinion as well. Stewart, however, had no interest in this proposal. Indeed, after an informal conversation with Stewart on March 20, Brennan was left with the impression that if Brennan was willing to return to the original draft that made no mention of "suspectness," Stewart would commit to join him in concluding in some later case that, taken together, *Reed* and *Frontiero* implicitly established gender as a suspect classification. However, Brennan found this proposal unacceptable, and the stalemate remained unresolved.[23]

Thus, although only Justice Rehnquist ultimately voted to uphold the challenged discrimination, no single opinion commanded the support of a majority of the justices. Brennan, Douglas, White, and Marshall joined in arguing for strict scrutiny, while Powell, Burger, and Blackmun relied on *Reed* and focused on the pendency of the ERA. Stewart also concurred separately in the result, citing *Reed* and asserting simply that the challenged statutes "worked an invidious discrimination."[24]

Frontiero marked the last major effort of the progressive justices to have sex branded formally as a suspect classification. Brennan's failure to obtain a majority for his position has sometimes been branded as an important setback for the cause of feminism more generally. However, the defeat was far from total. Although a majority of the Court did not explicitly abandon the rational basis test in gender discrimination cases, eight of the nine justices plainly signaled that they would view such discrimination with considerable suspicion. Thus, particularly when juxtaposed with contemporaneous decisions such as *Rodriguez* and *Kras*, the decision firmly established the proposition that gender was "special" for constitutional purposes and set the stage for enhanced scrutiny of sex discrimination in the future. Indeed, less than four years later, a majority of the justices formally announced that sex-based classifications would be subjected to an intermediate level of scrutiny, and thereafter the Court never upheld a classification that a majority of the justices characterized as discriminating against women.[25]

The plurality opinion in *Frontiero* is also noteworthy for its discussion of the justification for applying enhanced scrutiny more generally. The traditional structure of equal protection analysis had been shaped by the perception that the adoption of Section 1 of the Fourteenth Amendment, like the Thirteenth and Fifteenth Amendments, had been driven by a desire to protect African Americans from racial discrimination. Thus, all of the

Burger Court justices agreed that, as Justice Black observed in *Korematsu v. United States*, discrimination on the basis of race and national origin should be viewed as particularly suspect for constitutional purposes (at least where the targets of the discrimination were members of racial or ethnic minority groups).[26]

However, by 1973, Justice Rehnquist stood alone in adhering to the view that strict scrutiny should be applied *only* to discrimination based on race or national origin. The views of the other justices were clearly influenced by the *Carolene Products* footnote, in which Chief Justice Harlan Fiske Stone had implicitly associated judicial deference with faith in the operation of the legislative process and suggested that discrimination against "discrete and insular minorities" should be subject to more searching judicial review.[27] Thus, in 1971, speaking for eight justices in *Graham v. Richardson*, Justice Blackmun had embraced this theory in concluding that discrimination against aliens should generally be subjected to strict scrutiny, and after joining the Court, during the 1972 term Justice Powell explicitly endorsed this conclusion in *Sugarman v. Dougall*.[28]

Powell's 1972 opinion in *Weber v. Aetna Casualty and Surety Company* had suggested a different rationale for the use of enhanced scrutiny under the equal protection clause.[29] As already noted, in *Weber*, Powell spoke for seven members of the Court in striking down a Louisiana statute that denied unacknowledged illegitimate children access to workers' compensation benefits upon the death of their biological fathers. Although not formally holding that the constitutionality of discrimination against illegitimate children should be judged by a standard more stringent than the traditional rational basis test, Powell's conclusion rested in large measure on his assertion that "imposing disabilities on the illegitimate child is contrary to the basic concept of our system that legal burdens should bear some relationship to individual responsibility or wrongdoing."[30]

The rationales of both *Carolene Products* and *Weber* figured prominently in Brennan's argument for the application of strict scrutiny in *Frontiero*. First, although Brennan could not argue that women were formally barred from participation in the political process, he implicitly suggested that the decisions made by the process consistently undervalued the interests of women as a group. Brennan asserted that a widely shared attitude of "romantic paternalism" that had "in practical effect, put women not on a pedestal but in a cage" had resulted in "our statute books gradually be[coming] laden with gross, stereotyped distinctions between the sexes," and that although society had made progress against sex discrimination, "it can hardly be doubted that, in part because of the high visibility of the sex characteristic, women still face pervasive . . . discrimination in our educational institutions, in the job market, *and, perhaps most conspicuously, in the political arena.*"[31]

In addition, explicitly analogizing sex discrimination to discrimination on the basis of race and national origin, Brennan noted that sex is an "immutable characteristic based solely on the accident of birth." Quoting from the majority opinion in *Weber*, Brennan contended that sex discrimination was constitutionally suspect for the same reason Powell had condemned discrimination against illegitimate children in that case. Although Brennan could not plausibly argue that gender is never correlated with ability, he nonetheless asserted that sex discrimination was different from discrimination based on immutable characteristics such as intelligence or physical disability because sex "*frequently* bears no relation to ability to perform or contribute to society."[32]

Lastly, citing not only the ERA but also the prohibitions on sex discrimination embodied in the Equal Pay Act of 1963 and the Civil Rights Act of 1964, Brennan observed that, in recent years, "Congress itself has manifested an increased sensitivity to sex-based classifications." Thus, he declared that "Congress . . . has concluded that classifications based on sex are inherently invidious" and asserted confidently that "this conclusion of a coequal branch of government is not without significance [to the question of whether sex should be considered a suspect classification.]"[33]

This passage is in some respects the most revealing portion of the plurality opinion. From a distinctively legal perspective, the appeal to the actions of Congress in support of Brennan's analysis made little sense. The argument seemed to be that by taking a number of actions reflecting its disapproval of sex discrimination generally, Congress had somehow bypassed the formal amendment process and authorized the Court to change the substantive content of the Constitution without the approval of the requisite number of state legislatures. Indeed, the fact that Congress had acted on a number of occasions to protect women from discrimination actually undercut the claim that the political process did not adequately factor the needs of women into the lawmaking calculus.

However, at the same time, the overwhelming congressional support for the ERA in particular reflected the dramatic changes in social and political attitudes that had occurred in the short time between the 1961 decision in *Hoyt v. Florida* and the Court's consideration of *Frontiero*. At the time *Hoyt* was decided, most Americans accepted the premise that women should generally function as homemakers rather than breadwinners and that it was entirely appropriate for the structure of law to reflect that perspective. By 1973, however, support for that view had deteriorated to the point that most government officials were unwilling to fully embrace it in public. Both the congressional vote on the ERA and the Court's lopsided decision against the government in *Frontiero* are best understood as byproducts of this reality.

One month after *Frontiero* was decided, the strength of the justices' commitment to the principle of gender equality was tested in another context in *Pittsburgh Press Company v. Pittsburgh Commission on Human Relations.*[34] In *Pittsburgh Press,* a newspaper that divided help-wanted advertisements into "Male Help Wanted," "Female Help Wanted," and "Male-Female Help Wanted" sections had been cited for violating a city ordinance by aiding employers who sought to discriminate among applicants on the basis of sex. The newspaper argued that this application of the ordinance amounted to an unconstitutional infringement of the freedom of the press guaranteed by the First Amendment.

The nature of the issues presented by *Pittsburgh Press* forced a number of the justices to make difficult choices among competing values. In particular, Justices Brennan, Marshall, and Douglas, all of whom had argued in *Frontiero* that sex was a suspect classification, also generally supported an expansive view of the protections afforded by the First Amendment. Ultimately, by a five-to-four vote, the Supreme Court rejected the constitutional challenge to the application of the ordinance to newspaper advertisements.

The justices considered *Pittsburgh Press* against the backdrop not only of *Frontiero* but also of *Valentine v. Chrestensen,* a 1942 decision in which the Court's opinion had stated categorically that the "Constitution imposes no . . . restraint as to purely commercial advertising."[35] Thus, the *Pittsburgh Press* Court was called upon not only to define the scope of the commercial speech exception but also to determine whether the state's interest in preventing sex discrimination was sufficient to justify limiting speech that might otherwise have been viewed as protected by the First Amendment. The interaction between these two issues left the Court divided along lines that defied conventional ideological categorization. Douglas—the most progressive justice on the Court—joined Potter Stewart, Harry Blackmun, and the generally conservative Warren Burger in concluding that the application of the ordinance to newspaper advertising violated the First Amendment.

Burger, Douglas, and Stewart each filed separate opinions in *Pittsburgh Press.* Justice Douglas would simply have overruled *Chrestensen,* and speaking for himself and Justice Blackmun, Justice Stewart would at the very least have limited the decision to its facts. Stewart observed, "The motives behind the state law [in *Pittsburgh Press*] may have been to do good. But . . . history indicates that urges to do good have led to the burning of books and even to the burning of 'witches.'" By contrast, viewing the case as distinguishable from *Chrestensen,* Burger declared that *Pittsburgh Press* involved a "serious encroachment on the freedom of press guaranteed by the First Amendment."[36]

However, five justices saw *Pittsburgh Press* differently, creating a majority that rejected the constitutional challenge. At the conference at which the issue was discussed, Justice White gave no explanation for his position, while Justices Marshall and Rehnquist—an odd couple to be sure—both contended that the case involved nothing more than a simple application of the principles established in *Chrestensen.* Justice Brennan, by contrast, viewed *Pittsburgh Press* quite differently, asserting that the case was "very, very close" and necessitated a balancing of interests before ultimately concluding that the application of the ordinance was constitutional because of what he characterized as the government's "compelling" interest in combatting sex discrimination.[37]

However, having strongly resisted the effort to brand sex a suspect classification in *Frontiero,* Justice Powell was unwilling to implicitly endorse that characterization by asserting that the government had a compelling interest in ending such discrimination in *Pittsburgh Press.* Instead, his opinion for the majority relied on the theory that the format of the classified advertisements was unprotected because it constituted commercial speech. Analogizing advertisements that overtly discriminated on the basis of sex to proposals of criminal activity more generally, Powell emphasized the fact that "none [of the relevant advertisements] expresses a position on whether, as a matter of social policy, certain positions ought to be filled by members of one or the other sex, nor does any of them criticize the [antidiscrimination ordinance or its enforcement]." Instead, noting that each of the advertisements was "no more than a proposal of employment," he characterized them as "classic examples of commercial speech" and as such outside the protection of the First Amendment.[38]

Pittsburgh Press was much less widely discussed than the obscenity cases decided on the same day. Nonetheless, although the decision was a clear victory for opponents of sex discrimination, it predictably drew negative comments from some quarters. Thus, for example, an unnamed attorney who represented a major newspaper described the outcome as a "bad decision with dangerous implications" and asserted that "this decision stands for the proposition that the town council of Podunk can pass an ordinance decreeing what goes into a local newspaper."[39] In any event, one point is clear. Despite the unusual lineup in *Pittsburgh Press*, the case was one in a series of decisions in the 1972 term that generally disappointed those who pressed for an expansive reading of the protections for freedom of speech and the freedom of the press embodied in the First Amendment. By contrast, progressives were no doubt heartened by the Court's treatment of a different provision of the First Amendment—the constitutional prohibition on the establishment of religion.

Chapter Nine

Aid to Parochial Schools

The Burger era witnessed a significant change in the Court's attitude toward the constitutional issues raised by government aid to parochial schools. In the Warren Court's only major decision dealing with the issue, a majority of the justices indicated that the establishment clause of the First Amendment left the state and federal governments fairly wide latitude to provide such aid. By contrast, during the early 1970s, the Court consistently held that the government could provide only limited assistance either to church-related elementary and secondary schools or to the families of the children who attended those schools.[1] A series of cases resolved during the 1972 term played an important role in establishing this principle.

The government aid programs at issue in these cases were available to schools operated by people of a variety of different faiths as well as nondenominational private schools. However, all parties on both sides of the debate were well aware that the overwhelming majority of any government aid would inure to the benefit of schools operated by the Roman Catholic Church and the students that attended those schools. Thus, the dispute over the constitutionality of these programs is best understood as part of the long-running debate over the proper role of Catholic schools in the US educational system more generally.

The issue first became politically significant in the mid-nineteenth century, as an influx of immigrants from Germany and Ireland greatly increased the Catholic population of the United States. The new immigrants came to a nation where the curriculum in the public schools was often deeply infused with Protestant theology and practice. As Catholics gained political power, their leaders pressed hard for public support for the elementary and secondary schools operated by the church. These efforts were often resisted by Protestant leaders, who advocated the adoption of statutes and constitutional provisions to bar the distribution of public funds to religious institutions.

Against this background, in 1876 Congress narrowly failed to pass a proposed constitutional amendment that would have provided that "no money raised by taxation in any State for the support of public schools, or derived from any public fund therefor, nor any public lands devoted thereto, shall ever be under the control of any religious sect." However, the opponents of aid to parochial schools were more successful at the state level. By 1890, twenty-nine states had adopted constitutional amendments that barred the transfer of public funds to parochial schools.[2]

However, public funding was only part of the controversy surrounding parochial education. During the late nineteenth and early twentieth centuries, the very existence of Catholic elementary and secondary schools was viewed with suspicion by a significant number of Americans. The system of universal free public education was seen by many not only as a means for imparting knowledge to students but also as a vehicle to inculcate those students—particularly immigrants—with values seen as distinctively American. Some saw Catholicism itself as antithetical to those values. But in any event, the education of large numbers of children in Catholic schools was at times characterized not only as inimical to the mission of the public schools but also as a threat to the very existence of those schools. Sentiments such as these played a major role in the campaign that led to the adoption of the Oregon Compulsory Education Act of 1922, which would have required all parents in that state to send their children to public schools. However, in 1925, the Oregon statute was unanimously held unconstitutional by the Supreme Court in *Pierce v. Society of Sisters,* with Justice James C. McReynolds famously declaring that the statute "unreasonably interfere[d] with the liberty of parents and guardians to direct the upbringing and education of children."[3]

The four decades that followed brought explosive growth for Catholic schools in the United States. Between 1940 and 1963, the number of students attending such schools increased at a rate more than double the rate of increase in the number of students attending public schools. Thus, by 1960, over five million students—more than 10 percent of all elementary and secondary school students in the United States—attended Catholic schools. The concentration of Catholic school students was particularly high in the urban centers of the states of the Northeast and the upper Midwest. For example, in 1960, 37 percent of the school-aged children in New York attended Catholic schools.[4]

However, as the 1960s progressed, these same schools came under increasing financial stress for a variety of different reasons. Catholic schools were often housed in aging physical facilities that required either replacement or extensive renovation. Even more importantly, personnel costs increased dramatically as teachers and administrators were increasingly drawn from the lay population, rather than the nuns and priests who at one time had dominated the faculties of the schools. In 1950, the ratio of nuns to lay teachers was almost nine to one. By 1965, that ratio was less than two to one and declining rapidly.[5]

Faced with this new reality, the parochial schools increasingly sought to obtain government aid to help defray the costs associated with providing elementary and secondary education. While the idea of providing assistance became more popular in general in the early 1960s, the public remained deeply divided. Although some other religious groups that operated elementary and secondary schools supported the Catholic church in its efforts to have the government provide financial support, the opposition often included not only secular liberal groups such as the American Civil Liberties Union but also a wide variety of Protestant and Jewish organizations. The issue also divided the nation along lines of race and class. Nonwhites were far more likely than whites to support aid to parochial schools, and affluent, well-educated whites were significantly more likely to oppose such aid than were their working-class counterparts.[6]

Each side mounted a variety of policy arguments in support of its position. The supporters of aid to parochial schools contended that it was unfair to require the families of parochial school students to pay taxes to support public schools while at the same time bearing the full burden of financing their children's education at nonpublic schools. They also pointed out that the parochial schools in fact relieved the public schools of the financial costs that would otherwise be associated with providing education to parochial school students and that additional public funds would have to be raised if cost factors induced families to abandon nonpublic education in favor of the public schools.[7]

By contrast, opponents of aid to parochial schools argued that the total amount of government funding available for elementary and secondary education was limited and that any such funding that was diverted to nonpublic schools would therefore in effect rob the public schools of resources that were desperately needed to adequately perform their function. Critics also contended that providing government support for private schools would hamper efforts to integrate inner-city public schools by facilitating the exit of white students from those schools.[8]

At times, these objections reflected a deeper concern about the impact of parochial schools on the educational system as a whole. For example, one Methodist minister indicated that he believed government aid to parochial schools would threaten the ability of the public schools to function as "our effective national unifying influence." Like the critiques of Catholic education during the early twentieth century, such views were based on the theory that education at church-related schools was based on a set of values significantly different from and in some respects antithetical to those that underlay public education and that (by implication, at least) should guide US society as a whole. After he came to the Court, Harry Blackmun privately expressed a related concern, suggesting that a regime in which Catholic students were generally educated in church-related schools funded substantially with government resources would raise the "ghost of segregation."[9]

In addition, those opposed to providing government aid to parochial schools contended that the provision of such aid was barred by the Constitution. They consistently maintained that any government support for either church-related schools or the students who attended those schools violated the strictures of the establishment clause. As one commentator put it succinctly, opponents of aid contended that "constitutionally, there is no difference between using [government] funds to pay for parochial schools and using [government] funds to pay for racially segregated schools." By contrast, supporters argued that the provision of aid was constitutional as long as it was designed to provide a secular benefit for the students of the schools rather than the church institutions themselves. Moreover, they contended that government aid to families of parochial school students actually advanced the constitutional values protected by the free exercise clause by helping provide low-income families with a realistic option to choose to have their children receive their secular instruction in a religious context.[10]

Prior to 1968, the only Supreme Court case that had dealt directly with the issue was the 1947 decision in *Everson v. Board of Education*.[11] *Everson* was a challenge to the decision of the local officials in a New Jersey school district to supply free transportation to students attending the local parochial schools as well as those attending public school. With four justices dissenting, the Court rejected an establishment clause challenge to this practice. Speaking for the five-justice majority, Hugo Black conceded that the First Amendment was designed to establish a "'wall of separation between church and State'" that must be kept "high and impregnable." Nonetheless, he found no constitutional violation in *Everson*, analogizing the transportation of students to police and fire protection and observing that "[we must] be sure that we do not inadvertently prohibit New Jersey from extending its general state law benefits to all its citizens without regard to their religious belief."[12]

The justices did not revisit the question of the constitutionality of government aid to parochial schools for more than two decades after the decision in *Everson*. However, in 1963, the Court did more clearly articulate the constitutional standards for dealing with establishment clause issues generally in *School District of Abington Township v. Schempp*. In that case, speaking for the majority in concluding that the government could not constitutionally mandate reading the Bible out loud in the public schools, Justice Tom C. Clark declared that the "test may be stated as follows: what are the purpose and the primary effect of the enactment? If either is the advancement or inhibition of religion, then the enactment exceeds the scope of legislative power as circumscribed by the Constitution."[13] This test provided the foundation for the Court's analysis of all future establishment clause cases, including those involving challenges to government assistance to church-related schools.

Everson and *Schempp* left the constitutional status of many potential types of aid to parochial schools and students uncertain. The ambiguity of the relevant constitutional principles provided the backdrop for a series of bitter political struggles over such aid in the mid-1960s and the early 1970s. Proponents of government aid won a major victory at the federal level with the passage of the Elementary and Secondary School Act of 1965. The Catholic church had successfully opposed the passage of bills that would have appropriated federal support for elementary and secondary education in 1961 and 1963 because the bills would have provided support only to public schools. By contrast, the 1965 statute explicitly provided that states seeking federal grants for the purchase of schoolbooks and other instructional materials would be required to provide assurances that the materials would be made available to children and teachers in private schools "on an equitable basis."

In addition, a number of different states with large Catholic populations adopted measures that, although in form providing resources for private schools generally, were understood by all to be primarily aimed at providing support for both the Catholic schools as institutions and the families whose children attended those schools. Not surprisingly, the opponents of government aid to church-related schools turned to the federal courts in an effort to block the measures that provided such support. Although the Supreme Court never passed on the merits of the challenges to the federal statute, in 1968 the Warren Court squarely focused on the first of a series of challenges to the state statutes in *Board of Education v. Allen.*[14]

Allen was an attack on a 1965 New York statute that for the first time in state history required local boards of education to purchase textbooks approved by the board and to lend the books without charge to each child who attended an elementary or secondary school within the district, regardless of whether the school itself was private or affiliated with a religious institution. Speaking for the six-justice majority, Justice Byron White concluded that the regime established by the New York statute did not run afoul of the establishment clause.

Applying the purpose and primary effect test from *Schempp* and relying heavily on *Everson,* White observed that the express purpose of the statute was the "furtherance of the educational opportunities available to the young," that the benefits of the statute flowed directly to parents and students rather than to the schools themselves, that the local school boards were required to approve the books to be purchased, and that only secular books could be approved. Noting that the record contained no evidence to support the claim that the "processes of secular and religious training [in religious schools] are so intertwined that secular textbooks furnished to students by the public are, in fact, instrumental in the teaching of religion," White concluded that the statute passed the *Schempp* test.[15]

By contrast, Justice Black—the author of the majority opinion in *Everson*—joined William O. Douglas and Abe Fortas in arguing that the New York statute was unconstitutional. Black contended that whereas the statute at issue in *Everson* "merely provide[d] a general and nondiscriminatory transportation service in no way related to substantive religious views and beliefs," the New York statute would "us[e] funds levied from all of its citizens to purchase books for use by sectarian schools, which, although 'secular,' realistically will in some way inevitably tend to propagate the religious views of the favored sect." The dissenters emphasized the fact that the books to be loaned to students at religiously affiliated schools would initially be chosen by the officials of the schools themselves, with Justice Douglas asking rhetorically, "Can there be the slightest doubt that the head of the parochial school will select the book or books that best promote its sectarian creed?"[16]

Douglas also raised the specter of sectarian conflict over the approval of the selected books, asserting that "if the board of education supinely submits by approving and supplying the sectarian or sectarian-oriented textbooks, the struggle to keep church and state separate has been lost. If the board resists, then the battle line between church and state will have been drawn, and the contest will be on to keep the school board independent or to put it under church domination and control." Justice Black echoed the fear that others had expressed about the influence of organized religion over public policy generally, warning darkly that the "same powerful sectarian religious propagandists who have succeeded in securing passage of the present law to help religious schools carry on their sectarian religious purposes can, and doubtless will, continue their propaganda, looking toward complete domination and supremacy of their particular brand of religion."[17] Although the opinion did not mention any specific religion by name, in context the "powerful sectarian religious propagandists" to whom Black referred could only be understood to be the representatives of the Catholic church.

The substance and tone of the majority opinion in *Allen* heartened advocates for parochial schools, who continued to press for greater state aid for church-related educational institutions. For example, even before the Supreme Court had handed down its decision, in 1968 the Pennsylvania legislature had adopted a statute that allowed state officials to directly reimburse nonpublic schools for the cost of teachers' salaries, textbooks, and other instructional materials related to "secular" courses. The following year, the state of Rhode Island authorized the state government to provide a "supplement" for the salaries of those teaching such courses in private schools, and in 1970 the New York state legislature appropriated millions of dollars for the purpose of reimbursing nonpublic schools for the costs associated with the provision of a variety of state-mandated services including, but not limited to, "administration, grading, and the compiling and reporting of the results of tests and examinations." Not surprisingly, the passage of all of these measures was bitterly opposed by the same forces that had objected to the program whose constitutionality had been upheld in *Allen*, and each was challenged in federal court.

In 1971, the challenges to the Pennsylvania and Rhode Island plans were resolved by the Court in *Lemon v. Kurtzman* (*Lemon I*).[18] *Lemon I* clearly raised issues not resolved in *Allen*. As Justice Blackmun observed privately, although state and local governments could prescreen books to ensure that their content was not secular, money was fungible. Therefore, any state funds used to finance the teaching of purely secular subjects in a parochial school freed up the school's own funds to potentially finance the teaching of religious material.[19] The establishment clause problems associated with monetary subsidies were thus arguably more serious than those created by supplying books to parochial school students.

In dealing with these problems, the justices were forced to consider not only *Allen* but also the Court's 1970 decision in *Walz v. Tax Commission.*[20] *Walz* was a constitutional challenge to the common practice of granting property tax exemptions for property used exclusively for religious worship. With Warren Burger and Blackmun having replaced Earl Warren and Fortas, the Court concluded with only one dissent that the exemption did not run afoul of the establishment clause.

Speaking for the majority, Chief Justice Burger began his analysis by restating the standard approach to the treatment of establishment clause problems, asserting that "each value judgment under the Religion Clauses must . . . turn on whether particular acts in question are intended to establish or interfere with religious beliefs and practices or have the effect of doing so." Rejecting any intimation that the purpose of the tax exemptions was to advance religion, he observed that houses of worship were treated no differently than a wide variety of other nonprofit organizations and argued that the "legislative purpose of the property tax exemption is neither the advancement nor the inhibition of religion; it is neither sponsorship nor hostility. [Instead the government] has determined that certain entities that exist in a harmonious relationship to the community at large, and that foster its 'moral or mental improvement,' should not be inhibited in their activities by property taxation or the hazard of loss of those properties for nonpayment of taxes."[21]

The majority opinion then turned to an analysis of the effect of tax exemptions on religious institutions. But although he did not acknowledge that he was departing in any way from existing case law, Burger's articulation of the effects standard was in fact quite different from previous formulations and indeed his own phraseology from earlier in the opinion. Whereas cases such as *Schempp* and *Allen* had asked whether the primary effect of a challenged government action was to advance religion, in this portion of *Walz* Burger made no mention of advancing religion, instead asserting that "we must also be sure that the end result—the effect—is not an excessive government entanglement with religion." He observed that, from this perspective, the "exemption [from property taxes] creates only a minimal and remote involvement between church and state, and far less than taxation of churches. It restricts the fiscal relationship between church and state, and tends to complement and reinforce the desired separation insulating each from the other."[22] Thus, Burger concluded that granting the exemptions also did not run afoul of this aspect of establishment clause analysis and that the practice could therefore be continued.

At the time *Walz* was decided, some commentators expressed the belief that Burger's change in the phraseology of the effects test augured a relaxation of the Court's scrutiny of government aid to church-related organizations generally. Such assessments ignored a number of important points. First, in his majority opinion, Burger was careful to note that, even under his revised formulation, other types of aid might create greater constitutional problems. In particular, he observed that a direct money subsidy would be a relationship pregnant with involvement and, as with most governmental grant programs, could entail "sustained and detailed administrative relationships for enforcement of statutory or administrative standards."[23]

Even more importantly, the political context in which *Walz* was decided was very different from that which formed the backdrop of the Court's consideration of measures that provided aid to church-related schools. Tax exemptions benefited all religions equally. Thus, the only real opposition to such exemptions came from the most committed secularists in US society. By contrast, the debate over parochial school aid had generated an increasingly bitter political struggle pitting the largest single religious sect in the United States—the Roman Catholic Church—against not only secularists but also the representatives of most other mainstream religious organizations in the country. This dynamic in turn created problems for those who agreed with John Marshall Harlan, whose concurring opinion in *Walz* declared that "what is at stake [in establishment clause litigation is] preventing that kind and degree of government involvement in religious life that, as history teaches us, is apt to lead to strife and frequently strain a political system to the breaking point."[24]

These distinctions proved critical in *Lemon I*. With only Justice White dissenting, the Court concluded that neither the Pennsylvania nor the Rhode Island plans passed muster under the First Amendment. Speaking for the majority, Chief Justice Burger conceded that the purpose of the challenged statutes was to improve the quality of secular education generally rather than to advance religion. Moreover, he declined to express an opinion on the question of whether the primary effect of the statutes for constitutional purposes was to advance religion. Instead, he relied on an entirely different theory to invalidate the Pennsylvania and Rhode Island statutes.

In *Lemon I*, Burger took the view that, rather than simply redefining the nature of the primary effect test that had been articulated in *Schempp*, the reference to "excessive entanglement" in *Walz* had in effect added a new element to establishment clause analysis. He asserted that even if state aid to church-related institutions had both a secular purpose and a primarily secular effect, the First Amendment also required that the provision of the aid not create the danger of excessive entanglement between the state and religious institutions. Burger reasoned that because "comprehensive, discriminating, and continuing state surveillance" would be required to ensure that the funds provided by the state would not be used to support the inculcation of religious values, the Rhode Island and Pennsylvania statues inevitably created an unconstitutional degree of entanglement. In addition, referencing Harlan's concurrence in *Walz*, Burger emphasized what he characterized as the "political divisiveness related to religious belief and practice" inherent in the Rhode Island and Pennsylvania programs, arguing that the need to periodically reevaluate the amount that should be appropriated for each program would inevitably divide the community along religious lines.[25]

Justice Brennan's concurring opinion in *Lemon I* was also significant. Brennan had concurred silently in *Allen* and had also joined the majority opinion in *Walz*. However, Brennan's opinion in *Lemon I* made it clear that he viewed these cases as creating only limited exceptions to a general rule and that he would be skeptical of any further efforts to provide government aid either to parochial schools as institutions or to the families of the students who attended those schools. Relying on a three-part test he had first articulated in a concurring opinion in *Schempp*, Brennan argued that "'what . . . the Establishment Clause ha[s] forbidden, are those involvements of religious with secular institutions which (a) serve the essentially religious activities of religious institutions; (b) employ the organs of government for essentially religious purposes; or (c) use essentially religious means to serve governmental ends, where secular means would suffice.'" Noting that Catholic schools had been largely unsuccessful in their efforts to obtain public funding in the late nineteenth century and that most state constitutions prohibited the use of government funds to subsidize religious institutions, he asserted that "for more than a century, the consensus, enforced by legislatures and courts with substantial consistency, has been that public subsidy of sectarian schools constitutes an impermissible involvement of secular with religious institutions" and concluded that "my analysis of the operation, purposes, and effects of these statutes leads me inescapably to the conclusion that they . . . impermissibly involve the States . . . with the 'essentially religious activities' of sectarian educational institutions."[26]

In his dissent, Justice White contended that the majority had created an "insoluble paradox" for states seeking to provide aid to parochial schools to support the teaching of secular subjects. White complained that under Chief Justice Burger's analysis, the "State cannot finance secular instruction if it permits religion to be taught in the same classroom; but if it exacts a promise that religion not be so taught—a promise the school and its teachers are quite willing and, on this record, able, to give—and enforces it, it is then entangled in the 'no entanglement' aspect of the Court's Establishment Clause jurisprudence."[27]

The decision in *Lemon I* was a stinging defeat for those who believed that the government should provide financial assistance to parochial schools and the students who attended those schools. However, on the same day that *Lemon I* was decided, in *Tilton v. Richardson* a deeply divided Court reaffirmed the view that such assistance could be provided to church-related institutions under some circumstances.[28]

Tilton was a challenge to the use of the Higher Education Act of 1963 to provide construction grants to a number of church-related institutions. The act authorized federal grants and loans to "institutions of higher education" for the construction of a wide variety of "academic facilities." Although grants and loans were available to both public and nonpublic colleges and universities, the act expressly prohibited financial assistance for "any facility used or to be used for sectarian instruction or as a place for religious worship, or . . . any facility which . . . is used or to be used primarily in connection with any part of the program of a school or department of divinity." The statute also provided that the United States was to retain an interest in the buildings constructed with the aid for twenty years, after which the recipient would be granted unencumbered title, provided that the institution had not violated any of the conditions imposed by the statute during the twenty-year period. Thus, after twenty years, the institution would be free to use the building for any purpose it chose.

Noting that after twenty years the buildings constructed with government aid could be converted to purely religious purposes, all of the members of the *Lemon I* majority agreed that the removal of the use restriction after the expiration of that period violated the establishment clause. By contrast, the justices were deeply divided on the constitutionality of the remainder of the grant program insofar as it allowed the provision of government aid to church-related colleges and universities. Speaking for himself and Justices Black and Marshall, Justice Douglas observed that the sectarian institutions operated on a single budget and that therefore the use of public funds to support the teaching of even secular material necessarily had the effect of allowing such institutions to devote more resources to religious instruction. In addition, he argued that the same concerns about the need for government surveillance that had underlain *Lemon I* were equally present in *Tilton*. Justice Brennan also concluded that the aid funneled through the Higher Education Act could not be provided to sectarian colleges and universities, once again contending that the government could not constitutionally use religious means to achieve secular ends where secular means would suffice.[29]

However, Chief Justice Burger and Justices Harlan, Stewart, and Blackmun joined Justice White to form a majority that rejected the constitutional challenge to the provision of funds to church-related institutions of higher learning. On the critical entanglement issue, Burger's plurality opinion relied on a number of different factors to distinguish *Tilton* from *Lemon I*. First, he argued that, unlike sectarian primary and secondary schools, the main purpose of most church-related colleges and universities was not religious indoctrination, and that, in any event, college students were likely to be less susceptible to such indoctrination than their younger counterparts. In addition, Burger contended that the character of the aid being provided was different in *Tilton*. He noted that, whereas teachers might choose to indoctrinate students, there was no possibility that a building per se would attempt to convey an ideological or religious message. Moreover, he asserted that the need for government entanglement was reduced because, rather than creating ongoing complex relationships between the federal government and the institutions that benefited from the program, the Higher Education Act envisioned one-time grants to be used for specific purposes.[30]

During the 1972 term, the principles that had underlain the plurality opinion in *Tilton* were reaffirmed and expanded in *Hunt v. McNair*.[31] *Hunt* was a challenge to the effort of a church-related college to take advantage of a program established by the South Carolina Educational Facilities Act. The state statute created the Educational Facilities Authority, which had the power to issue revenue bonds to finance capital improvements at institutions of higher education within South Carolina. Institutions participating in the program would convey the buildings constructed with the funds raised by the issuance of the bonds to the authority, which would then lease the buildings back to the institutions. After the bonds were repaid through the use of the rental payments from the lease, the buildings were to be reconveyed to the institutions. Like the statute that had been at issue in *Tilton*, the Educational Facilities Act explicitly prohibited the use of the program to finance "any facility used or to be used for sectarian instruction or as a place of religious worship nor any facility which is used or to be used primarily in connection with any part of the program of a school or department of divinity for any religious denomination." In addition, the South Carolina statute required the documents reconveying the property after repayment of the bonds to contain a restriction against use for sectarian purposes.

Despite these safeguards, from an entanglement perspective the challengers could plausibly argue that the South Carolina program was more problematic than that established by the federal Higher Education Act. In *Tilton,* Chief Justice Burger had emphasized the fact that after making the grant, the federal government had no further involvement in the day-to-day operation of the facilities that were constructed. By contrast, the Educational Facilities Act vested the Educational Facilities Authority with broad powers to control the use of the buildings constructed with the proceeds from the revenue bonds. Justices Douglas, Brennan, and Marshall—all of whom had dissented in *Tilton*—seized upon this difference in arguing that the issuance of the revenue bonds in *Hunt* ran afoul of the establishment clause.[32]

However, the remaining six justices disagreed and concluded that the constitutional challenge should be rejected. The task of writing the majority opinion fell to Justice Powell, who had not yet come to the Court when *Tilton* was decided. Powell conceded that if there was a "realistic likelihood" that if all of the powers granted to the Educational Facilities Authority by the statute would actually be exercised, the entanglement problems created by the grant to the college in *Hunt* would "not be insignificant." However, after examining the proposed lease agreement itself, he determined that the possibility of entanglement arose only if the college defaulted on its contractual obligations. Under these circumstances, Powell concluded that it was inappropriate to find a First Amendment violation until the potentially offending powers were in fact exercised.[33]

Although the decision in *Hunt* was significant in both doctrinal and practical terms, the Court's further pronouncements on the issue of aid to elementary and secondary schools were far more eagerly awaited during the 1972 term. The reactions to *Lemon I* in 1971 had split along predictable lines. Spokespeople representing a wide variety of non-Catholic establishment institutions praised the Court's decision. For example, the *Washington Post* declared that the decision "serve[d] the cause of church independence and of the freedom of men of every faith to worship as they wish," and the *New York Times* hailed what it described as the maintenance of the wall of separation between church and state and also warned darkly against efforts to "erod[e] a basic principle through evasion and expediency." Similarly, although recognizing that *Lemon I* would lead to higher costs for both Catholic parents themselves and public schools that might be required to absorb a greater number of Catholic students, the more conservative *Wall Street Journal* observed that "perhaps it is good to be reminded from time to time that basic freedoms have a cost and thereby be apprised anew of their value."[34]

Not surprisingly, proponents of aid to parochial schools saw *Lemon I* quite differently. The defeat could hardly have come at a worse time for supporters of Catholic schools generally. The changing demographics of the membership of the church itself had made the financial situation of many parochial schools even more precarious. Like their counterparts of other faiths, by the late 1960s, many white Catholic families had abandoned the inner cities in favor of the suburbs. In addition to leaving the parochial schools in their former neighborhoods with significantly fewer students and financial support from tuition, the Catholic families who lived in the suburbs were more likely to choose the public schools in their new environs. Thus, by 1971—the peak year for the total number of students attending elementary and secondary schools in the United States—the number of students attending Catholic elementary and secondary schools had declined by more than 25 percent from its peak in the mid-1960s. Against this background, Catholic leaders became, if anything, even more anxious to obtain financial support from the government in order to avoid the need for tuition increases that would inevitably exacerbate the decline in parochial school attendance.[35]

This new reality was reflected in the tenor of the response of supporters of parochial schools to *Lemon I.* Almost immediately after the case was decided, Senator Hugh Scott of Pennsylvania, the leader of the Republicans in the US Senate, declared that the decision was "one that will haunt all of us." Less than two months later, Cardinal Terence Cooke, the Catholic archbishop of New York, launched a particularly fiery attack on *Lemon I* at a meeting of the Knights of Columbus. With President Richard Nixon in attendance, Cooke characterized the denial of government aid to parochial schools as "unreasonable and discriminatory." He also implicitly criticized Burger for emphasizing the likelihood that aid programs would create political conflict, asking rhetorically, "Are civil rights organizations guilty of divisiveness because occasionally unreasonable action or overreaction follows their legitimate political activity?" At the same time, Cooke recognized that, unless and until the Court changed course, the judiciary would measure the constitutionality of any aid program against the standards enunciated in Burger's opinion. Cooke concluded by calling for "practical means [to] be found . . . to assist the parents of non-public schoolchildren."[36]

Cooke was far from alone in his sentiments. He found support not only from fellow Catholics themselves but also from non-Catholic politicians who sought the support of Catholic voters. Thus, immediately after Cardinal Cooke's speech, Nixon declared, "You can count on my support." Similarly, in April 1972, the report of Nixon's panel on nonpublic education argued that Chief Justice Burger's opinion in *Lemon I* showed an "inadequate perception of realities in parochial schools," expressed the hope that public pressure would create a "more commodious judicial interpretation [of the establishment clause] in the future," and advocated measures that would provide aid in a manner that might be consistent with the standards outlined by the majority opinion in that case. In addition, the platforms of both political parties in the 1972 presidential election called for government aid to private and parochial schools, and on the eve of the election Nixon declared, "In my judgment, the Constitution does not prohibit tax inducements to encourage and maintain diversity in American education—and we are prepared to fight to guarantee that the diversity remains."[37]

However, despite Nixon's pronouncements, no additional federal initiatives providing aid to either parochial schools or the families of children attending such schools were in fact adopted in the early 1970s. By contrast, in reaction to *Lemon I,* the state legislatures of both New York and Pennsylvania promulgated new aid measures designed to satisfy the test that Burger had propounded. These programs provided the backdrop for a series of cases decided during the 1972 term in which the Court elaborated on the principles that had underlain *Lemon I.*

Proponents of government aid to parochial schools won an early victory on April 2, 1973, with the decision in the second incarnation of *Lemon v. Kurtzman* (*Lemon II*).[38] In *Lemon II,* the justices were called upon to review a district court's ruling that a state could reimburse parochial schools for services rendered before *Lemon I* had been handed down by the Court. With Justice Marshall not participating, the Court voted five to three to affirm a lower court judgment that allowed the state to make the payments.

For dissenters William O. Douglas, William Brennan, and Potter Stewart, *Lemon II* involved nothing more than a simple application of the principles that had been enunciated in *Lemon I.* Speaking for the three dissenters, Douglas declared that "there is as much a violation of the Establishment Clause of the First Amendment whether the payment from public funds to sectarian schools involves last year, the current year, or next year" and that "retroactivity of the decision in *Lemon I* goes to the very core of the integrity of the judicial process."[39] Conversely, White, who had been the sole dissenter in *Lemon I*, wrote no opinion in *Lemon II*, but not surprisingly voted to affirm the lower court judgment in the latter.

Unlike *Lemon I*, in *Lemon II* White was joined in his conclusion not only by the newly appointed Lewis Powell and William Rehnquist but also by Warren Burger and Harry Blackmun, both of whom had ascribed to the majority opinion in *Lemon I*. Speaking for this group in *Lemon II*, the chief justice emphasized the fact that the schools seeking reimbursement had incurred expenses in reliance on the Pennsylvania statute before any court had concluded that the state could not constitutionally make the payments contemplated by the statute. Burger also noted that the plaintiffs in *Lemon I* had made no effort to enjoin the implementation of the statutory program while their initial appeal had been pending in the Supreme Court and observed that, because the state government had already determined that the payments were for secular rather than religious programs, the making of the challenged payments would not require any further entanglement between the government and the religious schools.[40] Given these circumstances, he concluded that the district court had not abused its discretion by allowing the state to pay for services performed prior to the date of the decision in *Lemon I*.

Although supporters of government aid to parochial schools were no doubt pleased with the decision in *Lemon II*, the practical significance of the case was by its terms extremely limited. Thus, the ruling was not widely discussed by commentators. Instead, all parties to the dispute understood that the critical rulings would come later in the term, when the Court passed on the constitutionality of future aid based on state laws that both government officials and the operators of elementary and secondary parochial schools hoped would survive scrutiny under the standards that had been established in *Lemon I*. However, just as in 1971, a majority of the justices proved hostile to most government efforts to provide support to either the parochial schools themselves or the families of the children who attended such schools.

Admittedly, even among the members of this majority, there were some differences of opinion. These differences emerged clearly during the consideration of *Levitt v. Committee for Public Education and Religious Liberty*, a challenge to a New York program that reimbursed private schools for the cost of performing a variety of services mandated by the state, with the proviso that no payments were to be made for religious worship or instruction.[41] At the initial conference at which *Levitt* was considered, Justices Douglas, Brennan, Stewart, and Marshall argued that the establishment clause did not allow the state to reimburse parochial schools for any services, while Justices White and Rehnquist voted to reject the constitutional challenge in toto. By contrast, Harry Blackmun and Lewis Powell initially voted to allow reimbursement only for mandated tests whose content was created by the state itself, and Chief Justice Burger pronounced himself "not yet firm" on the appropriate disposition of the case.[42]

Ultimately, in *Levitt*, Burger was able to craft an opinion that all of the other justices except Justice White were willing to join. The opinion observed that the most expensive of the services for which reimbursement was available was the administration of a variety of tests and that although the content of some of these tests was established by the state, in most cases the tests were devised by the classroom teachers themselves.[43] Under these circumstances, he concluded that the statute was constitutionally infirm because it contained no mechanism to ensure that the tests would not be used or designed either consciously or unconsciously to inculcate religious values.

The justices differed more publicly over the constitutionality of the New York and Pennsylvania programs that provided tax credits or small grants to parents to defray part of the cost of tuition to nonpublic schools. Supporters of these measures, both of which had been passed in response to the decision in *Lemon I*, argued that because the aid was given to the families of students rather than to the schools themselves, the programs were more closely analogous to the transportation program that had given rise to *Everson* and the textbook loan program upheld in *Allen* than to the programs invalidated in *Lemon I*. In *Committee for Public Education and Religious Freedom v. Nyquist* and *Sloan v. Lemon*, Chief Justice Burger agreed with this assessment, observing that in each case it was the parent rather than the state itself that made the decision that might ultimately provide an indirect benefit to a religious institution.[44] Similarly, Justice Rehnquist contended that the programs at issue in *Nyquist* and *Sloan* were functionally indistinguishable not only from those held constitutional in *Allen* and *Everson* but also the tax exemption issue in *Walz v. Tax Commission*, and Justice White insisted that the programs in reality advanced the values embodied in the free exercise clause by facilitating parental decisions about the religious atmosphere (or lack thereof) in which their children would receive the secular instruction required by the state. In addition, both Burger and

White emphasized the fact that the state governments reaped fiscal benefits by having children educated in schools not financed with public funds.[45]

However, the remaining six justices disagreed, and both the New York and Pennsylvania programs were held to violate the establishment clause. Speaking for the majority in *Nyquist*, Justice Powell specifically addressed and rejected the claim that the aid programs advanced First Amendment values by helping preserve the ability of low-income families to choose between secular and church-related schools. Powell observed that "by reimbursing parents for a portion of their tuition bill, the State seeks to relieve their financial burdens sufficiently to assure that they continue to have the option to send their children to religion-oriented schools." Although professing sympathy for the plight of parents paying both taxes to support the public schools and tuition at parochial schools, Powell contended that the pursuit of such a goal was itself prohibited by the establishment clause, asserting that the "effect of the aid is unmistakably to provide desired financial support for nonpublic, sectarian institutions."[46]

Similarly, in his opinion for the Court in *Sloan*, Powell declared that the "State has singled out a class of its citizens for a special economic benefit. Whether that benefit be viewed as a simple tuition subsidy, as an incentive to parents to send their children to sectarian schools, or as a reward for having done so, at bottom its intended consequences is to preserve and support religion-oriented institutions." He argued that *Walz* was distinguishable because of the long historical pedigree of the practice of granting tax exemption to religious institutions and because religious institutions were part of a much larger class of analogous institutions granted tax exemptions.[47]

Supporters of government aid to parochial schools were understandably dismayed by the Court's actions in *Nyquist*, *Sloan*, and *Levitt*. Indeed, the superintendent of the Catholic schools in Memphis, Tennessee, went so far as to declare that the decisions were a "death blow to nonpublic schools." By contrast, the *New York Times* praised the Court for what it saw as "emphatically reaffirm[ing] the vital principle of church-state separation," and the *Washington Post* characterized the decisions as vindicating the "people's greatest guarantee of religious freedom." Moreover, once again, support for the decisions among non-Catholic elites cut across political lines. For example, the *Wall Street Journal*—a newspaper not normally associated with progressive causes that had expressed cautious support for the Court's resolution of the obscenity issue—praised the Court's actions as "perfectly consistent with the spirit and intent of the Founding Fathers" and asserted that "it is difficult to see how the Court could have taken any other course without creating . . . complex problems of both a constitutional and a practical nature."[48]

Against the background of *Levitt, Sloan,* and *Nyquist,* the opponents of aid to parochial schools declared that the political struggle over such aid was over. One such opponent asserted, "It is time for politicians to stop deceiving Catholic leaders and Catholic parents into thinking that they are going to get tax money for their schools."[49] However, the final chapter in the struggle over aid to parochial schools during the early Burger years was not written until two year later, with the decision in *Meek v. Pittenger.*[50]

Meek was a challenge to two Pennsylvania statutes that had been passed in the interim between the decision in *Lemon I* and the 1972 decisions dealing with aid to parochial schools. Act 194 provided for the provision of "auxiliary [secular] services" to students in nonpublic schools, including "counseling, testing, and psychological services, speech and hearing therapy, teaching and related services for exceptional children, for remedial students, and for the educationally disadvantaged." Act 195, on the other hand, authorized the state government to allow such students to borrow without charge textbooks approved by the state for use in public schools. In addition, Act 195 allowed the nonpublic schools themselves to borrow "instructional materials and equipment useful to the education of nonpublic school children." The "instructional materials" covered by the statute included periodicals, photographs, maps, charts, sound recordings, and films, while the category of "instructional equipment" encompassed projection equipment, recording equipment, and laboratory equipment.

The Court gave supporters of aid to parochial schools a minor victory by rejecting the constitutional challenge to the textbook loan provision of Act 195. Justices Douglas, Brennan, and Marshall intimated that in their view *Allen* should be overruled and contended that, in any event, the Pennsylvania loan program was distinguishable from the New York program the Court had upheld. However, the remaining six justices disagreed, concluding that this aspect of *Meek* was controlled by *Allen.*[51]

A majority of the justices took a quite different view of the remainder of Act 195. Given the possibility that the instructional materials and equipment described in Act 195 could easily be turned to sectarian uses, the outcome of the constitutional challenge to that portion of the statute was virtually preordained by the Court's earlier decisions in cases such as *Lemon I* and *Nyquist.* Not surprisingly, with only Justices White and Rehnquist dissenting, the Court held that this provision violated the establishment clause.

By contrast, the fate of Act 194 had at least arguably been left open by the Court's precedents. The authorization for the provision of auxiliary services at issue in *Meek* differed from the regime that the Court struck down in *Lemon I* in one critical respect. The Court's major objection to the reimbursement system that had been challenged in *Lemon I* was that the government would be required to become deeply involved in supervising the school employees delivering the services to ensure that government funds were not being used to subsidize religious teachings and that such involvement in turn would create excessive entanglement between the government and religion. By contrast, under Act 194, the services were to be provided by people selected by the state government itself rather than employees of church-related schools. Chief Justice Burger and Justices White and Rehnquist argued that there was no particular reason to believe that the state employees would engage in religious indoctrination under the guise of providing secular services. Thus, in their view, there would be no need for outside government supervision and thus no excessive entanglement between church and state.[52]

However, the remaining justices disagreed, concluding that Act 194 ran afoul of the establishment clause. Speaking for the majority, Justice Stewart did not explicitly discuss the potential differences between the attitudes of church employees and government employees. Instead, he simply stated flatly that the state could not "rely . . . entirely on the good faith and professionalism of the secular teachers and counselors functioning in church-related schools to ensure that a strictly nonideological posture is maintained" in the provision of auxiliary services. Therefore, he concluded that, for constitutional purposes, Act 194 was indistinguishable from the program that had been invalidated in *Lemon I*.[53]

Nyquist and *Meek* basically ended all hope for anything more than token government assistance to either parochial schools below the college level or the families of the elementary and secondary students who attended those schools. Although *Everson* and *Allen* remained formally intact as precedents, *Allen* in particular had essentially been limited to its facts. The decisions of the early 1970s made it clear that, with only the most minor exceptions, a majority of the justices would not countenance the provision of state resources that might underwrite the instructional process, even if the use of those resources was limited to secular purposes by law. In short, the cases produced a near total victory for the secularists and their allies in the non-Catholic establishment over the Catholic church and other supporters of church-related schools.

The dispute over aid to parochial schools was not the only constitutional issue that aroused religious passions during the early 1970s. By their nature, cases such as *Nyquist* and *Sloan* required the Court to focus specifically on the relationship between the government and religious institutions. However, even when not explicitly dealing with this relationship, judicial decisions can implicate fundamental aspects of religious doctrine. *Roe v. Wade* provides a classic example of this phenomenon.[54]

Chapter Ten

The Abortion Conflict

During the 1972 term, the Supreme Court confronted a wide variety of important political and social issues. The decisions that dealt with issues such as criminal procedure, pornography, school finance, and school desegregation not only were jurisprudentially significant but also elicited passionate reactions and had major public policy implications. Nonetheless, it was the Court's treatment of the question of abortion rights that would ultimately prove to have the greatest political and jurisprudential impact.[1]

Like many of the disputes resolved by the Court during the 1972 term, the abortion cases had their roots in the political and cultural upheaval that roiled the nation in the 1960s and early 1970s.[2] During the period from the late nineteenth century through 1967, states uniformly prohibited abortions except in cases in which the mother's life was in danger. To be sure, beginning in the 1930s, groups of reformers challenged the existing regime. Moreover, they won an important symbolic victory in 1959 by persuading the American Law Institute to include a more liberal abortion statute in the Model Penal Code. However, it was not until 1967 that advocates of liberalization, who described themselves as "prochoice," broke through with legislative triumphs in California, Colorado, and North Carolina.

The period from 1967 through 1972 brought a series of intense political struggles at the state level. The prochoice forces, typically allied with feminist groups, pressed hard for the reform or repeal of antiabortion statutes, whereas equally passionate opponents of abortion, who characterized their position as "prolife," tenaciously defended the status quo. By 1972, the pre-1967 consensus had been replaced by a patchwork of different laws. Although some states left their existing abortion laws unchanged, others adopted a variety of different reforms, ranging from some variant on the

Model Penal Code provision to the abolition of all restrictions on abortions up to some stage of the woman's pregnancy.

During the early 1970s, the abortion issue also gained increasing prominence in national politics. As part of his effort to appeal to Catholic voters, as the presidential election of 1972 approached, Richard Nixon took an increasingly strong prolife stance. Thus, for example, on April 3, 1971, he reversed a US Department of Defense ruling that required military hospitals throughout the United States and around the world to provide abortions to servicewomen in all cases where two medical doctors or one doctor and one psychiatrist agreed that the procedure was necessary. Nixon ordered that, instead, military hospitals should be bound by the restrictions imposed by the laws of the states in which they were located, declaring that "I consider abortion an unacceptable method of population control" and that "he could not square unrestricted abortion policies or abortion on demand . . . with my personal belief in the sanctity of the human life, including the life of the yet unborn." Similarly, in June 1972, after the White House Commission on Population Growth had recommended that states allow abortion on demand, Nixon persuaded officials of the US Department of Health, Education, and Welfare to reject the recommendation.[3]

However, Nixon's most dramatic intervention in the debate over abortion came in connection with the ongoing struggle in the state of New York. Prior to 1970, New York had been one of those states that prohibited all abortions except in cases in which the mother's life was endangered. However, in that year, after a fierce, impassioned debate in both houses, the state legislature had replaced the restrictive statute with a measure that essentially allowed abortion on demand prior to the twenty-fourth week of pregnancy. Led by the Catholic church but also supported by a variety of other groups, the prolife forces counterattacked, launching a vigorous campaign to repeal the 1970 statute and reinstate the legal regime that had previously been in place. The repeal effort came to a crescendo during the 1972 legislative session.

In the midst of this political conflict, President Nixon dispatched a letter to Cardinal Terrence Cooke voicing full support for the prolife campaign. Although recognizing that the issue was one that each state had the power to decide for itself, Nixon declared, "The unrestricted abortion policies now recommended by some Americans and the liberal abortion policies in effect in some sections of this country seem to me impossible to reconcile with either our religious traditions or our Western heritage. . . . In recent years, the right to life of literally hundreds of thousands of unborn children has been destroyed—legally—but in my judgment without anything approaching adequate justification."[4]

The reaction to Nixon's letter broke down along predictable lines. One prochoice state legislator declared that he was "shocked" and asserted, "It's just inappropriate for the President to be doing this." Similarly, the *New York Times* characterized what it described as "President Nixon's dismaying interference with the legislative process of this state" as a "blatant misuse of his high position." By contrast, prolife legislators were delighted and expressed the hope that Nixon's statement would sway enough votes to reinstate the pre-1970 curbs of legal abortions.[5]

The resolution of the struggle in New York reflected the complexities of the political crosscurrents surrounding the abortion issue in the early 1970s. The prolife forces were ultimately able to muster enough support in both houses of the state legislature to pass a bill repealing the 1970 statute and reinstating the legal regime that had existed prior to the passage of that statute. However, Republican governor Nelson Rockefeller—the state chair of Nixon's reelection campaign in New York—vetoed the repeal bill, thus leaving the provisions of the liberalization measure intact.[6]

Democrats were also deeply divided on the abortion question in the early 1970s. For example, although many elements of the party opposed restrictions on abortions, in April 1971 Democratic senator Edmund S. Muskie of Maine—then viewed as the frontrunner for the Democratic presidential nomination in 1972—suggested that he believed that all but the earliest term abortions should be legally restricted. Nonetheless, at the Democratic National Convention that met in July 1972, feminists pressed hard for the inclusion of a prochoice plank in the party platform. However, their efforts were rebuffed by the forces of Senator George McGovern, who by that time was guaranteed to be the presidential nominee of the party. During the presidential campaign itself, McGovern, who on other issues had shown no hesitation in openly supporting other progressive initiatives, refused to take a position on the question of whether antiabortion laws should be repealed, insisting that the matter was one for each state to decide for itself. At the same time, he acknowledged that his "personal position" was that the decision to terminate a pregnancy should be left to families and doctors. Against this background, as part of its effort to paint McGovern as the embodiment of radical elements that were seeking to destroy the traditional values that underlay US society, the Nixon campaign labeled him the candidate of "Acid, Amnesty, and Abortion."[7] Ironically, however, unbeknownst to the Republican presidential candidate, Nixon appointee Harry

Blackmun was already well on his way to becoming the judicial face of the prochoice movement.

Roe v. Wade and its companion case, *Doe v. Bolton,* first came before the Court during the 1971 term. Prior to its consideration of these cases, the Court had addressed the constitutionality of government regulation of the reproductive process in a variety of different contexts. The 1927 decision in *Buck v. Bell*—the first major case that focused on the issue—gave short shrift to the claim that such regulations raised serious constitutional concerns. In *Buck,* with only one dissent, the Court rejected a challenge to a Virginia statute that provided for the sterilization of residents of state institutions found afflicted with "hereditary forms of insanity [or] imbecility." Brushing aside the contention that the statute violated the due process rights of those who were sterilized, Justice Oliver Wendell Holmes analogized the statute to mandatory vaccination requirements, asserting, "The principle that sustains compulsory vaccination is broad enough to cover cutting the Fallopian tubes."[8]

Fifteen years later, the Court struck a quite different note in *Skinner v. Oklahoma,* in which the justices unanimously struck down a state statute that provided for the sterilization of people convicted of committing certain felonies. Speaking for the Court, Justice William O. Douglas purported to give the state's judgment "large deference," but at the same time also declared, "We are dealing here with legislation which involves one of the basic civil rights of man. Marriage and procreation are fundamental to the very existence and survival of the race." Against this background, Douglas asserted that "when the law lays an unequal hand on those who have committed intrinsically the same quality of offense and sterilizes one and not the other, it has made as invidious a discrimination as if it had selected a particular race or nationality for oppressive treatment." He concluded that the Oklahoma statute violated the equal protection clause because the state had not provided adequate reasons to differentiate the crimes that could be punished by sterilization from other felonies for which that penalty could not be imposed.[9]

For more than two decades, the potential broader implications of Douglas's assertion that strict scrutiny should be applied to regulation of marriage and procreation remained largely unexplored. In 1961, the Court faced a constitutional challenge to a Connecticut statute that prohibited the use of contraceptives in *Poe v. Ullman,* but the case was dismissed on procedural grounds, with only Douglas and John Marshall Harlan choosing to discuss the merits.[10] However, when the same statute once again came under attack four years later in *Griswold v. Connecticut*, all members of the Court reached the merits, and seven of the nine justices concluded that the statute was unconstitutional.[11]

The structure of a number of the opinions in *Griswold* was shaped by the brooding omnipresence of memories of the jurisprudence of the *Lochner* era, which had covered roughly the first third of the twentieth century. During that period, the Court had deployed the doctrine of substantive due process to strike down a variety of economic and social legislation. However, beginning in the late 1930s, the Court had systematically overturned most of the precedents that had been based on the use of substantive due process, and by 1965, the prospect of even being accused of reviving the jurisprudence of the *Lochner* era was anathema to most of the justices.[12]

For Hugo Black and Potter Stewart, the distaste for *Lochner*-era jurisprudence was the overriding factor in determining their positions in *Griswold*. Both Black and Stewart explicitly noted their disagreement with the policy judgments that underlay the statute, with Black declaring that "the law is every bit as offensive to me as it is to my Brethren [who voted to find the law unconstitutional]" and Stewart labeling the statute an "uncommonly silly law." Nonetheless, specifically referencing a number of the discredited decisions from the early twentieth century and invoking the specter of judges "roam[ing] at will in the limitless area of their own beliefs as to reasonableness, and actually select[ing] policies," both Black and Stewart concluded that the constitutional challenge to the prohibition on the use of contraceptives should be rejected.[13]

Unlike Black and Stewart, the seven justices in the majority were unwilling to countenance the Connecticut statute. The members of the majority deployed a variety of different strategies to deal with the claim that they were replicating the errors of the *Lochner* era. Despite the widespread criticism of the concept of substantive due process, both Harlan and Byron White explicitly relied on that concept to find the Connecticut statute unconstitutional, with Harlan asserting that the statute violated values that were "'implicit in the concept of ordered liberty'" and White relying on *Skinner* to support the proposition that the right of married couples to have access to contraceptives was "among 'the basic civil rights of man.'" By contrast, the remaining five justices joined an opinion by Justice Douglas that specifically eschewed reliance on the idea of substantive due process per se and instead insisted that the Connecticut statute violated a right to privacy that could be found in the "penumbra" of the specific provisions of the Bill of Rights. In addition, in a concurring opinion joined by Chief Justice

Warren and Justice Brennan, Arthur Goldberg argued that a right to privacy could be derived from the language of the Ninth Amendment, which provides that the enumeration of specific rights in the Constitution "shall not be construed to deny or disparage others retained by the people."[14]

Obviously, the *Griswold* majority's embrace of the basic concept of a constitutionally protected right to privacy created a jurisprudential platform from which attacks on a variety of government regulations of decisions related to reproduction might conceivably be launched. Yet at the time the decision was announced in 1965, it was also entirely possible to view the case as being of only limited long-term significance. Like the statute in *Skinner*, the statute at issue in *Griswold* was an outlier. By the mid-1960s, the use of contraceptive drugs and devices was a widely accepted and publicly discussed practice in US society, and Connecticut was the only state that completely banned the use of contraceptives by law. Moreover, although some of the language of the majority opinion could plausibly have been read to be based on the theory that the Constitution protected a right of access to contraception generally, other parts of the opinion suggested a narrower interpretation.

In particular, much of the opinion focused specifically on the impact the Connecticut statute had on the relationship of married people to one another. Thus, for example, in defending his contention that the Constitution should be interpreted to protect a right of privacy, Douglas observed, "We deal with a right of privacy older than the Bill of Rights—older than our political parties, older than our school system. Marriage is a coming together for better or for worse, hopefully enduring, and intimate to the degree of being sacred." Similarly, noting that the Connecticut statute prohibited the use of contraceptives rather than their manufacture or sale, he asked rhetorically, "Would we allow the police to search the sacred precincts of marital bedrooms for telltale signs of the use of contraceptives?" He insisted that the "very idea is repulsive to the notions of privacy surrounding the marriage relationship." Sounding a related note, Justice Goldberg's concurring opinion rested on the theory that the Ninth Amendment protected a right of "*marital* privacy." The concurring opinions of Justices Harlan and White also emphasized the impact of the Connecticut statute on the rights of married couples specifically.[15]

Whatever the intentions of the members of the *Griswold* majority might have been in 1965, subsequent efforts to limit reproductive rights to married couples would be undermined by the sexual revolution of the late 1960s. During this period, the idea that women could openly have sexual relations outside of marriage became more socially acceptable. Nonetheless, US society in general remained firmly committed to the concept that, at least in theory, women should not bear children out of wedlock. Taken together, these two concepts led almost inevitably to the conclusion that access to contraceptives should not be limited to married couples. The 1972 decision in *Eisenstadt v. Baird* firmly ensconced this principle into constitutional law.[16]

Eisenstadt was a constitutional challenge to a Massachusetts statute that provided that only doctors and pharmacists could dispense contraceptives without cost and that even they could only distribute free contraceptives to married people The case was argued before Justices Powell and Rehnquist were confirmed and thus was decided by a seven-member Court. With only Chief Justice Burger dissenting, the justices concluded that the Massachusetts statute ran afoul of the Fourteenth Amendment.

Justices White and Blackmun argued that the statute was unconstitutional because it burdened the right of married people to obtain nonprescription contraceptives. By contrast four of the seven participating justices—including perhaps most notably Justice Stewart, who had dissented in *Griswold*—concluded that the statute violated the equal protection clause by discriminating against unmarried people. Speaking for the majority, although Justice Brennan's opinion purported to apply the rational basis test in reaching that conclusion, the opinion also relied heavily on *Griswold* and declared that "if the right of privacy means anything, it is the right of the individual, married or single, to be free from unwarranted governmental intrusion into matters so fundamentally affecting a person as the decision whether to bear or beget a child."[17]

The decoupling of procreative rights from the marital relationship had obvious implications for the dispute over abortion. One year before *Eisenstadt* was decided, the Court had begun to grapple with the issue in *United States v. Vuitch*.[18] *Vuitch* was a challenge to a District of Columbia statute that prohibited abortions except when "necessary for the preservation of the mother's life or health." The federal district court held that the law violated the due process clause of the Fourteenth Amendment because the statutory language was unconstitutionally vague. Rather than seeking to have this judgment overturned by a federal appellate court, the government appealed the judgment directly to the Supreme Court.

Contending that the Court lacked jurisdiction over the case, Justices Brennan and Marshall argued that the appeal should simply have been dismissed.[19] Although neither Brennan nor Marshall chose to express any views on the merits of the challenge in *Vuitch*, this course of action would have had the effect of leaving intact the district court's holding invalidating the law. However, five justices concluded that the Court did in fact have jurisdiction over the appeal, and seven justices took positions on the merits.

Among those who reached the merits, only Justice Douglas would have affirmed the judgment of the lower court. By contrast, Chief Justice Burger and Justices Harlan, White, and Blackmun joined an opinion by Justice Black that asserted that, properly construed, the District of Columbia statute allowed abortions when either the mental or physical health of the woman was at stake, and that, given this interpretation, the law provided a constitutionally adequate description of the circumstances under which abortions could be legally performed. Conversely, while evincing some sympathy for the vagueness argument, Justice Stewart would have obviated the problem by interpreting the limitations of the statute even more narrowly so that "'a competent licensed practitioner of medicine' [would be] wholly immune from being charged with the commission of a criminal offense under this law."[20]

Although the Court rejected the constitutional challenge in *Vuitch*, the structure of Justice Black's majority opinion brought some cheer to the pro-choice forces. The opinion emphasized the importance of interpreting the District of Columbia statute in a manner that recognized the importance of allowing the physician to exercise reasonable professional judgment. Thus, Dr. Milan Vuitch, the target of the indictment that gave rise to the decision, observed, "What the Supreme Court did was throw the whole mess on the shoulders of American physicians, and that is the correct position."[21] In any event, partisans on all sides of the debate understood that *Vuitch* would only be a prelude to a much broader ruling on the constitutional issues raised by statutes that regulated abortions. On April 22, 1971—the day after *Vuitch* was decided—the justices set the stage for such a ruling by voting to grant certiorari in *Roe v. Wade* and *Doe v. Bolton*.[22]

The state laws involved in the two cases were very different. *Roe* was a challenge to a Texas statute that prohibited all abortions except those performed to save the life of the mother. By contrast, the Georgia statute at issue in *Doe* followed the outlines of the Model Penal Code, allowing abortions in cases of rape or incest and those in which the fetus would be born deformed or the mother's physical or mental health was at stake. The Georgia statute also required that the abortions be performed in a hospital accredited by the Joint Commission on the Accreditation of Hospitals (JCAH) and be approved by a hospital committee and also that the performing physician's judgment be confirmed by two other physicians. In both cases, those challenging the relevant state statute argued that it violated both the Ninth Amendment and the due process clause of the Fourteenth Amendment.

Although petitions for certiorari in both cases had actually reached the Court in 1970, the justices decided to postpone action on the petitions until after *Vuitch* was decided. At the time that the petitions were granted, the Court had its full complement of nine justices. However, before the date on which the cases were scheduled to be argued, Justices Black and Harlan had resigned from the Court. In the wake of the resignations, Chief Justice Burger charged Justices Stewart and Blackmun with the task of screening the docket to determine which cases might best be postponed until after replacements were seated to give the Court its full complement of justices. Blackmun would later recall ruefully that they came to the conclusion that *Roe* and *Doe* might appropriately be considered by a seven-member Court because Stewart believed the decisions in the two cases would turn primarily on jurisdictional issues.[23] Thus, only a few days before Justices Powell and Rehnquist were confirmed, *Roe* and *Doe* were argued before a seven-member Court on December 13, 1971.

At the conference that followed the argument, it quickly became clear all of the justices were prepared to reach the merits of both cases. Five of the seven justices voiced the opinion that the Texas statute at issue in *Roe* should be found unconstitutional, and the comments of Chief Justice Burger were somewhat equivocal. Only Justice White appeared to take the opposing view, and even he seemed less than firm in his convictions.[24]

The discussions surrounding *Doe* revealed a more complicated dynamic. Not surprisingly, Justice White would have rejected the challenge to the Georgia statute. However, unlike in *Roe*, in *Doe* he was at least tentatively joined in this conclusion by Chief Justice Burger, who stated that he was "inclined to hold the [Georgia] statute constitutional."[25]

By contrast, Justices Brennan and Marshall were clearly convinced that both state laws were unconstitutional. Brennan complained that the procedural requirement of the Georgia statute "overrides a good faith determination by the attending M.D." In addition, both he and Marshall also contended that the statute unconstitutionally discriminated against poor women who might live in rural areas and be unable to travel to the only kind of facilities in which the statute allowed abortions to be performed.

Potter Stewart also voted to strike down the Georgia statute. Given his position in *Griswold*, one might well have predicted that Stewart would vote to uphold restrictions on abortions. However, he would ultimately file an opinion that asserted *Griswold* had definitively established the proposition that "freedom of personal choice in matters of marriage and family life is one of the liberties protected by the Due Process Clause of the Fourteenth Amendment" and that the statutes at issue in both *Roe* and *Doe* violated the Constitution by infringing on that freedom.[26]

Despite expressing some of the same concerns as Brennan and Marshall, Justices Douglas and Blackmun expressed more uncertainty about the proper disposition of *Doe*. While describing the Georgia law as "troublesome," Douglas also characterized it as a "better statute than [that of] Texas." Blackmun initially seemed even more hesitant to invalidate the Georgia statute, having privately expressed the opinion that the statute was "pretty good and strikes a good balance of the asserted interests." Douglas and Blackmun suggested the possibility that the Court might send *Doe* back to the district court for findings about how the law operated in practice.[27]

The apparent ambiguity in the positions of Justices Douglas and Burger led to a heated debate between them over the authority to assign the opinions in the abortion cases. Taking the position that there was no clear majority for any single disposition of *Doe*, Burger exercised what he viewed as his prerogative as chief justice to assign Harry Blackmun the task of writing the majority opinions in both *Roe* and *Doe*. Douglas, by contrast, complained that he believed the conference discussions had indicated that a majority of the justices were in favor of invalidating the Georgia statute and that because Burger would have rejected the constitutional challenge in *Doe*, Douglas, as the senior associate justice in the majority, should have been the one to assign the opinion. Burger shot back a reply that not only disputed Douglas's characterization of the conference deliberations but also suggested he would move to set the abortion cases down for reargument after Powell and Rehnquist took their seats on the Court. However, at the time, Burger made no formal effort to follow through on this threat, and although Douglas quickly wrote a draft of an opinion on the merits, after consultation with Brennan, he decided not to circulate it. Thus, Blackmun became the central figure in what was to become a protracted struggle over the proper approach to the constitutional problems associated with abortion regulations.[28]

Almost from the beginning, Blackmun was uncomfortable with the idea of having *Roe* and *Doe* decided by a seven-member Court. Thus, on January 18, 1972, after Chief Justice Burger asked for nominations for cases to be reargued in the wake of the confirmation of Justices Powell and Rehnquist, Blackmun nominated the abortion cases because, in his view,

"The importance of the issue is such that the cases merit[ed] treatment by a full Court." However, he would later recall that "the suggestion was not enthusiastically received" and that "it was the consensus . . . that [he] produce some drafts and we would see what reactions ensued."[29]

With a majority of his colleagues apparently convinced that the abortion cases should be resolved without further argument, Blackmun began his task with the premise that *Doe* should be the primary vehicle for the discussion of the constitutional status of abortion generally. Because he viewed *Roe* as a relatively easy case, and in the conference only White had expressed the view that the Texas statute was constitutional, Blackmun hoped to attract White's vote and achieve unanimity by resting the opinion in that case on the theory that the statute was void for vagueness. However, when Blackmun circulated a tentative draft opinion embodying that theory on May 18, 1972, White quickly dashed Blackmun's hope of avoiding dissent by responding with a draft dissent arguing that Blackmun's position was foreclosed by *Vuitch* and reaffirming his allegiance to the decision in that case.[30]

One week later, Blackmun circulated a draft of his opinion on *Doe*. In sharp contrast to the *Roe* draft, the *Doe* opinion explicitly rejected the claim that the Georgia statute was void for vagueness. Nonetheless, he concluded that much of the statute was unconstitutional for other reasons.

Blackmun relied on the right to travel to invalidate the statutory residency requirement. By contrast, the opinion's treatment of the other sections of the statute rested squarely on the theory that the right to make the "fundamental personal decision whether or not to bear an unwanted child" was a privacy interest protected by the Ninth and Fourteenth Amendments. In making this argument, Blackmun relied heavily on decisions such as *Griswold* and *Eisenstadt*. Nonetheless, he also observed that the abortion cases raised issues that were "inherently different" from those the Court had faced in the contraception cases because "somewhere, either forthwith at conception, or at quickening, or at birth, or at some other point in between, another being becomes involved." Thus, Blackmun conceded that the "woman's personal right . . . is not unlimited [but] must be balanced against the state's interest."[31]

Although the draft opinion purported to rest on an assessment of the extent of the woman's privacy interest, the structure of the opinion was plainly influenced by other considerations as well. In particular, the language of the opinion clearly reflected the reverence for the medical profession that Blackmun had developed in his position as general counsel to the

Mayo Clinic. The opinion is replete with discussions of the significance of the role the woman's attending physician played in abortion decisions and the importance of the physician's interest in having the freedom to properly perform his or her function.[32] Thus, in essence, Blackmun took the view that any justification for abortion regulation must be sufficiently strong to outweigh the interests of both the pregnant woman and her physician.

Against this background, Blackmun had no trouble in concluding that the requirement that abortions be performed in a JCAH-accredited hospital was unconstitutional. He observed that many of the requirements for JCAH accreditation were simply irrelevant to the safety of abortions and that, in any event, the state of Georgia did not impose the same requirements for other types of surgery. By contrast, the draft opinion would have left intact the requirement that abortions be performed only in hospitals licensed by the state. Although acknowledging in a memorandum accompanying the draft that some members of the majority no doubt wished to have the hospital requirement stricken in its entirety, Blackmun also observed, "I have seen abortion mills in operation and the general misery they have caused despite their being run by otherwise 'competent' technicians."[33]

In the same memorandum, Blackmun observed that the decision on the constitutionality of the abortion committee provision was "not the easiest for me to reach," noting that "I have worked closely with hospital supervisory committees set up by the medical profession itself [and] can state with complete conviction that they serve a high purpose in maintaining standards and in keeping the overzealous surgeon's knife sheathed." Nonetheless, although observing that each hospital could, if it wished, establish just such a committee, the draft opinion concluded that the statutory requirement was unconstitutional, asserting that the "imposition of the hospital abortion committee is unnecessary and is unduly restrictive of the patient's rights and needs that . . . have been medically delineated and substantiated by her personal physician."[34]

Blackmun also emphasized the role of the pregnant woman's personal physician in his treatment of the propriety of the requirement that the appropriateness of the abortion be confirmed by two other physicians. Noting that such confirmation was not required by law for any other procedure, Blackmun characterized the requirement as having "no rational connection with the patient's needs and unduly infring[ing] on the physician's right to practice" and asserted that the "attendant physician will know when a consultation is advisable. . . . Physicians have followed this routine for decades and know its usefulness and benefit."[35]

Although Justices Douglas, Brennan, Stewart, and Marshall were not enthusiastic about the tone of the draft opinion in *Doe*, by May 30 it appeared Blackmun had a solid majority for his general approach. On that day, after a private conversation with Blackmun, Stewart circulated a memorandum declaring himself "in basic agreement with the [draft opinion] subject to modifications which I understand you intend to make." However, the next day, events took a dramatically different turn when Blackmun renewed his suggestion that both abortion cases be reargued before a nine-member Court, once again noting the importance of the issues involved and also his uncertainty about the proper resolution of questions such as the constitutionality of requiring abortions to be performed in hospitals. Having by this time also come to the conclusion that a majority of the justices would vote to strike down the death penalty in *Furman*, Blackmun stated that he "didn't think the country could have the death penalty and abortion laws declared unconstitutional on the same day."[36]

Not surprisingly, the motion for reargument was immediately seconded by Chief Justice Burger and Justice White. By contrast, the justices who had voted to strike down the Georgia statute were understandably alarmed by the notion that the abortion cases should be reargued. They believed that both Powell and Rehnquist would join Burger and White in voting to reject the constitutional challenge in *Doe*. Moreover, given the tone of the draft opinion, they feared that after reargument, Blackmun might be persuaded to change his position and vote to uphold the Georgia statute. Thus, on May 31—the same day Blackmun moved for reargument—Douglas, Brennan, and Marshall each circulated memoranda opposing the motion. Both Douglas and Brennan emphasized the fact that the result in *Doe* was supported by five justices, enough to form a majority even if the Court had had a full complement of justices at the time the case was initially argued.

In addition, Douglas sought to downplay the significance of the objections that the other members of the majority had raised to Blackmun's drafts in *Roe* and *Doe*, describing the proposed opinions as "creditable jobs of craftsmanship [that] will, I think, stand the test of time" and asserting that "while we could sit around and make pages of suggestions, I really don't think that is important. The important thing is to get them down." Douglas was even more emphatic in a memorandum distributed the following day, declaring that if a majority of the justices voted to reargue the abortion cases, he would file a statement "telling what is happening to us and the tragedy it entails."[37]

On June 1, Justice Powell entered the fray. He observed that although both he and Justice Rehnquist had been confirmed before Justice Blackmun first suggested in January that the abortion cases should be reargued, both of them had believed at the time that it was inappropriate for them to take a position in the discussion. By contrast, after having served on the Court for more than half a term, Powell now took the view that he should participate in the consideration of the motion for reargument. Both he and Rehnquist supported Blackmun's motion, creating a majority to mandate reconsideration of the abortion cases during the 1972 term. Douglas was irate and drafted an opinion dissenting from the order for reargument and explicitly impugning Burger's integrity. However, Douglas ultimately decided not to publish the opinion, instead simply noting without explanation that he dissented from the decision to have *Roe* and *Doe* reargued.[38]

When the justices returned to the consideration of the abortion issue early in the 1972 term, it quickly became clear that the fears of the members of the original *Doe* majority about the potential impact of reconsideration had been unfounded. At the conference that followed the reargument on October 11, Rehnquist did indeed join White in voting to reject the constitutional challenges to both the Texas and Georgia statutes. However, rather than joining Rehnquist and White, Powell took the position that both laws were unconstitutional. Both he and Stewart urged Blackmun to make *Roe* the lead case and abandon the vagueness rationale, with Powell suggesting an approach that would characterize abortion as a "medical problem broadly defined" and Stewart arguing that the opinion should rely on the right to privacy that Brennan had articulated in *Eisenstadt* and Blackmun himself had embraced in his analysis of *Doe* during the previous term.[39]

With his majority thus fortified in both *Roe* and *Doe,* Blackmun accepted the idea that *Roe* should be the lead case and turned to the task of producing a revised opinion. On November 22, he circulated a new draft that focused on the privacy analysis. The draft—much of which would be incorporated in the majority opinion that was ultimately issued—began by quoting Oliver Wendell Holmes's famous observation that the Constitution "'is made for people of fundamentally differing views, and the accident of our finding certain opinions natural and familiar or novel and even shocking ought not to conclude our judgment upon the question whether statutes embodying them conflict with the Constitution of the United States.'"[40] However, whereas Holmes was advocating judicial restraint, much of the remainder of Blackmun's opinion in *Roe* was devoted to an argument for judicial intervention against existing state abortion laws.

After concluding that procedural issues did not bar the Court from considering the merits in *Roe*, Blackmun observed that the "restrictive laws in effect in a majority of States today are of relatively recent vintage." He then essayed a detailed discussion of the history of societal attitudes and legal restraints on abortion, beginning with the approach of the Persian empire and ending with the official positions taken in the late twentieth century by professional organizations such as the American Medical Association, the American Public Health Association, and the American Bar Association. After dismissing any intimation that modern restrictions on abortion could be justified as means to discourage sexual promiscuity among women, Blackmun conceded that government might have two legitimate interests in imposing such restrictions. First, he observed that despite medical advances that had lessened the potential hazards associated with abortions, the government still had an interest in ensuring that the procedures were performed safely. Second, Blackmun recognized that, however one characterized the fetus, the state had a legitimate interest in preserving "potential life."[41] The draft opinion thus implicitly conceded that even the Texas statute would have passed constitutional muster under the traditional rational basis test.

However, Blackmun argued that the rational basis test was not in fact the applicable standard of review in *Roe*. Citing a variety of potential consequences for women forced to carry an unwanted pregnancy to term, he contended that the right to choose whether to terminate a pregnancy was an aspect of the fundamental right of privacy that had underlain decisions such as *Skinner* and *Griswold*. Thus, Blackmun concluded that restrictions on the ability to obtain an abortion could pass constitutional muster only if necessary to serve a compelling governmental interest.[42]

The defenders of the Texas law, however, argued that it served the compelling governmental interest of preserving the life of the fetus. Some of the defenders contended that the fetus was a "person" for purposes of the equal protection clause of the Fourteenth Amendment. Others, by contrast, simply claimed that the Constitution left each state free to define the point at which human life began for its own purposes.[43]

In responding to these and similar arguments, Blackmun sought to steer a middle course. He observed that the "pregnant woman cannot be isolated in her privacy [because] she carries an embryo and later, a fetus" and conceded that, at some point, the interest in preserving fetal life became compelling for constitutional purposes. But at the same time, he flatly rejected the claim that fetuses were persons for purposes of the Fourteenth

Amendment, noting that when the Constitution referred to persons in other contexts, "The use of the term is such that it has application only post-natally." In addition, although acknowledging that the Catholic church and some others believe that human life begins at conception, Blackmun once again emphasized the wide variety of views on this subject and, asserting that "we need not resolve the difficult problem of when life begins" in order to decide *Roe*, declared, "Texas [cannot] override the rights of the pregnant woman that are at stake" simply "by adopting one theory of life."[44]

To this point, the November 22 draft created little controversy among the members of the *Roe* majority. However, the balance of the draft generated considerable disagreement. Asserting that the interest of the state in protecting "potential life" grew as the pregnancy progressed, the draft concluded that the interest became "compelling" at the end of the first trimester. Prior to that point, Blackmun maintained that "if the attending physician determines in consultation with his patient that in his best medical judgment her pregnancy should be terminated, that judgment is sufficient." Conversely, the opinion also concluded that, after the end of the first trimester, the "State may . . . choose a point beyond which it limits abortions to stated therapeutic categories." On the same day, Blackmun also circulated a briefer draft opinion in *Doe* that concluded that the procedural requirements imposed by the Georgia statute violated the Fourteenth Amendment as well.[45]

The choice of the end of the first trimester as the date beyond which the states would be largely free to regulate abortions was not entirely satisfactory to some members of the *Roe* majority. On November 29, at the urging of his law clerk, Lewis Powell sent Blackmun a private note asking whether Blackmun was wedded to this position. Noting that in the memorandum accompanying the draft Blackmun himself had described this line as arbitrary, Powell suggested that drawing the line at viability might be more "defensible in logic and biologically [*sic*] than perhaps any other single time." Blackmun responded to Powell on December 4, indicating a willingness to accept viability as the dividing line but expressing a preference for the first-trimester approach because of concerns about the need to ensure the safety of second-trimester abortions and the fear that a majority of the justices might not accept an opinion that focused on viability.[46]

Despite these concerns, on December 11, Blackmun submitted a memorandum to the other justices requesting their input on Powell's suggestion. Blackmun stated that he had chosen the first trimester in large measure because he thought that it would be more easily accepted not only by the other members of the majority but by the public at large and also noted his concern about ensuring that the facilities in which second-trimester abortions were performed were adequate. But at the same time, he also conceded that a focus on the second trimester had logical and biological justifications and observed that some women, "particularly younger girls," might refuse to accept the fact that they were pregnant and "for one reason or another" not seek medical advice until the first trimester had already passed.[47]

Justice Douglas immediately responded by stating his preference for the position taken in the draft opinion, whereas Justice Powell reiterated his view that viability was the appropriate dividing line. Justice Marshall took the same basic view as Powell but also suggested that some of the concerns mentioned in Blackmun's memorandum could be addressed by allowing state regulations directed specifically at protecting the health and safety of the mother. It was this approach that ultimately became the basis of the final majority opinion in *Roe*.[48]

Justices White and Rehnquist each filed separate dissents. White asserted that the "Court simply fashions and announces a new constitutional right for pregnant mothers and, with scarcely any reason or authority for its action, invests that right with sufficient substance to override most existing state abortion statutes." Similarly, once again taking an originalist perspective, Rehnquist complained that "to reach its result, the Court necessarily has had to find within the scope of the Fourteenth Amendment a right that was apparently completely unknown to the drafters of the Amendment."[49]

Although joining the opinion of the Court, Chief Justice Burger and Justices Douglas and Stewart chose to file separate opinions as well. Burger sought to dispel any notion that the reasoning of the majority required states to allow "abortion on demand" and also declared that he would be willing to countenance a requirement that two doctors confirm the need for an abortion as long as the procedure for confirmation was less cumbersome than that prescribed by the statute at issue in *Doe v. Bolton*.

Stewart's opinion was plainly designed to address the apparent dissonance between his dissent in *Griswold* and his decision to join the majority in the abortion cases. His concurrence in *Roe* noted that, despite his dissent, *Griswold* had established the principle that the due process clause had a substantive component, and that, given this reality, cases such as *Skinner* and *Eisenstadt* stood for the proposition that the right to choose whether to bear a child was entitled to special constitutional protection. By contrast, Douglas saw the privacy right recognized by the majority as part of a much broader set of rights he characterized as fundamental for constitutional purposes, including "freedom to walk, stroll, or loaf."[50]

From a purely jurisprudential perspective, the decision in *Roe* was most important for its rehabilitation of the concept of substantive due process. Although Stewart asserted in his concurring opinion in *Roe* that *Griswold* was best understood in substantive due process terms, the majority opinion in that case had taken pains to justify the decision (however unconvincingly) by reference to the specific provisions of the Bill of Rights. By contrast, Blackmun's open embrace of substantive due process opened the door for the use of the doctrine in other contexts as well—perhaps most notably in the contemporary dispute over gay rights.[51]

However, *Roe* was even more significant for its impact on the political debate. To be sure, even before the Court's decision, state legislators were wrestling with the abortion question, and the question had played some role in the presidential campaign of 1972. However, by focusing public attention on the issue, *Roe* dramatically raised the profile of the debate, bringing the abortion controversy to the center of US political life.

Not surprisingly, the prochoice forces were exultant at the Court's action. For example, the president of the Planned Parenthood Federation of America characterized *Roe* as a "wise and courageous stroke for the right to privacy and the protection of a woman's physical and emotional health," and another high-profile crusader for abortion rights hailed what he described as "a triumph that culminated a long struggle." Leaders of the prolife movement were no less passionate in their denunciation of the Court's action. Thus, Cardinal John Krol condemned what he described as an "unspeakable tragedy for this nation," and the head of the Bronx chapter of Right to Life proclaimed that "it is ironic that at a time when this country is trying to improve the lot of so many people and is so opposed to violence [that] the Court should sanction the destruction of human life."[52]

The state legislative responses to the abortion decisions reflected the depth of the feelings surrounding the issue. For obvious reasons, no legislative action was taken in states where prochoice forces dominated the political process. By contrast, *Roe* forced prolife legislators to take the offensive in other states, and they often moved aggressively to promulgate a wide range of new restrictions on abortion that might conceivably have been viewed as constitutional under the standards established in *Roe*. Thus, for example, in 1974, the Missouri state legislature passed a statute that, among other things, (1) required married women to obtain the consent of their husbands before obtaining abortions, (2) required minors to obtain parental consent before obtaining abortions, and (3) outlawed the use of the most common procedure for second-trimester abortions on the theory that safer methods were available. In 1976, over the dissents of Chief Justice Burger and Justices White and Rehnquist, the Court found almost all of the restrictions in the Missouri statute unconstitutional in *Planned Parenthood v. Danforth.*[53] However, Justices Stewart, Powell, and Stevens later joined the *Danforth* dissenters in concluding that a state could presumptively require parental consent for minors seeking abortions as long as that state also provided for a judicial procedure in which a minor could contest a parent's refusal to grant consent.[54]

The impact of the abortion decisions was equally apparent at the level of national politics. On one hand, an energized prolife movement made a nationwide effort to mobilize support for a constitutional amendment that would effectively overturn *Roe*. On the other hand, support for *Roe* became a litmus test for any politician seeking the support of the burgeoning feminist community.

Initially, the lines between the two national political parties on the abortion issues were somewhat fluid. Thus, in 1976, Ellen McCormack became one of the most visible symbols of the prolife movement by becoming the first woman to qualify for federal matching funds while campaigning for president on an antiabortion platform in twenty Democratic state primaries and earning the support of twenty-two delegates, and the Democratic Party platform ultimately took a somewhat lukewarm prochoice position. Conversely, in 1976 the Republican Party platform took an equally equivocal prolife stance.[55]

However, by 1980, each party had become clearly identified with one side of the dispute over *Roe*. Prolife activists became an important element of the Republican coalition that ultimately brought Ronald Reagan to power, whereas prochoice feminists and their allies assumed an equally significant role in national Democratic politics. Thus, in every presidential election since 1980, the Republican platform has advocated a constitutional amendment to overturn *Roe*, and the Democratic platform has included a strong endorsement of the prochoice position.[56]

The significance of the abortion issue has been perhaps most apparent in the selection of nominees to the Supreme Court. Republican presidents have attempted to choose justices who would overrule *Roe*, whereas no person suspected of prolife sympathies could have any hope of being nominated to the Court by a Democratic president. Although the performance of Democratic nominees has been uniformly satisfactory to the prochoice forces, in practice the voting pattern of Republican nominees in abortion cases has been uneven. Indeed, in the 1992 decision in *Planned Parenthood v. Casey,* two justices nominated by Ronald Reagan and one chosen by his successor, George H. W. Bush, joined to pen the plurality opinion that reaffirmed the basic principle that the Constitution provides strong protection for the right of a woman to choose whether to have an abortion.[57] Thus, despite being modified in *Casey, Roe* continues to be the signature example of judicial activism not only of the 1972 term but also of the Burger era more generally.

Chapter Eleven

Conclusion

The overall performance of the Supreme Court during the 1972 term might be evaluated from a variety of different perspectives. In some ways, the term can be viewed as heralding what was once famously described as the "counter-revolution that wasn't."[1] By the end of the term, it had become clear that, with the notable exception of William Rehnquist, none of the members of the Burger Court were willing to either consistently commit themselves to the idea of judicial deference or to embrace a formalistic approach to constitutional interpretation. Instead, all of the other justices—even Chief Justice Warren Burger—at times either implicitly or explicitly invoked the idea of the "living Constitution" to invalidate statutes they viewed as fundamentally unjust. In this sense, the performance of the Nixon appointees in particular confirmed rather than undermined the long-term significance of the constitutional innovations of the Warren era.

But while the basic commitment to judicial activism survived the appointment of the Nixon justices, the orientation of that activism changed significantly. In large measure, this change in orientation reflected the impact of exogenous factors beyond the control of any of the justices themselves. For example, a change in the outcome of the presidential election of 1968 would undoubtedly have had a dramatic impact on the development of constitutional doctrine. A shift in fewer than two hundred thousand votes out of the more than seventy million that were cast could have led to a victory by Hubert Humphrey rather than Richard Nixon. In that case, Humphrey rather than Nixon would then have had the opportunity to select four new members of the Court, and the justices chosen by Humphrey almost certainly would have established a solid progressive majority not only for the 1972 term but also for a significant number of years thereafter. Rather than discussing a failed counterrevolution, commentators would then no doubt have been faced with the task of analyzing the ongoing expansion of progressive constitutional doctrine.

After the Nixon appointments, however, the makeup of the Supreme Court during the 1972 term was in many respects typical of what one would normally expect over time. From an ideological perspective, the early Burger Court was far more diverse than that which preceded it. Whereas the Court of the late Warren era was thoroughly dominated by progressives, beginning in 1972 the Court included justices whose viewpoints spanned virtually the entire spectrum of US politics, with three justices who were committed progressives, two justices who were equally committed conservatives, and four justices whose political perspectives were less easily described. The decisions rendered by the Court as a whole were the by-product of coalitions among these different groups.

The decisions of the 1972 term reflected both the nature and the limitations of the changes wrought by the Nixon appointees on the dominant political culture of the Court. Like holdover Potter Stewart, these appointees uniformly rejected the progressive narrative of the period from the mid-1960s through the late 1970s, which held that US society was in need of fundamental structural change. Nonetheless, once again with the exception of Rehnquist, all of the Nixon justices were willing to concede that even a well-functioning system would on occasion produce profoundly unjust political decisions and that the Court ought to redress those injustices.[2]

Not surprisingly, the reconfigured Court was less willing than its immediate predecessor to conclude that the Constitution affirmatively protected progressive values. However, contrary to the assertions of some commentators, the activism of the early Burger era cannot be characterized as either "rootless" or simply pragmatic.[3] Rather, in cases such as *Frontiero v. Richardson*, *Committee for Public Education and Religious Freedom v. Nyquist*, and *Roe v. Wade*, a majority of the justices deployed the Constitution in support of values embraced not only by progressives but also more generally by many members of the affluent, well-educated Protestant community from which all of the centrist judges were drawn.[4] Conversely, members of that same community were less likely to support the approach urged by the progressive dissenters in the obscenity cases.[5]

At the same time, the centrist justices were in general more reluctant than their progressive compatriots to support decisions that would disrupt the established institutional structures of government in the United States. This reality was reflected clearly in the decisions dealing with school finance and school desegregation. Thus, for example, while Justice Powell's majority opinion in *San Antonio Independent School District v. Rodriguez* implicitly conceded that school financing systems based on property taxes resulted in an unjust distribution of resources, he argued that judicial intervention was inappropriate because of the need to preserve state and local control over the operation of the school systems.[6] Similarly, the refusal to order cross-district transportation of students in *Bradley v. State Board of Education* was based primarily on the perceived need to respect the jurisdictional boundaries established by the state government.[7]

The same forces that produced decisions such as *Roe* and *Rodriguez* continued to strongly influence the evolution of constitutional doctrine throughout the tenure of Burger as chief justice. Although on occasion a majority of the justices deployed the Constitution to advance the conservative political agenda, progressives continued to be the more likely beneficiaries of judicial activism even after the retirement of William O. Douglas in 1975.[8] But while the Warren Court progressives at times sought to fundamentally restructure the governmental decision-making process and US society generally, the centrists who controlled the Burger Court believed that the Court should focus almost exclusively on the injustice of individual decisions made by the government and generally resisted efforts to involve the Court in major structural reforms.[9] More than any specific doctrinal innovation, this change in emphasis—clearly evident by the end of the 1972 term—was the most important jurisprudential development of the Burger era.

Selected Cases

Abington School District v. Schempp, 374 U.S. 203 (1963)
Adams v. Williams, 407 U.S. 142 (1972)
Adkins v. Children's Hospital, 261 U.S. 525 (1923)
Alberts v. California, 354 U.S. 476 (1957)
Almeida-Sanchez v. United States, 413 U.S. 266 (1973)
Apodaca v. Oregon, 406 U.S. 404 (1972)
Baker v. Carr, 369 U.S. 186 (1962)
Barker v. Wingo, 407 U.S. 514 (1972)
Board of Education v. Allen, 392 U.S. 236 (1968)
Boddie v. Connecticut, 401 U.S. 371 (1971)
A Book Named "John Cleland's Memoirs of a Woman of Pleasure" v. Attorney General of Massachusetts, 383 U.S. 413 (1966)
Bradley v. Milliken, 484 F.2d 215 (6th Cir. 1973)
Bradley v. Milliken, 433 F.2d 897 (6th Cir. 1970)
Bradley v. School Board of Richmond, 412 U.S. 92 (1973)
Bradley v. School Board of Richmond, 338 F. Supp. 67 (E.D. Va. 1972)
Bradley v. School Board of Richmond, 325 F. Supp. 828 (E.D. Va. 1971)
Bradley v. State Board of Education, 412 U.S. 92 (1973)
Bradwell v. Illinois, 83 U.S. 130 (1873)
Branzburg v. Hayes, 408 U.S. 665 (1972)
Breedlove v. Suttles, 302 U.S. 207 (1937)
Broadrick v. Oklahoma, 413 U.S. 601 (1973)
Brown v. Board of Education, 347 U.S. 483 (1954)
Brown v. Board of Education, 394 U.S. 294 (1955)
Buck v. Bell, 274 U.S. 200 (1927)
Bumper v. North Carolina, 391 U.S. 543 (1968)
Burns v. Fortson, 410 U.S. 686 (1973)
Burton v. Wilmington Housing Authority, 365 U.S. 725 (1961)
Carter v. Carter Coal Co., 298 U.S. 238 (1936)
Chaplinsky v. New Hampshire, 315 U.S. 568 (1942)
City of Rome v. United States, 446 U.S. 156 (1980)

Colegrove v. Green, 328 U.S. 549 (1946)
Committee for Public Education and Religious Freedom v. Nyquist, 413 U.S. 756 (1973)
Cooper v. Aaron, 358 U.S. 1 (1958)
Craig v. Boren, 429 U.S. 190 (1976)
Dandridge v. Williams, 397 U.S. 471 (1970)
Doe v. Bolton, 410 U.S. 179 (1973)
Douglas v. California, 373 U.S. 353 (1963)
Dunn v. Blumstein, 405 U.S. 330 (1972)
Escobedo v. Illinois, 378 U.S. 478 (1964)
Everson v. Board of Education, 330 U.S. 1 (1947)
Fay v. Noia, 372 U.S. 391 (1963)
Frontiero v. Richardson, 411 U.S. 677 (1973)
Furman v. Georgia, 408 U.S. 238 (1972)
Gaffney v. Cummings, 412 U.S. 735 (1973)
Gilbert v. California, 388 U.S. 263 (1967)
Ginsberg v. New York, 390 U.S. 629 (1968)
Ginzburg v. United States, 383 U.S. 463 (1966)
Goldberg v. Kelly, 397 U.S. 254 (1970)
Graham v. Richardson, 403 U.S. 365 (1971)
Green v. County School Board of New Kent County, 391 U.S. 430 (1968)
Griffin v. County School Board of Prince Edward County, 377 U.S. 218 (1964)
Griswold v. Connecticut, 381 U.S. 479 (1965)
Hadley v. Junior College School District, 397 U.S. 50 (1970)
Harper v. Virginia Board of Elections, 383 U.S. 663 (1966)
H. L. v. Matheson, 450 U.S. 398 (1981)
Hoyt v. Florida, 368 U.S. 57 (1961)
Hunt v. McNair, 413 U.S. 734 (1973)
Jacobellis v. Ohio, 378 U.S. 184 (1964)
Jefferson v. Hackney, 406 U.S. 535 (1972)
Jenkins v. Georgia, 415 U.S. 153 (1974)
Kaufman v. United States, 394 U.S. 217 (1969)
Keyes v. School District No. 1, 396 U.S. 1215 (1969)
Keyes v. School District No. 1, 402 U.S. 182 (1971)
Keyes v. School District No. 1, 413 U.S. 189 (1973)
Keyes v. School District No. 1, 445 F.2d 990 (10th Cir. 1971)
Kirby v. Illinois, 406 U.S. 682 (1972)
Kirkpatrick v. Preisler, 394 U.S. 526 (1969)
Korematsu v. United States, 333 U.S. 214 (1944)
Kramer v. Union Free School District, 395 U.S. 621 (1969)
Labine v. Vincent, 401 U.S. 535 (1971)
Lassiter v. Northhampton County Board of Elections, 360 U.S. 45 (1959)

Lawrence v. Texas, 539 U.S. 558 (2003)
Lemon v. Kurtzman, 403 U.S. 602 (1971)
Lemon v. Kurtzman, 411 U.S. 192 (1973)
Levitt v. Committee for Public Education and Religious Liberty, 413 U.S. 472 (1973)
Levy v. Louisiana, 391 U.S. 68 (1968)
Lloyd v. Tanner, 407 U.S. 551 (1972)
Mahan v. Howell, 410 U.S. 315 (1973)
Marston v. Lewis, 410 U.S. 679 (1973)
McDonald v. State Board of Election Commissioners, 394 U.S. 802 (1969)
McGautha v. California, 402 U.S. 183 (1971)
Meek v. Pittenger, 421 U.S. 349 (1975)
Miller v. California, 413 U.S. 15 (1973)
Milliken v. Bradley, 418 U.S. 717 (1974)
Miranda v. Arizona, 384 U.S. 436 (1966)
Mishkin v. New York, 383 U.S. 502 (1966)
Moose Lodge v. Irvis, 407 U.S. 163 (1972)
Morehead v. New York ex rel. Tipaldo, 298 U.S. 597 (1936)
New York Times Co. v. Sullivan, 376 U.S. 54 (1964)
New York Times Co. v. United States, 403 U.S. 703 (1971)
Paris Adult Theater No. 1 v. Slaton, 413 U.S. 48 (1973)
Penn Central Transportation Co. v. City of New York, 438 U.S. 104 (1978)
Pierce v. Society of Sisters, 268 U.S. 510 (1925)
Pittsburgh Press Co. v. Pittsburgh Commission on Human Relations, 413 U.S. 376 (1973)
Planned Parenthood v. Casey, 505 U.S. 833 (1992)
Planned Parenthood v. Danforth, 428 U.S. 52 (1976)
Poe v. Ullman, 367 U.S. 497 (1961)
Pope v. Williams, 193 U.S. 621 (1904)
Redrup v. New York, 386 U.S. 767 (1967)
Reed v. Reed, 404 U.S. 71 (1971)
Reitman v. Mulkey, 387 U.S. 369 (1967)
Reynolds v. Sims, 377 U.S. 533 (1964)
Roe v. Wade, 410 U.S. 113 (1973)
Rosario v. Rockefeller, 410 U.S. 752 (1973)
Roth v. United States, 354 U.S. 476 (1957)
Rudolph v. Alabama, 375 U.S. 889 (1963)
Salyer Land Co. v. Tulare Lake Basin Water District, 410 U.S. 719 (1973)
San Antonio Independent School District v. Rodriguez, 411 U.S. 1 (1973)
Schecter Poultry Corp. v. United States, 295 U.S. 495 (1935)
Schneckloth v. Bustamonte, 412 U.S. 218 (1973)
School District of Abington Township v. Schempp, 374 U.S. 204 (1963)
Serrano v. Priest, 483 P.2d 1241, 5 Cal.3d 584 (1971)

Shapiro v. Thompson, 394 U.S. 618 (1969)
Skinner v. Oklahoma, 316 U.S. 535 (1942)
Sloan v. Lemon, 413 U.S. 825 (1973)
Stanley v. Georgia, 394 U.S. 557 (1969)
Stanley v. Illinois, 405 U.S. 645 (1972)
Starns v. Malkerson, 401 U.S. 985 (1971)
Stone v. Powell, 428 U.S. 465 (1976)
Stovall v. Denno, 388 U.S. 293 (1967)
Sugarman v. Dougall, 413 U.S. 634 (1973)
Swann v. Charlotte-Mecklenburg Board of Education, 402 U.S. 1 (1971)
Tilton v. Richardson, 403 U.S. 672 (1971)
Tinker v. Des Moines Community Independent School District, 393 U.S. 503 (1969)
Trop v. Dulles, 359 U.S. 86 (1958)
United States Civil Service Commission v. National Association of Letter Carriers, 413 U.S. 548 (1973)
United States Department of Agriculture v. Moreno, 413 U.S. 528 (1973)
United States Department of Agriculture v. Murry, 413 U.S. 508 (1973)
United States v. 12,200-ft. Reels of Film, 413 U.S. 123 (1973)
United States v. Ash, 413 U.S. 300 (1973)
United States v. Carolene Products Co., 304 U.S. 144 (1938)
United States v. Kras, 409 U.S. 434 (1973)
United States v. Orito, 413 U.S. 139 (1973)
United States v. Reidel, 402 U.S. 351 (1971)
United States v. Vuitch, 402 U.S. 62 (1971)
United States v. Wade, 388 U.S. 218 (1967)
Valentine v. Chrestensen, 316 U.S. 52 (1942)
Village Books Inc. v. Marshall, 418 U.S. 930 (1974)
Vlandis v. Kline, 412 U.S. 441 (1973)
Walz v. Tax Commission, 397 U.S. 664 (1970)
Weber v. Aetna Casualty and Surety Co., 406 U.S. 164 (1972)
Wesberry v. Sanders, 376 U.S. 1 (1964)
White v. Regester, 412 U.S. 755 (1973)
White v. Weiser, 412 U.S. 783 (1973)
Witherspoon v. Illinois, 391 U.S. 510 (1968)
Wright v. Council of the City of Emporia, 407 U.S. 451 (1972)

Abbreviations

BRW	Byron R. White
BRWP	Byron R. White Papers, Manuscript Division, Library of Congress
HAB	Harry A. Blackmun
HABP	Harry A. Blackmun Papers, Manuscript Division, Library of Congress
LFP	Lewis F. Powell, Jr.
LFPP	Lewis F. Powell, Jr., Papers, Powell Archives, Washington and Lee University School of Law, http://law2.wlu.edu/powellarchives/page.asp?pageid=1279
PS	Potter Stewart
PSP	Potter Stewart Papers, Manuscript and Archives Division, Yale University
TM	Thurgood Marshall
TMP	Thurgood Marshall Papers, Manuscript Division, Library of Congress
WEB	Warren E. Burger
WHR	William Hobbes Rehnquist
WJB	William J. Brennan, Jr.
WJBP	William J. Brennan, Jr., Papers, Manuscript Division, Library of Congress
WOD	William O. Douglas
WODP	William O. Douglas Papers, Manuscript Division, Library of Congress

Notes

Preface

1. Roe v. Wade, 410 U.S. 113 (1973).

Chapter 1. The Making of the Burger Court

1. For detailed discussions of the jurisprudence of the Warren Court, see, for example, Morton J. Horwitz, *The Warren Court and the Pursuit of Justice* (New York: Hill and Wang, 1998); Lucas A. Powe, Jr., *The Warren Court and American Politics* (Cambridge, MA: Belknap Press of Harvard University Press, 2000); Bernard Schwartz, ed., *The Warren Court: A Retrospective* (New York: Oxford University Press, 1996); Mark V. Tushnet, ed., *The Warren Court in Historical and Political Perspective* (Charlottesville: University Press of Virginia, 1993).

2. Brown v. Board of Education, 347 U.S. 483 (1954).

3. "Supreme Court Statistics," *Harvard Law Review* 82 (November 1968): 306; "Supreme Court Statistics," *Harvard Law Review* 83 (November 1969): 278.

4. See, for example, Green v. County School Board of New Kent County, 391 U.S. 430 (1968); Reynolds v. Sims, 377 U.S. 433 (1964); Miranda v. Arizona, 384 U.S. 436 (1966); Harper v. Virginia Board of Elections, 383 U.S. 663 (1966).

5. Griswold v. Connecticut, 381 U.S. 479 (1965); Abington School District v. Schempp, 374 U.S. 203 (1963); Jacobellis v. Ohio, 378 U.S. 184 (1964).

6. Compare Herbert Wechsler, "Toward Neutral Principles of Constitutional Law," *Harvard Law Review* 73 (November 1959): 1–35 with Frank I. Michelman, "The Supreme Court, 1968 Term: Foreword—on Protecting the Poor through the Fourteenth Amendment," *Harvard Law Review* 83 (November 1969): 7–59.

7. *New York Times*, May 31, 1968, 18.

8. The struggle over the Fortas nomination and the circumstances that led to his resignation are described in detail in Laura Kalman, *Abe Fortas: A Biography* (New Haven, CT: Yale University Press, 1990); Bruce Allen Murphy, *Fortas: The Rise and Ruin of a Supreme Court Justice* (New York: Morrow, 1988).

9. Kevin J. McMahon, *Nixon's Court: His Challenge to Political Liberalism and Its Political Consequences* (Chicago: University of Chicago Press, 2011).

10. See, for example, *Wall Street Journal*, September 24, 1971, 3; *Washington Post*, September 24, 1971, A1.

11. See, for example, Gideon v. Wainwright, 372 U.S. 335 (1963).

12. Robert H. Bork, "Neutral Principles and Some First Amendment Problems," *Indiana Law Journal* 47 (1971): 1–35.

13. Much of what follows is taken from Earl M. Maltz, *The Chief Justiceship of Warren Burger, 1969–1986* (Columbia: University of South Carolina Press, 2000), 8–23. The justices are also profiled in Vincent Blasi, ed., *The Burger Court: The Counter-Revolution That Wasn't* (New Haven, CT: Yale University Press, 1983), 239–256; Charles M. Lamb and Steven C. Halpern, eds., *The Burger Court: Political and Judicial Profiles* (Champaign: University of Illinois Press, 1991).

14. Leon Friedman, "Warren E. Burger," in *The Justices of the Supreme Court: Their Lives and Major Opinions*, ed. Leon Friedman and Fred L. Israel (New York: Chelsea House, 1997) provides detailed biographical information on Burger.

15. William O. Douglas's life and career are chronicled in his two-volume autobiography, Douglas, *Go East, Young Man: The Early Years—The Autobiography of William O. Douglas* (New York: Random House, 1974); Douglas, *The Court Years, 1939–1975: The Autobiography of William O. Douglas* (New York: Random House, 1980). James F. Simon, *Independent Journey: The Life of William O. Douglas* (New York: Harper and Row, 1980) provides a different perspective.

16. Bernard Schwartz, *The Ascent of Pragmatism: The Burger Court in Action* (Reading, MA: Addison-Wesley, 1990).

17. The standard biography of Brennan is Seth Stern and Stephen Wermeil, *Justice Brennan: Liberal Champion* (Boston: Houghton Mifflin Harcourt, 2010). In addition, see Hunter C. Clark, *Mr. Justice Brennan, the Great Conciliator* (New York: Birch Lane, 1995); Kim Isaac Eisler, *The Last Liberal: William J. Brennan and the Decisions That Transformed America* (Washington, DC: Beard Books, 2003).

18. "Supreme Court Statistics," *Harvard Law Review* 82 (1968): 306; "Supreme Court Statistics," *Harvard Law Review* 83 (1969): 278.

19. "Supreme Court Statistics," *Harvard Law Review* 87 (1973): 303.

20. Marshall's life is the subject of a vast literature. Among the more notable works are Howard Ball, *A Defiant Life: Thurgood Marshall and the Persistence of Racism in America* (New York: Crown, 1998); Mark V. Tushnet, *Making Civil Rights Law: Thurgood Marshall and the Supreme Court, 1936–1961* (New York: Oxford University Press, 1994); Tushnet, *Making Constitutional Law: Thurgood Marshall and the Supreme Court, 1961–1991* (New York: Oxford University Press, 1997); Juan Williams, *Thurgood Marshall: American Revolutionary* (New York: Times Books, 1998).

21. For a detailed biographical sketch, see "Potter Stewart," in *The Justices of the Supreme Court: Their Lives and Major Opinions*, vol. 5, ed. Leon Friedman and Fred L. Israel (New York: Chelsea House, 1997), 1546–1573. Stewart's jurisprudence

is described in Gayle Binion, "Justice Potter Stewart: The Unpredictable Vote," *Journal of Supreme Court History* (1992): 99–108.

22. Dennis J. Hutchinson, *The Man Who Once Was Whizzer White: A Portrait of Justice Byron R. White* (New York: Free Press, 1998) provides a detailed account of White's life and jurisprudence.

23. "Supreme Court Statistics," *Harvard Law Review* 87 (1973): 303, 304.

24. The conflict surrounding the Haynsworth nomination is discussed in detail in Edward N. Beiser, "The Haynsworth Affair Reconsidered: The Significance of Conflicting Perspectives of the Judicial Role," *Vanderbilt Law Review* 23 (1970): 263–292; Stephen L. Wasby and Joel B. Grossman, "Judge Clement F. Haynsworth, Jr.: New Perspective on His Nomination to the Supreme Court," *Duke Law Journal* (1990): 74–80.

25. The considerations that led Nixon to nominate Carswell and the factors that led to the defeat of the nomination in the Senate are described in Bruce H. Kalk, "The Carswell Affair: The Politics of a Supreme Court Nomination in the Nixon Administration," *American Journal of Legal History* 42 (1998): 262–287.

26. Blackmun's life and career are discussed in Linda Greenhouse, *Becoming Justice Blackmun: Harry Blackmun's Supreme Court Journey* (New York: Times Books, 2005); Tinsley Yarbrough, *Harry A. Blackmun, the Outsider Justice* (New York: Oxford University Press, 2008).

27. *Newsweek*, April 27, 1970, 28; *U.S. News and World Report*, April 27, 1970, 22.

28. The standard account of Powell's life is John C. Jeffries, Jr., *Justice Lewis F. Powell, Jr.* (New York: Scribner's, 1994).

29. "Supreme Court Statistics," *Harvard Law Review* 87 (1973): 303.

30. Georgia v. United States, No. 72-75, Lewis F. Powell, Jr. (LFP) to Potter Stewart (PS), March 30, 1973, case file, pt. 1, WJBP, 300.

31. For very different perspectives on Rehnquist, compare John A. Jenkins, *The Partisan: The Life of William Rehnquist* (Jackson, TN: Public Affairs, 2012) with Sue Davis, *Justice Rehnquist and the Constitution* (Princeton, NJ: Princeton University Press, 1989) and Herman Obermayer, *Rehnquist: A Personal Profile of the Distinguished Chief Justice of the United States* (New York: Threshold, 2009).

32. See, for example, City of Rome v. United States, 446 U.S. 156, 206–221 (1980) (Rehnquist, J. dissenting) (constitutionality of application of preclearance requirement in Voting Rights Act); Penn Central Transportation Co. v. City of New York, 438 U.S. 104, 138–153 (1978) (Rehnquist, J., dissenting) (property rights).

Chapter 2. Prelude: The 1971 Term

1. *New York Times*, January 9, 1972, E10; *New York Times*, January 8, 1972, 1; *Boston Globe*, January 8, 1972, 16.

2. Moose Lodge v. Irvis, 407 U.S. 163 (1972).

3. See Moose Lodge No. 107 v. K. Leroy Irvis, No. 70-75, brief of appellee K. Leroy Irvis, (1971).

4. Burton v. Wilmington Housing Authority, 365 U.S. 725 (1961); Reitman v. Mulkey, 387 U.S. 369 (1967).

5. *Moose Lodge*, 406 U.S. at 175.

6. Ibid., at 186 (Brennan, J., dissenting); 182–183 (Douglas, J., dissenting); 187–189 (Brennan, J., dissenting).

7. Kirby v. Illinois, 406 U.S. 682 (1972). The process by which the Court reached its decision in *Kirby* is discussed in Bernard Schwartz, *The Ascent of Pragmatism: The Burger Court in Action* (Reading, MA: Addison-Wesley, 1990), 321–322.

8. United States v. Wade, 388 U.S. 218 (1967); Gilbert v. California, 388 U.S. 263 (1967).

9. *Wade*, 388 U.S. at 236–237 (footnote omitted), quoting Powell v. Alabama, 287 U.S. 45, 57 (1932); *Gilbert*, 388 U.S. at 273.

10. Escobedo v. Illinois, 378 U.S. 478 (1964).

11. Kirby v. Illinois, case history, Box II: 6, Folder 13, WJBP, cxxv.

12. Ibid., cxv–cxvii.

13. Ibid.

14. Kirby v. Illinois, No. 70-5061, conference notes, case file, LFPP; *Kirby*, 407 U.S. at 687–691 (plurality opinion).

15. Stovall v. Denno, 388 U.S. 293 (1967).

16. *Kirby*, 406 U.S. at 688, 689–690 (plurality opinion); 691–704 (Brennan, J., dissenting).

17. Ibid., at 691 (Burger, C.J., concurring); 705 (White, J., dissenting).

18. *Kirby*, memorandum to file, March 21, 1972, LFP case file, LFPP, 1, 2; *Kirby*, argument notes, March 21, 1972, LFP case file, LFPP.

19. *Kirby*, Lewis F. Powell, Jr. (LFP), to Larry A. Hammond, May 8, 1972, LFP case file, LFPP; *Kirby*, LFP to Potter Stewart, May 8, 1972, LFP case file, LFPP; *Kirby*, 406 U.S. at 691 (Powell, J., concurring in the result).

20. For example, during the 1971 term, the Court also rejected the arguments of progressives in a variety of other criminal procedure cases. Examples include Barker v. Wingo, 407 U.S. 514 (1972); Adams v. Williams, 407 U.S. 142 (1972); Apodaca v. Oregon, 406 U.S. 404 (1972).

21. Furman v. Georgia, 408 U.S. 238 (1972).

22. The Court's treatment of the death penalty in general and *Furman* in particular has been the subject of a vast literature. See, for example, Lee Epstein and Joseph F. Kobylka, *The Supreme Court and Legal Change: Abortion and the Death Penalty* (Chapel Hill: University of North Carolina Press, 1992); D. J. Herda, Furman v. Georgia*: The Death Penalty Case* (Lawrence: University Press of Kansas, 2010); Evan Mandery, *A Wild Justice: The Death and Resurrection of Capital Punishment in America* (New York: Norton, 2013). Bob Woodward and Scott Armstrong, *The Brethren: Inside the Supreme Court* (New York: Simon and Schuster, 1979), 247–266, purports to describe the internal deliberations of the Court.

23. Jeffrey M. Jones, "Americans' Support for Death Penalty Stable," http://www.gallup.com/poll/178790/americans-support-death-penalty-stable.aspx.

24. Trop v. Dulles, 359 U.S. 86, 99 (1958) (opinion of Warren, C.J.).

25. Ibid., at 101.

26. Rudolph v. Alabama, 375 U.S. 889 (1963) (Goldberg, J., dissenting from denial of certiorari).

27. Witherspoon v. Illinois, 391 U.S. 510 (1968).

28. Ibid., at 520 (footnote omitted).

29. McGautha v. California, 402 U.S. 183 (1971).

30. Ibid., at 196, 203, 248 (Brennan, J., dissenting); 207 (footnote omitted).

31. *Furman*, case history, Box II: 6, Folder 13, WJBP, cxxxv.

32. Aikens v. California, No. 68-5027, conference notes, LFP case file, Folders 1 and 2, LFPP.

33. *Furman*, 408 U.S. at 240–257 (Douglas, J., concurring); 257–306 (Brennan, J., concurring); 306–310 (Stewart, J., concurring); 310–314 (White, J., concurring); 314–374 (Marshall, J., concurring).

34. Ibid., 408 U.S. at 286, 291, 300 (opinion of Brennan, J.).

35. Ibid., at 302, 303.

36. Ibid., at 331, 353 (opinion of Marshall, J.).

37. Ibid., at 362, 363 (emphasis added).

38. Ibid., at 365, 369.

39. *Aikens*, case file, LFPP, 6 (draft opinion of Douglas, J., dissenting from grant of certiorari).

40. *Furman*, 408 U.S. at 248, 258 (opinion of Douglas, J.).

41. *Furman*, case history, WJBP, cxliv.

42. Ibid., cxlix.

43. Ibid.; *Furman*, 408 U.S. at 307, 308 (opinion of Stewart, J.), 310, 312 (opinion of White, J.), 313.

44. *Furman*, 408 U.S. at 375–404 (Burger, C.J., dissenting); 415–465 (Powell, J., dissenting).

45. Ibid., at 466, 468 (Rehnquist, J., dissenting), 470; 388, 402 (Burger, C.J., dissenting).

46. Ibid., at 405, 406, 410 (Blackmun, J., dissenting).

47. Ibid., at 417, 418, 462.

48. *Washington Post*, June 30, 1972, A13.

49. Weber v. Aetna Casualty and Surety Co., 406 U.S. 164 (1972). The evolution of the Court's approach to discrimination based on illegitimacy is discussed in detail in Earl M. Maltz, "Illegitimacy and Equal Protection," *Arizona State Law Journal* (1980): 831–851; Robert L. Stenger, "The Supreme Court and Illegitimacy: 1968–1977," *Family Law Quarterly* 11 (1978): 365–405.

50. Levy v. Louisiana, 391 U.S. 68, 72 (1968).

51. Labine v. Vincent, 401 U.S. 535, 539–540 (1971).

52. *Weber*, 406 U.S. at 177–186 (Rehnquist, J., dissenting).

53. Ibid., at 176–177 (Blackmun, J., concurring in the result); 175 (majority opinion).

Chapter 3. Reapportionment and Voting Rights

1. Detailed studies of the background and consequences of the Warren Court's reapportionment decisions include Gordon E. Baker, *The Reapportionment Revolution: Representation, Political Power, and the Supreme Court* (New York: Random House, 1966); Robert B. Mackay, *Reapportionment: The Law and Politics of Equal Representation* (New York: Twentieth Century Fund, 1965); J. Douglas Smith, *On Democracy's Doorstep: How the Supreme Court Brought "One Person, One Vote" to the United States* (New York: Hill and Wang, 2014).
2. See, for example, Smiley v. Holm, 283 U.S. 355 (1932).
3. Colegrove v. Green, 328 U.S. 549 (1946).
4. Pope v. Williams, 193 U.S. 621 (1904).
5. Ibid., at 632 (citation omitted).
6. Lassiter v. Northampton County Board of Elections, 360 U.S. 45 (1959).
7. Ibid., at 50 (citation omitted).
8. Baker v. Carr, 369 U.S. 186 (1962).
9. Wesberry v. Sanders, 376 U.S. 1 (1964).
10. Reynolds v. Sims, 377 U.S. 433 (1964).
11. Ibid., at 562, 565.
12. Kirkpatrick v. Preisler, 394 U.S. 526 (1969).
13. Ibid., at 531.
14. Harper v. Virginia State Board of Elections, 383 U.S. 663 (1966); Breedlove v. Suttles, 302 U.S. 207 (1937).
15. Kramer v. Union Free School District, 395 U.S. 621 (1969).
16. Ibid., at 626 (citation omitted), 630.
17. Hadley v. Junior College School District, 397 U.S. 50 (1970).
18. Ibid., at 53–54.
19. Dunn v. Blumstein, 405 U.S. 30 (1972).
20. Ibid., at 363 (Burger, C.J., dissenting).
21. Ibid., at 343 (citations omitted), 348.
22. Marston v. Lewis, 410 U.S. 679 (1973) (per curiam); Burns v. Fortson, 410 U.S. 686 (1973) (per curiam).
23. Gerald Gunther, "The Supreme Court, 1971 Term: Foreword—in Search of Evolving Doctrine on a Changing Court: A Model for a Newer Equal Protection," *Harvard Law Review* 86 (1972): 8.
24. *Marston*, 410 U.S. at 682–684 (Marshall, J., dissenting); *Burns*, 410 U.S. at 688–689 (Marshall, J., dissenting).
25. Salyer Land Co. v. Tulare Lake Basin Water District, 410 U.S. 719 (1973).

26. Ibid., at 735–742 (Douglas, J., dissenting); 727–728, quoting *Hadley*, at 53–54 (1970).

27. Rosario v. Rockefeller, 410 U.S. 752 (1973).

28. Ibid., at 764 (Powell, J., dissenting), 765, 771.

29. Ibid., at 760.

30. Mahan v. Howell, 410 U.S. 315 (1973).

31. Ibid., at 333–349 (Brennan, J., concurring in part and dissenting in part).

32. Ibid., at 320, 322.

33. Gaffney v. Cummings, 412 U.S. 735 (1973); White v. Regester, 412 U.S. 755 (1973).

34. Gaffney v. Cummings, No. 71-1741, draft opinion concurring in part and dissenting in part, May 1, 1973, case file, LFPP.

35. *Burns*, 410 U.S. at 687.

36. *Mahan*, 410 U.S. at 330–333.

37. White v. Weiser, 412 U.S. 783 (1973).

38. White v. Weiser, No. 71-1623, conference notes, LFP case file, LFPP.

39. See *Mahan*, 410 U.S. at 323.

40. *Weiser*, No. 71-1623, memorandum from Byron R. White to Warren E. Burger, March 5, 1973, case file; *Weiser*, 412 U.S. at 790.

41. *Weiser*, 412 U.S. at 793 (Powell, J., concurring).

Chapter 4. The Battle over Obscenity

1. New York Times Co. v. Sullivan, 376 U.S. 54 (1964).

2. Tinker v. Des Moines Community Independent School District, 393 U.S. 503 (1969).

3. New York Times Co. v. United States, 403 U.S. 703 (1971).

4. Branzburg v. Hayes, 408 U.S. 665 (1972).

5. Lloyd v. Tanner, 407 U.S. 551 (1972).

6. Broadrick v. Oklahoma, 413 U.S. 601 (1973); United States Civil Service Commission v. National Association of Letter Carriers, 413 U.S. 548 (1973).

7. Miller v. California, 413 U.S. 15 (1973); Paris Adult Theater No. 1 v. Slaton, 413 U.S. 48 (1973). The Court's role in the dispute over the regulation of sexually explicit material is discussed in detail in Lane V. Sunderland, *Obscenity: The Court, the Congress, and the President's Commission* (Washington, DC: American Enterprise Institute for Public Policy Research, 1974).

8. Chaplinsky v. New Hampshire, 315 U.S. 568, 572 (1942) (footnote omitted).

9. Roth v. United States, 354 U.S. 476 (1957); Alberts v. California, 354 U.S. 476 (1957).

10. *Roth*, 457 U.S. at 483, 484, 487 n. 20.

11. Ibid., at 508–514 (Douglas, J., dissenting); 494–496 (Warren, C.J., concurring); 497–504 (Harlan, J., concurring in part and dissenting in part).

12. Ibid., at 496 (Warren, C.J., concurring).

13. Ibid., at 497–498, 502 (Harlan, J., concurring in part and dissenting in part).

14. Jacobellis v. Ohio, 378 U.S. 184 (1964).

15. Ibid., at 198 (Goldberg, J., concurring); 194 (opinion of Brennan, J.).

16. Ibid., at 196 (Black, J., concurring); 203–204 (Harlan, J., dissenting); 196 (Stewart, J., concurring).

17. Ibid., at 188–190.

18. Ibid., at 191 (opinion of Brennan, J., citation and footnote omitted).

19. Ibid., at 193, quoting Manual Enterprises Inc. v. Day, 378 U.S. 478, 480 (1962).

20. Ibid., at 200 (Warren, C.J., dissenting), 201.

21. Ibid., at 200–201, 202, 203.

22. Ginzburg v. United States, 383 U.S. 463 (1966); Mishkin v. New York, 383 U.S. 502 (1966).

23. A Book Named "John Cleland's Memoirs of a Woman of Pleasure" v. Attorney General of Massachusetts, 383 U.S. 413 (1966).

24. *Ginzburg*, 383 U.S. at 476–482 (Black, J., dissenting); 482–492 (Douglas, J., dissenting); 498, 500 (Stewart, J., dissenting); 493–497 (Harlan, J., dissenting).

25. *Mishkin*, 383 U.S. at 508 (footnote omitted); *Ginzburg*, 383 U.S. at 468, 470, 475.

26. *Memoir*, 418 U.S. at 418, 420 (opinion of Brennan, J.).

27. Ibid., at 461, 462 (opinion of White, J.).

28. Ibid., at 442, 446–451.

29. "The Ginzburg Decision," *New York Times*, March 24, 1966, 21.

30. William B. Lockhart and Robert C. McClure, "Liberty, the Law of Obscenity, and the Constitution," *Minnesota Law Review* 38 (1972): 387.

31. PL 90-100.

32. See Bruce Allen Murphy, *Fortas: The Rise and Ruin of a Supreme Court Justice* (New York: Morrow, 1988), 442–445.

33. "Recommendations of Panel on Pornography," *Washington Post*, October 1, 1970, A12.

34. *New York Times*, October 1, 1970, 20.

35. Ibid., 29; *New York Times*, October 21, 1971, 71; *New York Times*, October 1, 1970, 50; 116 Congressional Record 36478 (1970).

36. Ginsberg v. New York, 390 U.S. 629 (1968).

37. Stanley v. Georgia, 394 U.S. 557 (1969).

38. United States v. Reidel, 402 U.S. 351 (1971).

39. Ibid., at 357.

40. Redrup v. New York, 385 U.S. 767, 771 (1967).

41. Miller v. California, No. 70-73, conference notes, Lewis F. Powell (LFP) case file, Box 1, LFPP.

42. United States v. 12,200-ft. Reels of Film, 413 U.S. 123 (1973); United States v. Orito, 413 U.S. 139 (1973). Bob Woodward and Scott Armstrong, *The Brethren:*

Inside the Supreme Court (New York: Simon and Schuster, 1979), 231–246, 294–306, provides an account of the Court's deliberations on the obscenity cases.

43. United States v. Orito, No. 70-69, conference notes, LFP case file, LFPP.

44. United States v. 12,200-ft. Reels of Film, No. 70-2, draft opinion of Warren E. Burger (WEB), HAB case file, Box 150, File 8, HABP; *12,200-ft. Reels*, No. 70-2, draft opinion of Byron R. White, HAB case file, Box 150, File 8, HABP; *12,200-ft. Reels*, No. 70-2, draft opinion of William O. Douglas, HAB case file, Box 150, File 8, HABP.

45. *12,200-ft. Reels*, No. 70-2, WEB to the conference, March 16, 1972, HAB case file, Box 150, File 8, HABP.

46. *Orito*, No. 70-69, WEB to the conference, June 14, 1972, case file, WEBP, 15.

47. Ibid., 13.

48. Ibid., 10, 11.

49. Ibid., 10–11, 14.

50. *12,200-ft. Reels*, No. 70-2, case history, Box II: 6, Folder 14, WJBP, xxxi–xxxiv.

51. Miller v. California, No. 70-73, William J. Brennan (WJB) to the conference, May 22, 1972, LFP case file, LFPP.

52. *Miller*, No. 70-73, WJB to the conference, June 13, 1972, LFP case file, LFPP, 6.

53. Ibid., 8, 10–11, 11–12.

54. Ibid., 16.

55. *Miller*, No. 70-73, notes on October 24 conference on obscenity cases, LFP case file, LFPP.

56. *Miller*, No. 70-73, WEB to the conference, October 31, 1972, LFP case file, LFPP, 9, 10–11.

57. Ibid., 6, 21–22, 23.

58. *12,200-ft. Reels*, No. 70-2, Byron R. White (BRW) to the conference, November 16, 1972, HAB case file, Box 150, Folder 7, HABP; *12,200-ft. Reels*, No. 70-2, Harry A. Blackmun (HAB) to the conference, November 16, 1972, HAB case file, Box 150, Folder 7, HABP; *Miller*, No. 70-73, William H. Rehnquist (WHR) to WEB, November 27, 1972, LFP case file, LFPP.

59. *12,200-ft. Reels*, No. 70-2, case history, WJBP, xxxix.

60. *Miller*, No. 70-73, memorandum from LFP to Messrs. Larry A. Hammond et al., June 8, 1972, LFP case file, LFPP, 1, 2.

61. Ibid., 2, 3.

62. Paris Adult Theater No. 1 v. Slaton, No. 71-1051, LFP to Larry A. Hammond, September 20, 1972, LFP case file, LFPP, 3.

63. *Paris Adult Theater*, No. 71-1051, memorandum from LFP to Larry A. Hammond, December 12, 1972, LFP case file; *Miller*, No. 70-73, memorandum from LFP to WEB, November 14, 1972, LFP case file, LFPP.

64. *Paris Adult Theater*, No. 71-1051, LFP to WJB, December 12, 1972, LFP case file, LFPP; *Paris Adult Theater*, No. 71-1051, HAB to WJB, January 9, 1973, LFP case file, LFPP.

65. *Paris Adult Theater*, 413 U.S. at 63.

66. *Miller*, 413 U.S. at 25, 27; *Miller*, No. 70-73, BRW to WEB, April 16, 1972, LFP case file, pt. 2, LFPP.

67. *Miller*, No. 70-73, fourth draft of opinion, LFP case file, pt. 2, LFPP, 6; *Miller*, No. 70-73, LFP to WEB, April 16, 1973, LFP case file, pt. 2, LFPP; *Miller*, No. 70-73, HAB to WEB, May 9, 1973, LFP case file, pt. 2, LFPP; *Paris Adult Theater*, No. 71-1051, LFP to WEB, February 3, 1973, LFP case file, LFPP.

68. *Paris Adult Theater*, 413 U.S. at 992–993 (citation omitted, Brennan, J., dissenting).

69. *Miller*, 413 U.S. at 29 (footnote and citation omitted).

70. *Miller*, No. 70-73, handwritten comments of LFP on eighth draft, LFP case file, pt. 2, LFPP.

71. *Washington Post*, June 23, 1973, B9, C2.

72. *New York Times*, June 23, 1973, 14.

73. *Jenkins v. Georgia*, 415 U.S. 153, 161 (1974).

74. Ibid., 161, 163 (Brennan, J., concurring in the result).

75. See, for example, Village Books Inc. v. Marshall, 418 U.S. 930, 930 fn. * (1974) (Brennan, J., dissenting from denial of certiorari).

Chapter 5. Criminal Procedure

1. Almeida-Sanchez v. United States, 413 U.S. 266 (1973).

2. See, for example, United States v. Biswell, 406 U.S. 311 (1972); Camara v. Municipal Court, 387 U.S. 523 (1967).

3. Almeida-Sanchez v. United States, No. 71-6278, conference notes, Lewis F. Powell (LFP) case file, LFPP.

4. *Almeida-Sanchez*, 413 U.S. at 291 (White, J., dissenting); *Almeida-Sanchez*, No. 71-6278, draft opinion of Potter Stewart, May 11, 1973, LFP case file, LFPP, 7.

5. *Almeida-Sanchez*, No. 71-6278, LFP to Byron R. White (BRW) and Potter Stewart (PS), May 10, 1973, LFP case file, LFPP; *Almeida-Sanchez*, 413 U.S. at 275 (Powell, J., concurring); *Almeida-Sanchez*, No. 71-6278, draft opinion of Lewis Powell concurring in the result, June 11, 1973, LFP case file, LFPP, 10.

6. *Almeida-Sanchez*, 413 U.S. at 279 (Powell, J., concurring).

7. *Almeida-Sanchez*, No. 71-6278, BRW to Warren E. Burger (WEB), Harry A. Blackmun (HAB), and William H. Rehnquist (WHR), June 11, 1973, LFP case file, LFPP; *Almeida-Sanchez*, No. 71-6278, WHR to BRW, June 12, 1973, LFP case file, LFPP.

8. *Almeida-Sanchez*, 413 U.S. at 275–285 (Powell, J., concurring); 288 (White, J., concurring).

9. United States v. Ash, 413 U.S. 300 (1973). *Ash* is discussed in detail in Yale Kamisar, "The Warren Court (Was It Really So Defense-Minded?), the Burger

Court (Is It Really So Defense-Oriented?), and Police Investigatory Practices," in *The Burger Court: The Counter-Revolution That Wasn't*, ed. Vincent Blasi (New Haven, CT: Yale University Press, 1983), 62–92.

10. *Ash*, 413 U.S. at 326–344 (Brennan, J., dissenting)

11. Ibid., at 326.

12. Ibid., at 306–313, 313–321 (majority opinion); 324 (Stewart, J., concurring in the judgment).

13. Schneckloth v. Bustamonte, 412 U.S. 218 (1973).

14. Fay v. Noia, 372 U.S. 391 (1963).

15. Kaufman v. United States, 394 U.S. 217 (1969).

16. *Schneckloth*, 412 U.S. at 277 (Brennan, J., dissenting); Bumper v. North Carolina, 391 U.S. 543, 548 (1968); *Schneckloth*, 412 U.S. at 283–285 (Marshall, J., dissenting); *Schneckloth*, 412 U.S. at 248–249 (majority opinion).

17. *Schneckloth*, 412 U.S. at 250–275 (Powell, J., concurring).

18. Ibid., at 249 (Blackmun, J., concurring); 249 n. 38.

19. Stone v. Powell, 428 U.S. 465 (1976).

Chapter 6. School Desegregation

1. Brown v. Board of Education (*Brown I*), 347 U.S. 483 (1954).

2. Brown v. Board of Education (*Brown II*), 394 U.S. 294 (1955).

3. *Brown II*, brief for appellants, 10, 301.

4. The evolution of the Warren Court's approach to remedial issues in school desegregation cases is described in detail in Frank T. Read, "Judicial Evolution of the Law of School Integration since *Brown v. Board of Education*," *Law and Contemporary Problems* 39 (1975): 7–49.

5. Cooper v. Aaron, 358 U.S. 1 (1958).

6. Griffin v. County School Board of Prince Edward County, 377 U.S. 218, 221–222 (1964).

7. The description of the facts that follows is taken from ibid., at 222–225.

8. Ibid., at 231.

9. J. Harvie Wilkinson III, *From* Brown *to* Bakke: *The Supreme Court and School Integration, 1954–1978* (New York: Oxford University Press, 1979), 102.

10. "School Desegregation and Equal Educational Opportunity," http://www.civilrights.org/resources/civilrights101/desegregation.html.

11. Green v. County School Board of New Kent County, 391 U.S. 430 (1968).

12. Ibid., at 437–438, 439.

13. Ibid., at 441–442.

14. *New York Times*, November 3, 1969, 1.

15. Republican Party Platform of 1964, http://www.presidency.ucsb.edu/ws/?pid–25840#axzz2j3P9astp; *New York Times*, October 4, 1968, 1.

16. *New York Times*, September 13, 1968, 50.
17. *New York Times*, March 25, 1970, 27.
18. Ibid., 28; *New York Times*, March 26, 1968, 29.
19. Swann v. Charlotte-Mecklenburg Board of Education, 402 U.S. 1 (1971). The account of the background of the *Swann* decision that follows is taken from Bernard Schwartz, *Swann's Way: The School Busing Case and the Supreme Court* (New York: Oxford University Press, 1986).
20. Swann v. Charlotte-Mecklenburg Board of Education, 431 F.2d 138 (4th Cir. 1969).
21. The deliberations of the Court are described in Schwartz, *Swann's Way*.
22. *Swann*, 402 U.S. at 25, 24.
23. Wright v. Council of the City of Emporia, 407 U.S. 451 (1972).
24. Wright v. Council of the City of Emporia, 442 F.2d 570 (4th Cir. 1971).
25. Ibid., at 473 (Burger, C.J., dissenting).
26. *Emporia*, 407 U.S. at 459, 464, 466.
27. *New York Times*, April 22, 1971, 1; *New York Times*, February 15, 1970, 156.
28. *Washington Post*, April 21, 1971, A10; *New York Times*, April 21, 1971, 1.
29. *Washington Post*, April 15, 1971, A1; *Washington Post*, April 22, 1971, A6.
30. *New York Times*, April 23, 1971, 1; *New York Times*, March 17, 1972, 1; *New York Times*, June 9, 1972, 1.
31. *Washington Post*, February 16, 1972, A15.
32. *Washington Post*, March 20, 1972, 37; Democratic Party Platform of 1972, http://www.presidency.ucsb.edu/ws/?pid=29605#axzz2j8kKvHgu; Republican Party Platform of 1972, http://www.presidency.ucsb.edu/ws/index.php?pid=25842#axzz2j8kKvHgu.
33. Keyes v. School District No. 1, 413 U.S. 189 (1973).
34. Keyes v. School District No. 1, 445 F.2d 990 (10th Cir. 1971).
35. Keyes v. School District No. 1, 396 U.S. 1215 (1969).
36. John C. Jeffries, Jr., *Justice Lewis F. Powell, Jr.* (New York: Scribner's, 1994), 302; Keyes v. School District No. 1, 402 U.S. 182 (1971) (per curiam).
37. Keyes v. School District No. 1, No. 71-507, conference notes, Lewis F. Powell, Jr. (LFP) basic file, LFPP.
38. *Keyes*, No. 71-507, fourth draft opinion, printed draft opinions 1 of 2, LFP case file, LFPP, 8, 17, 19.
39. *Keyes*, No. 71-507, Thurgood Marshall (TM) to William J. Brennan (WJB), December 1, 1972, LFP basic case file, LFPP; *Keyes*, No. 71-507, William O. Douglas (WOD) to WJB, December 5, 1972, LFP basic case file, LFPP; *Keyes*, No. 71-507, Potter Stewart (PS) to WJB, December 7, 1972, LFP basic case file, LFPP.
40. *Keyes*, 413 U.S. at 257 (Rehnquist, J., dissenting).
41. Powell's actions during the immediate post-*Brown* era are described in detail in Jeffries, *Justice Lewis F. Powell*, 131–183.

42. *Swann*, 402 U.S. at 281, brief for Commonwealth of Virginia, amicus curiae, 23.

43. Ibid., at 24.

44. *Keyes*, No. 71-507, LFP to file, December 28, 1972, LFP basic case file, LFPP; *Keyes*, No. 71-507, LFP to J. Harvie Wilkinson III, January 6, 1973, LFP basic case file, LFPP, 3. Powell's analysis of the issues presented by *Keyes* is described in detail in Jeffries, *Justice Lewis F. Powell*, 292–305.

45. *Keyes*, No. 71-507, LFP to J. Harvie Wilkinson III, October 7, 1972, LFP basic case file, LFPP, 1; *Keyes*, No. 71-507, LFP to J. Harvie Wilkinson III, July 31, 1972, LFP basic case file, LFPP, 1–2.

46. *Keyes*, 413 U.S. at 218–219, 232 (Powell, J., concurring and dissenting), 253.

47. Ibid., at 223, 226.

48. Ibid., at 253.

49. *Keyes*, No. 71-507, WJB to the conference, April 3, 1973, LFP basic case file, LFPP.

50. *Keyes*, No. 71-507, LFP to the conference, April 4, 1973, LFP basic case file, LFPP.

51. Ibid.

52. *Keyes*, No. 71-507, Harry A. Blackmun (HAB) to WJB, May 30, 1973, LFP basic case file, LFPP.

53. *New York Times*, June 26, 1973, 44; *Washington Post*, June 22, 1973, A22.

54. Bradley v. School Board of Richmond, 412 U.S. 92 (1973).

55. Bradley v. School Board of Richmond, 325 F. Supp. 828 (E.D. Va. 1971).

56. Bradley v. School Board of Richmond, 338 F. Supp. 67 (E.D. Va. 1972).

57. Ibid., at 67, 90.

58. Bradley v. School Board of Richmond, 462 F.2d 1058 (4th Cir. 1972) (en banc).

59. Ibid., at 1064 (citations omitted), 1068, 1069, 1070.

60. Bradley v. School Board of Richmond, No. 72-549, conference notes, HAB case file, Box 168, Folder 4, HABP; *Bradley*, No. 72-549, HAB to Warren E. Burger (WEB), April 25, 1973, HAB case file, Box 168, Folder 4, HABP.

61. *Bradley*, No. 72-549, HAB case file, HABP, 2.

62. *Bradley*, No. 72-549, undated memorandum, WJB to the conference, HAB case file, HABP, 4.

63. *Bradley*, No. 72-549, WEB to HAB, April 26, 1973, HAB case file, HABP; *Bradley*, No. 72-549, WEB to the conference, April 26, 1973, HAB case file, HABP; *Bradley*, No. 72-549, WEB to the conference, May 10, 1973, HAB case file, HABP.

64. *Bradley*, No. 72-549, William H. Rehnquist (WHR) to the conference, May 3, 1973, HAB case file, Box 168, Folder 4, HABP, 2, 8; *Bradley*, No. 72-549, memorandum from HAB to WHR, May 11, 1973, HAB case file, Box 168, Folder 4, HABP.

65. All facets of *Milliken* are discussed extensively in Joyce A. Baugh, *The Detroit School Busing Case:* Milliken v. Bradley *and the Dispute over School Desegregation* (Lawrence: University Press of Kansas, 2011).

66. The factual context that gave rise to *Milliken* is described in detail in Bradley v. Milliken, 338 F. Supp. 582 (E.D. Mich. 1971).

67. Bradley v. Milliken, 433 F.2d 897 (6th Cir. 1970).

68. Bradley v. Milliken, 484 F.2d 215 (6th Cir. 1973).

69. *Keyes*, No. 71-507, WEB to WJB, December 18, 1972, LFP basic case file, LFPP; *Keyes*, No. 71-507, WEB to WJB, May 30, 1973, LFP basic case file, LFPP; *Keyes*, No. 71-507, WJB to WEB, May 30, 1973, LFP basic case file, LFPP.

70. Milliken v. Bradley, No. 73-434, HAB memorandum to file, February 25, 1974 , HAB case file, Box 187, Folder 4, HABP, 3–4.

71. Ibid., 4, 6.

72. *Milliken*, No. 73-434, undated notes, LFP case file, Folder 2, LFPP.

73. *Milliken*, No. 73-434, draft opinion, May 31, 1974, LFP case files, LFPP.

74. *Milliken*, No. 73-434, PS to WEB, June 17, 1974, LFP case file, LFPP; *Milliken*, No. 73-434, HAB to WEB, June 18, 1974, LFP case file, LFPP; *Milliken*, No. 73-434, WHR to WEB, June 3, 1974, LFP case file, LFPP; *Milliken*, No. 73-434, LFP to WEB, June 3, 1974, LFP case file, LFPP; *Milliken*, No. 73-434, memorandum from LFP to WEB, June 5, 1974, Folder 3, LFP case file, LFPP.

75. *Milliken*, No. 73-434, LFP to John Buckley, June 14, 1974, LFP case file, LFPP.

76. Milliken v. Bradley, 418 U.S. 717, 738, 744–745 (1974).

77. Ibid., at 758–762 (Douglas, J., dissenting); 781 (White, J., dissenting).

78. Ibid., at 782–815 (Marshall, J., dissenting).

79. Ibid., at 814, 782, 783, 808 (citation omitted).

80. *New York Times*, July 27, 1974, 60; *New York Times*, July 26, 1974, 17; *New York Times*, July 28, 1974, 172; *Wall Street Journal*, July 26, 1974, 2.

Chapter 7. Equal Protection and Wealth Discrimination

1. See, for example, Carter v. Carter Coal Co., 298 U.S. 238 (1936); Schecter Poultry Corp. v. United States, 295 U.S. 495 (1935).

2. See, for example, Charles G. Haines, *The American Doctrine of Judicial Supremacy* (New York: Russell and Russell, 1959), 467–499.

3. Frank I. Michelman, “The Supreme Court, 1968 Term: Foreword—on Protecting the Poor through the Fourteenth Amendment,” *Harvard Law Review* 83 (1969): 7–59.

4. Gerald Gunther, “Foreword: In Search of Evolving Doctrine on a Changing Court—a Model for a Newer Equal Protection,” *Harvard Law Review* 86 (1972): 8.

5. Douglas v. California, 373 U.S. 353, 357–358 (1963).

6. Harper v. Virginia Board of Elections, 383 U.S. 663 (1966).

7. Ibid., at 668 (citation omitted); McDonald v. State Board of Election Commissioners, 394 U.S. 802, 807 (1969).

8. Boddie v. Connecticut, 401 U.S. 371 (1971).

9. Ibid., at 383–386 (Douglas, J., concurring in the result); 386–389 (Brennan, J., concurring in part).

10. *Boddie*, 401 U.S. at 383, 376 (citations omitted).

11. United States v. Kras, 409 U.S. 434 (1973).

12. United States v. Kras, No. 71-749, Harry A. Blackmun (HAB) memorandum to file, October 10, 1972, case file, Box 156, Folder 5, HABP; *Kras*, No. 71-749, conference notes, Lewis F. Powell, Jr. (LFP) case file, LFPP.

13. *Kras*, No. 71-749, argument notes, LFP case file, LFPP; *Kras*, No. 71-749, conference notes, LFP case file, LFPP.

14. *Kras*, 409 U.S. at 442 (quoting *Boddie*, 401 U.S. at 382).

15. Ibid., at 444, 445, 450–451 (Burger, C.J., concurring).

16. Ibid., at 449.

17. Ibid., at 455 (Stewart, J., dissenting); 458 (Douglas, J., dissenting); 461 (Marshall, J., dissenting).

18. Ibid., at 460 (Marshall, J., dissenting).

19. *Kras*, No. 71-749, Byron R. White (BRW) to HAB, December 7, 1972, BRW case file, Box 242, Folder 3, BRWP.

20. *Kras*, note from BRW to HAB, December 14, 1972, HAB case file, HABP; *Kras*, HAB note to file, HAB case file, HABP.

21. San Antonio Independent School District v. Rodriguez, 411 U.S. 1 (1973). Both the dispute that gave rise to *Rodriguez* and the Supreme Court's treatment of the case are described in detail in Paul A. Sracic, San Antonio v. Rodriguez *and the Pursuit of Equal Education* (Lawrence: University Press of Kansas, 2006). For other perspectives, see, for example, Michael Heise, "The Story of *San Antonio Independent School Dist. v. Rodriguez:* School Finance, Local Control, and Constitutional Limits," in *Education Law Stories,* ed. Michael Olivas and Ronna Schneider (New York: Foundation, 2007); Richard Schragger, "*San Antonio v. Rodriguez* and the Legal Geography of School Finance Reform," in *Civil Rights Stories,* ed. Myriam Gilles and Risa Goluboff (New York: Foundation, 2008).

22. Serrano v. Priest, 483 P.2d 1241, 5 Cal.3d 584 (1971).

23. *New York Times*, March 7, 1972, 1.

24. Furman v. Georgia, 408 U.S. 238, 448 (1972) (Powell, J., dissenting); San Antonio School District v. Rodriguez, No. 71-1332, conference notes, LFP case file, LFPP, 2.

25. *Rodriguez*, No. 71-1332, HAB memorandum to file, October 11, 1972, HAB case file, Box 161, Folder 4, HABP, 4; Stephen R. Goldstein, "Interdistrict Inequalities in School Financing: A Critical Analysis of *Serrano v. Priest* and Its Progeny," *University of Pennsylvania Law Review* 120 (1972): 504–544.

26. Brown v. Board of Education, 347 U.S. 487, 493 (1954); *Rodriguez*, No. 71-1332, conference notes, LFP case file, LFPP.

27. *Rodriguez*, No. 71-1332, LFP to J. Harvie Wilkinson III, August 30, 1972, LFP case file, LFPP.

28. *Rodriguez*, No. 71-1332, LFP to Larry F. Hammond, October 12, 1972, LFP case file, LFPP, 15–16; *Rodriguez*, No. 71-1332, conference notes, LFP case file, LFPP, 4.

29. *Rodriguez*, No. 71-1332, LFP to Larry F. Hammond, October 9, 1972, LFP case file, LFPP, 4; *Rodriguez*, No. 71-1332, LFP to Hammond, October 12, 1972, LFP case file, LFPP, 4–5.

30. *Rodriguez*, No. 71-1332, LFP to Larry F. Hammond, October 1972, LFP case file, LFPP, 6; *Rodriguez*, No. 71-1332, HAB memorandum to file, HAB case file, HABP, 5.

31. *Rodriguez*, No. 71-1332, LFP to Hammond, October 12, 14; HAB memorandum, HABP, 4.

32. *Rodriguez*, No. 71-1332, LFP to Hammond, October 12, HABP, 12; *Rodriguez*, No. 71-1332, HAB memorandum to file, HABP, 5; *Rodriguez*, No. 71-1332, LFP to Hammond, October 9, HABP, 2–3.

33. *Rodriguez*, No. 71-1332, LFP conference notes, LFPP.

34. *Rodriguez*, No. 71-1332, Potter Stewart (PS) to LFP, February 8, 1973, LFP basic case file, LFPP; *Rodriguez*, No. 71-1332, memorandum from PS to LFP, February 26, 1973, LFP basic case file, LFPP.

35. *Rodriguez*, 411 U.S. at 28.

36. Ibid., at 32, 35–38.

37. Ibid., at 43, 49.

38. Ibid., at 59 (Stewart, J., concurring); 63 (Brennan, J., dissenting); 64 (White, J., dissenting).

39. Ibid., at 71–72 (Marshall, J., dissenting, citation omitted), 98–99.

40. *Washington Post*, March 22, 1973, A16.

41. For differing scholarly perspectives on *Rodriguez*, see Judith Areen and Leonard Ross, "The *Rodriguez* Case: Judicial Oversight of School Finance," *Supreme Court Review* (1973): 33–56; Robert W. Bennett, "The Burger Court and the Poor," in *The Burger Court: The Counter-Revolution That Wasn't*, ed. Vincent Blasi (New Haven, CT: Yale University Press, 1983), 53–55; Richard Y. Funston, *Constitutional Counter-Revolution? The Warren Court and the Burger Court: Judicial Policy Making in Modern America* (New York: Wiley, 1977), 66–73.

42. See, for example, Robinson v. Cahill, 62 N.J. 473, 303 A.2d 273 (1973).

43. Vlandis v. Kline, 412 U.S. 441 (1973); United States Department of Agriculture v. Murry, 413 U.S. 508 (1973); United States Department of Agriculture v. Moreno, 413 U.S. 528 (1973).

44. Shapiro v. Thompson, 394 U.S. 618 (1969); Dunn v. Blumstein, 405 U.S. 330 (1972).

45. Starns v. Malkerson, 401 U.S. 985 (1971); Vlandis v. Kline, No. 72-493, conference notes, LFP case file, LFPP.

46. *Vlandis*, No. 72-493, William J. Brennan (WJB) to PS, May 14, 1973, LFP case file, LFPP; *Vlandis*, No. 72-493, LFP to PS, May 15, 1973, LFP case file, LFPP.

47. *Vlandis*, 412 U.S. at 456–458 (White, J., concurring in the result).

48. Ibid., at 446–453.

49. Stanley v. Illinois, 405 U.S. 645 (1972).

50. Ibid., at 651, 652.

51. Ibid., at 652, 653, 656–657.

52. *Vlandis*, 412 U.S. at 449, 451 (citation omitted), 452.

53. See, for example, William Van Alstyne, "The Demise of the Right-Privilege Distinction in Constitutional Law," *Harvard Law Review* 81 (1968): 1439–1464.

54. *Shapiro*, at 627, 629.

55. Ibid., at 629–632.

56. Goldberg v. Kelly, 397 U.S. 254 (1970).

57. Ibid., at 275 (Black, J., dissenting).

58. Ibid., at 264.

59. Ibid., at 264–265.

60. See, for example, *Washington Post*, March 24, 1970, A11.

61. Dandridge v. Williams, 397 U.S. 471 (1970).

62. Ibid., at 485, 486.

63. Ibid., at 490–508 (Douglas, J., dissenting); 508–530 (Marshall, J., dissenting).

64. Jefferson v. Hackney, 406 U.S. 535 (1972).

65. *Moreno*, 413 U.S. at 531–532.

66. United States Department of Agriculture v. Moreno, No. 72-534, conference notes, LFP case file, LFPP; *Moreno*, 413 U.S. at 546.

67. *Moreno*, 413 U.S. at 534, 537, 538.

68. *Murry*, 413 U.S. at 509–511.

69. Ibid., 413 U.S. at 520–522 (Blackmun, J., dissenting); United States Department of Agriculture v. Murry, No. 72-848, conference notes, LFP case file, LFPP; *Murry*, No. 72-848, LFP to PS, June 9, 1973, LFP case file, LFPP; *Murry*, 413 U.S. at 522–528 (Rehnquist, J., dissenting).

70. *Murry*, 413 U.S. at 514–517 (Stewart, J., concurring); 517–520 (Marshall, J., concurring).

71. Ibid., at 514.

72. See, for example, City of Cleburne v. Cleburne Living Center, 473 U.S. 432 (1985).

73. Frontiero v. Richardson, 411 U.S. 677 (1973).

Chapter 8. The Problem of Sex Discrimination

1. For a detailed, perceptive discussion of the evolution of the legal theories of supporters of women's rights, see Serena Mayeri, *Reasoning from Race: Feminism,*

Law, and the Civil Rights Revolution (Cambridge, MA: Harvard University Press, 2011).

2. *Chicago Tribune*, March 23, 1972, 7.

3. *New York Times*, June 24, 1973, 53–54, 55.

4. Frontiero v. Richardson, 411 U.S. 677 (1973). For a comprehensive discussion of all aspects of *Frontiero*, see Serena Mayeri, "'When the Trouble Started': The Story of *Frontiero v. Richardson*," in *Women and the Law Stories*, ed. Elizabeth M. Schneider and Stephanie M. Wildman (New York: Foundation, 2011).

5. See, for example, Morehead v. New York ex rel. Tipaldo, 298 U.S. 597 (1936); Adkins v. Children's Hospital, 261 U.S. 525 (1923).

6. Bradwell v. Illinois, 83 U.S. 130, 141 (1873) (Bradley, J., concurring in the result)

7. Ibid., at 142.

8. Hoyt v. Florida, 368 U.S. 57, 62 (1961).

9. Reed v. Reed, 404 U.S. 71 (1971).

10. Ibid., at 76–77.

11. Gerald Gunther, "Foreword: In Search of Evolving Doctrine on the Supreme Court—a Model for a Newer Equal Protection," *Harvard Law Review* 86 (1972): 1.

12. Frontiero v. Richardson, No. 71-1694, argument notes, Frontiero v. Laird, Lewis F. Powell, Jr. (LFP) case file, 1 of 2, LFPP; *Frontiero*, No. 71-1694, conference notes, Frontiero v. Laird, LFP case file, 1 of 2, LFPP.

13. *Frontiero*, No. 71-1694, LFP conference notes, Frontiero v. Laird.

14. *Frontiero*, No. 71-1694, draft opinion of William J. Brennan (WJB), Frontiero v. Laird, February 14, 1973, LFP case file, 1 of 2, LFPP, 5.

15. Ibid., 8 (citation omitted).

16. *Frontiero*, No. 71-1694, WJB to the conference, February 14, 1973, LFP case file, 1 of 2, LFPP; *Frontiero*, No. 71-1694, third draft opinion, February 28, 1973, LFP case file, 1 of 2, LFPP.

17. *Frontiero*, No. 71-1694, William O. Douglas (WOD) to WJB, February 28, 1973, in LFP case file, 1 of 2, LFPP; *Frontiero*, No. 71-1694, Thurgood Marshall (TM) to WJB, March 1, 1972, LFP case file, 1 of 2, LFPP; *Frontiero*, No. 71-1694, Byron R. White (BRW) to WJB, February 15, 1973, Harry A. Blackmun (HAB) case file, Box 163, Folder 9, HABP.

18. Weber v. Aetna Casualty and Surety Co., 406 U.S. 164, 177–186 (1972) (Rehnquist, J., dissenting); *Frontiero*, No. 71-1694, Warren E. Burger (WEB) to WJB, March 7, 1973, in LFP case file, 1 of 2, LFPP; *Frontiero*, No. 71-1694, Potter Stewart (PS) to WJB, February 16, 1973, LFP case file, 1 of 2, LFPP.

19. *Frontiero*, No. 71-1694, LFP to WJB, March 2, 1973, LFP case file, 1 of 2, LFPP.

20. Ibid.; *Frontiero*, No. 71-1694, HAB to WJB, March 5, 1973, LFP case file, 1 of 2, LFPP.

21. *Frontiero,* No. 71-1694, WJB to LFP, March 6, 1973, LFP case file, 1 of 2, LFPP.

22. *Frontiero,* No. 71-1694, LFP to William C. Kelly, Jr., March 8, 1973, LFP case file, 1 of 2, LFPP; *Frontiero,* No. 71-1694, first draft of opinion concurring in the result, March 12, 1973, LFP case file, 2 of 2, LFPP.

23. *Frontiero,* No. 71-1694, WJB case histories, Box II: 6, Folder 14, WJBP, lxxxv–lxxxvi.

24. *Frontiero*, 411 U.S. at 678–691 (opinion of Brennan, J.); 691–692 (Powell, J., concurring in the judgment); 691 (statement of Stewart, J., concurring in the judgment).

25. Craig v. Boren, 429 U.S. 190 (1976). In some cases, the justices disagreed over the question of whether a gender-based classification should be considered discrimination against women or discrimination against men. See, for example, Califano v. Goldfarb, 430 U.S. 199 (1977).

26. Korematsu v. United States, 333 U.S. 214, 216 (1944).

27. United States v. Carolene Products Co., 304 U.S. 144, 152 n. 4 (1938).

28. Graham v. Richardson, 403 U.S. 365, 372 (1971); Sugarman v. Dougall, 413 U.S. 634 (1973).

29. *Weber*, at 164.

30. Ibid., at 175.

31. *Frontiero*, 411 U.S. at 684, 685, 686 (opinion of Brennan, J., citations omitted, emphasis added).

32. Ibid., at 686 (citation omitted, emphasis added).

33. Ibid., at 687–688 (citations omitted).

34. Pittsburgh Press Company v. Pittsburgh Commission on Human Relations, 413 U.S. 376 (1973).

35. Valentine v. Chrestensen, 316 U.S. 52, 54 (1942).

36. *Pittsburgh Press*, 413 U.S. at 397–400 (Douglas, J., dissenting); 403 (Stewart, J., dissenting, citation omitted); 393 (Burger, C.J., dissenting).

37. Pittsburgh Press Company v. Pittsburgh Commission on Human Relations, No. 72-419, conference notes, LFP case file 1, LFPP.

38. *Pittsburgh Press*, 413 U.S. at 385.

39. *New York Times*, June 24, 1973, 33.

Chapter 9. Aid to Parochial Schools

1. For detailed discussions of the Burger Court's treatment of the issue of aid to parochial schools, see, for example, Joseph E. Bryson and Samuel H. Houston, Jr., *The Supreme Court and Public Funds for Religious Schools: The Burger Years, 1969–1986* (Jefferson, NC: McFarland, 1990); Leo Pfeffer, *Religion, State, and the Burger Court* (Buffalo, NY: Prometheus Books, 1984).

2. Andy Smarick, "Can Catholic Schools Be Saved?" *National Affairs* (Spring 2011): 116.

3. Pierce v. Society of Sisters, 268 U.S. 510 (1925), 534.

4. Smarick, "Can Catholic Schools Be Saved?" 117.

5. Ibid., 118; *New York Times*, July 1, 1973, 15.

6. Richard E. Morgan, "The Establishment Clause and Sectarian Schools: A Final Establishment?" *Supreme Court Review* (1973): 59–60.

7. *New York Times*, January 31, 1965, SM11–13.

8. *New York Times*, February 12, 1970, 36; *New York Times*, August 23, 1966, 23.

9. Lemon v. Kurtzman, No. 89, memo to file, February 26, 1971, Harry A. Blackmun (HAB) case file, Box 124, Folder 2, HABP.

10. *New York Times*, January 10, 1965, 61; *New York Times*, January 31, 1965, SM13.

11. Everson v. Board of Education, 330 U.S. 1 (1947).

12. Ibid., at 17.

13. School District of Abington Township v. Schempp, 374 U.S. 204, 222 (1963).

14. Board of Education v. Allen, 392 U.S. 236 (1968).

15. Ibid., at 243, 248.

16. Ibid., at 253, 252 (Black, J., dissenting); 256 (Douglas, J., dissenting).

17. Ibid., at 256; *Allen*, 392 U.S. at 251 (Black, J., dissenting).

18. Lemon v. Kurtzman (*Lemon I*), 403 U.S. 602 (1971).

19. *Lemon*, No. 89, HAB memorandum to file, HAB case file, HABP.

20. Walz v. Tax Commission, 397 U.S. 664 (1970).

21. Ibid., at 669, 672.

22. Ibid., at 674, 676.

23. Wilbur G. Katz, "Radiations from Church Tax Exemption," *Supreme Court Review* (1970): 93–108; *Walz*, 397 U.S. at 675.

24. *Walz*, 397 U.S. at 694 (opinion of Harlan, J.).

25. *Lemon I*, 403 U.S. at 619, 622–224.

26. Ibid., at 643 (citation omitted), 648–649, 657.

27. Ibid., at 668 (opinion of White, J.).

28. Tilton v. Richardson, 403 U.S. 672 (1971).

29. Ibid., at 689–697 (Douglas, J., dissenting in part); *Lemon I*, 403 U.S. at 642–661 (opinion of Brennan, J.).

30. *Tilton*, 403 U.S. at 676–689 (opinion of Burger, C.J.)

31. Hunt v. McNair, 413 U.S. 734 (1973).

32. Ibid., at 749–755 (Brennan, J., dissenting).

33. Ibid, at 747, 748–749.

34. *Washington Post*, June 30, 1971, A22; *New York Times*, June 29, 1971, 36; *Wall Street Journal*, June 30, 1971, 10.

35. Smarick, "Can Catholic Schools Be Saved?" 118.

36. *New York Times*, June 30, 1971, 29; *New York Times*, August 18, 1971, 1.

37. *New York Times*, August 1, 1971, 1; *Washington Post*, April 21, 1972, A10; Republican Party Platform of 1972, http://www.presidency.ucsb.edu/ws/?pid=25842#axzz2iPKubwxn; Democratic Party Platform of 1972, http://www.presidency.ucsb.edu/ws/?pid=29605#axzz2iPKubwxn; *Washington Post*, July 7, 1973, A15.

38. Lemon v. Kurtzman (*Lemon II*), 411 U.S. 192 (1973).

39. Ibid., at 209, 211 (Douglas, J., dissenting).

40. Ibid., at 195–196, 202.

41. Levitt v. Committee for Public Education and Religious Liberty, 413 U.S. 472 (1973).

42. Levitt v. Committee for Public Education and Religious Freedom, No. 72-269, conference notes, LFP case file, LFPP.

43. *Levitt*, 413 U.S. at 475–476.

44. Committee for Public Education and Religious Freedom v. Nyquist, 413 U.S. 756 (1973); Sloan v. Lemon, 413 U.S. 825 (1973).

45. *Nyquist*, 413 U.S. at 798–805 (Burger, C.J., concurring in part and dissenting in part); *Sloan*, 413 U.S. at 798–813 (Burger, C.J., dissenting); *Nyquist*, 413 U.S. at 805–813 (Rehnquist, J., dissenting in part); *Sloan*, 413 U.S. at 813–824 (White, J., dissenting).

46. *Nyquist*, 413 U.S. at 783.

47. *Sloan*, 413 U.S. at 832.

48. *New York Times*, June 27, 1973, 19; *New York Times*, June 29, 1973, 36; *Washington Post*, July 2, 1973, A22; *Wall Street Journal*, July 2, 1973, 10.

49. *Washington Post*, July 7, 1973, A15.

50. Meek v. Pittenger, 421 U.S. 349 (1975).

51. Ibid., at 373–385 (Brennan, J., concurring in part and dissenting in part); 359–362 (opinion of Stewart, J.); 387–396 (Rehnquist, J., concurring in the judgment in part and dissenting in part).

52. Ibid., at 385–387 (Burger, C.J., concurring in the judgment in part and dissenting in part); 391 (Rehnquist, J., concurring in the judgment in part and dissenting in part).

53. *Meek*, 421 U.S. at 369.

54. Roe v. Wade, 410 U.S. 113 (1973).

Chapter 10. The Abortion Conflict

1. The abortion decisions have been the subject of a vast secondary literature. For examples of different perspectives, see, for example, Marian Faux, Roe v. Wade: *The Untold Story of the Supreme Court Decision That Made Abortion Legal* (New York: Cooper Square, 2000); Clarke D. Forsythe, *Abuse of Discretion: The Inside Story of* Roe v. Wade (Jackson, TN: Encounter Books, 2013); David J.

Garrow, *Liberty and Sexuality: The Right to Privacy and the Making of* Roe v. Wade (New York: Macmillan, 1994); N. E. H. Hull and Peter Charles Hoffer, Roe v. Wade: *The Abortion Rights Controversy in American History* (Lawrence: University Press of Kansas, 2010).

2. The summary that follows is taken from Garrow, *Liberty and Sexuality*, 270–389; Hull and Hoffer, Roe v. Wade, 11–134.

3. *New York Times*, April 4, 1971, 28; *New York Times*, June 21, 1972, 48.

4. *New York Times*, May 7, 1972, 1.

5. Ibid., 9; *New York Times*, May 8, 1972, 1, 36.

6. *New York Times*, May 14, 1972, 62.

7. *New York Times*, April 7, 1971, 43; *Washington Post*, July 13, 1972, A14; *New York Times*, July 13, 1972, 25; *Washington Post*, April 27, 1972, A23.

8. Buck v. Bell, 274 U.S. 200, 207 (1927, citation omitted).

9. Skinner v. Oklahoma, 316 U.S. 535, 541 (1942).

10. Poe v. Ullman, 367 U.S. 497 (1961).

11. Griswold v. Connecticut, 381 U.S. 479 (1965).

12. See, for example, Williamson v. Lee Optical Co., 383 U.S. 483 (1955).

13. *Griswold*, 381 U.S. at 507 (Black, J., dissenting); 527 (Stewart, J., dissenting); 525–526 (Black, J., dissenting).

14. *Griswold*, 381 U.S. at 500 (Harlan, J., concurring in the judgment, citation omitted); 503 (White, J., concurring in the judgment, citation omitted); 484 (majority opinion); 486–499 (Goldberg, J., concurring).

15. *Griswold*, 381 U.S. at 486, 485–486, 487 (Goldberg, J., concurring, emphasis added); 500 (Harlan, J., concurring in the judgment, by implication); 503 (White, J., concurring in the judgment).

16. Eisenstadt v. Baird, 405 U.S. 438 (1972).

17. Ibid., at 460–465 (White, J., concurring in the result); 447, 453 (majority opinion).

18. United States v. Vuitch, 402 U.S. 62 (1971).

19. Ibid., at 81–96 (Harlan, J., dissenting as to jurisdiction).

20. Ibid., at 74–80 (Douglas, J., dissenting in part); 67–73 (majority opinion); 96–97 (Stewart, J., dissenting in part).

21. *Washington Post*, April 22, 1971, A1.

22. Roe v. Wade, 410 U.S. 113 (1973); Doe v. Bolton, 410 U.S. 179 (1973).

23. Linda Greenhouse, *Becoming Justice Blackmun: Harry Blackmun's Supreme Court Journey* (New York: Times Books, 2005) 80.

24. Roe v. Wade, No. 70-18, conference notes, December 17, 1971, Harry A. Blackmun (HAB) case file, Box 151, Folder 9, HABP.

25. Ibid.

26. Ibid.

27. Ibid.

28. Roe v. Wade, No. 70-18, Warren E. Burger (WEB) to William O. Douglas

(WOD), January 27, 1972, HAB case file, Box 151, Folder 8, HABP; Roe v. Wade, No. 70-18, case history, Box II: 6, Folder 14, HABP, xli–xliii.

29. Roe v. Wade, No. 70-18, HAB to WEB, LFP basic case file, LFPP; Roe v. Wade, No. 70-18, HAB to the conference, May 31, 1972, LFP basic case file, LFPP.

30. Roe v. Wade, No. 70-18, draft opinion of HAB, May 18, 1972, LFP basic case file, LFPP; Roe v. Wade, No. 70-18, draft opinion of Byron R. White (BRW), May 29, 1972, LFP basic case file, LFPP.

31. Doe v. Bolton, No. 70-40, draft opinion of HAB, May 25, 1972, LFP case file, LFPP.

32. See, for example, ibid., 12–13.

33. Doe v. Bolton, No. 70-40, HAB to the conference, LFP case file, LFPP.

34. Doe v. Bolton, No. 70-40, draft opinion of HAB, May 25, 17.

35. Ibid., 19.

36. Roe v. Wade, No. 70-18, Potter Stewart (PS) to HAB, May 30, 1972, LFP basic case file, LFPP; Roe v. Wade, No. 70-18, HAB to the conference, May 31, 1972, LFP basic case file, LFPP; Roe v. Wade, No. 70-18, case history, William J. Brennan (WJB) case histories, 1971 term, WJBP, cxlvi.

37. Roe v. Wade, No. 70-18, WEB to the conference, May 31, 1972, LFP basic case file, LFPP; Roe v. Wade, No. 70-18, BRW to the conference, June 2, 1972, LFP basic case file, LFPP; Roe v. Wade, No. 70-18, WOD to the conference, May 31, 1972, LFP basic case file, LFPP; Roe v. Wade, No. 70-18, WJB to the conference, May 31, 1972, LFP basic case file, LFPP; Roe v. Wade, No. 70-18, memorandum from Thurgood Marshall (TM) to the conference, May 31, 1972, LFP basic case file, LFPP; Roe v. Wade, No. 70-18, WOD to the conference, June 1, 1972, LFP basic case file, LFPP.

38. Roe v. Wade, No. 70-18, LFP to the conference, June 1, 1972, LFP basic case file, LFPP; Roe v. Wade, No. 70-18, William H. Rehnquist (WHR) to the conference, June 1, 1972, LFP basic case file, LFPP; Roe v. Wade, No. 70-18, draft opinion of WOD, June 13, 1972, LFP basic case file, LFPP.

39. Roe v. Wade, No. 70-18, conference notes, LFP basic case file, LFPP.

40. *Roe*, 410 U.S. at 117 (citation omitted).

41. Ibid., at 129–148, 148–151.

42. Ibid., at 153, 155.

43. Ibid., at 156–157.

44. Ibid., at 157, 159, 162.

45. Roe v. Wade, No. 70-18, second draft, November 22, 1973, in LFP case file opinions, LFPP, 47, 48.

46. Roe v. Wade, No. 70-18, LFP to HAB, November 29, 1972, LFP basic case file, LFPP.

47. Roe v. Wade, No. 70-18, HAB to LFP, December 4, 1972, LFP basic case file, LFPP.

48. Roe v. Wade, No. 70-18, HAB to the conference, December 11, 1972, LFP

basic case file, LFPP; Roe v. Wade, No. 70-18, WOD to HAB, December 11, 1972, LFP basic case file, LFPP; Roe v. Wade, No. 70-18, TM to HAB, December 12, 1972, LFP basic case file, LFPP.

49. *Roe*, 410 U.S. at 221–222 (White, J., dissenting); 174 (Rehnquist, J., dissenting).

50. Doe v. Bolton, 410 U.S. at 208 (Burger, C.J., concurring); *Roe*, 410 U.S. at 167–171 (Stewart, J., concurring); *Doe*, 410 U.S. at 209–221 (Douglas, J., concurring).

51. See Lawrence v. Texas, 539 U.S. 558 (2003).

52. *New York Times*, January 23, 1973, 81.

53. Planned Parenthood v. Danforth, 428 U.S. 52 (1976).

54. H. L. v. Matheson, 450 U.S. 398 (1981).

55. *New York Times*, March 25, 2011, A25; Democratic Party Platform of 1976, http://www.presidency.ucsb.edu/ws/index.php?pid=29606#axzz2ixMUnkUs; Republican Party Platform of 1976, http://www.presidency.ucsb.edu/ws/index.php?pid=25843#axzz2ixMUnkUs.

56. See, for example, Republican Party Platform of 1980, http://www.presidency.ucsb.edu/ws/?pid=25844#axzz2fLYQqYR4; Democratic Party Platform of 1980, http://www.presidency.ucsb.edu/ws/index.php?pid=29607#axzz1nV70qf65.

57. Planned Parenthood v. Casey, 505 U.S. 833 (1992).

Chapter 11. Conclusion

1. Vincent Blasi, ed., *The Burger Court: The Counter-Revolution That Wasn't* (New Haven, CT: Yale University Press, 1983).

2. This theme is developed in Mark V. Tushnet, "The Burger Court in Historical Perspective: The Triumph of Country-Club Republicanism," in *The Burger Court: Counter-Revolution or Confirmation?* ed. Bernard Schwartz (New York: Oxford University Press, 1998), 203–215.

3. See Vincent Blasi, "The Rootless Activism of the Burger Court," in Blasi, ed., *Burger Court*, 198–217; Bernard Schwartz, *The Ascent of Pragmatism: The Burger Court in Action* (Reading, MA: Addison-Wesley, Longman, 1990). For a very different perspective, see Mark Tushnet, "'. . . And Only Wealth Will Buy You Justice': Some Notes on the Supreme Court, 1972 Term," *Wisconsin Law Review* (1974): 177–197.

4. Frontiero v. Richardson, 411 U.S. 677 (1973); Committee for Public Education and Religious Freedom v. Nyquist, 413 U.S. 756 (1973); Roe v. Wade, 410 U.S. 113 (1973); George W. Gallup, *The Gallup Poll: Public Opinion, 1972–1977*, vol. 1 (Wilmington, DE: Scholarly Resources, 1978), 375–378.

5. Gallup, *Gallup Poll*, vol. 1, 142–143.

6. San Antonio Independent School District v. Rodriguez, 411 U.S. 1 (1973).

7. Bradley v. State Board of Education, 412 U.S. 92 (1973).

8. Examples of activist decisions that advanced the conservative agenda after the 1972 term include United Trust Co. of New Jersey v. New York, 431 U.S. 1 (1977); Wygant v. Jackson Board of Education, 476 U.S. 267 (1986). Activist decisions with a progressive orientation include Batson v. Kentucky, 476 U.S. 79 (1986); Plyler v. Doe, 457 U.S. 402 (1981).

9. See, for example, Davis v. Bandemer, 478 U.S. 189 (1986).

Bibliography

Papers of the Justices

Blackmun, Harry A., Papers, Manuscript Division, Library of Congress
Brennan, William J., Jr., Papers, Manuscript Division, Library of Congress
Douglas, William O., Papers, Manuscript Division, Library of Congress
Marshall, Thurgood, Papers, Manuscript Division, Library of Congress
Powell, Lewis F., Jr., Papers, Powell Archives, Washington and Lee University School of Law, http://law2.wlu.edu/powellarchives/page.asp?pageid=1279
Stewart, Potter, Papers, Manuscript and Archives Division, Yale University
White, Byron R., Papers, Manuscript Division, Library of Congress

Contemporary Periodicals

Boston Globe
Newsweek
New York Times
U.S. News and World Report
Wall Street Journal
Washington Post

Other Primary Sources

Democratic Party Platform of 1972, http://www.presidency.ucsb.edu/ws/?pid=29605#axzz2j8kKvHgu.
Democratic Party Platform of 1976, http://www.presidency.ucsb.edu/ws/index.php?pid=29606#axzz2ixMUnkUs.
Republican Party Platform of 1964, http://www.presidency.ucsb.edu/ws/?pid=25840#axzz2j3P9astp.

Republican Party Platform of 1972, http://www.presidency.ucsb.edu/ws/index.php?pid=25842#axzz2j8kKvHgu.

Republican Party Platform of 1976, http://www.presidency.ucsb.edu/ws/index.php?pid=25843#axzz2ixMUnkUs.

Selected Secondary Sources

Aranella, Peter. "Foreword: Rethinking the Functions of Criminal Procedure—the Warren and Burger Courts' Competing Ideologies." *Georgetown Law Journal* 72 (1983): 185–248.

Areen, Judith, and Leonard Ross. "The *Rodriguez* Case: Judicial Oversight of School Finance." *Supreme Court Review* (1973): 33–56.

Baker, Gordon E. *The Reapportionment Revolution: Representation, Political Power, and the Supreme Court.* New York: Random House, 1966.

Ball, Howard. *A Defiant Life: Thurgood Marshall and the Persistence of Racism in America.* New York: Crown, 1998.

Baugh, Joyce A. *The Detroit School Busing Case:* Milliken v. Bradley *and the Dispute over School Desegregation.* Lawrence: University Press of Kansas, 2011.

Beiser, Edward N. "The Haynsworth Affair Reconsidered: The Significance of Conflicting Perspectives of the Judicial Role." *Vanderbilt Law Review* 23 (1970): 263–292.

Bennett, Robert W. "The Burger Court and the Poor." In *The Burger Court: The Counter-Revolution That Wasn't.* Edited by Vincent Blasi. New Haven, CT: Yale University Press, 1983, 53–55.

Berg, Thomas C. "*Lemon v. Kurtzman:* The Parochial School Crisis and the Establishment Clause." In *Law and Religion Cases in Context.* Edited by Leslie Griffin. New York: Aspen, 2010.

Binion, Gayle, "Justice Potter Stewart: The Unpredictable Vote." *Journal of Supreme Court History* (1992): 99–108.

Bland, Russell W. *Justice Thurgood Marshall: Crusader for Liberalism—His Judicial Biography.* Bethesda, MD: Academica, 2001.

Blasi, Vincent, ed. *The Burger Court: The Counter-Revolution That Wasn't.* New Haven, CT: Yale University Press, 1983.

———. "The Rootless Activism of the Burger Court." In *The Burger Court: The Counter-Revolution That Wasn't.* New Haven, CT: Yale University Press, 1983, 198–217.

Boles, Donald E. *Mr. Justice Rehnquist: Judicial Activist.* Ames: Iowa State University Press, 1987.

Bork, Robert H. "Neutral Principles and Some First Amendment Problems." *Indiana Law Journal* 47 (1971): 1–35.

Bryson, Joseph E., and Samuel H. Houston, Jr. *The Supreme Court and Public Funds for Religious Schools: The Burger Years, 1969–1986*. Jefferson, NC: McFarland, 1990.

Casper, Gerhard. "Apportionment and the Right to Vote: Standards of Judicial Scrutiny." *Supreme Court Review* (1973): 1–32.

Clark, Hunter C. *Mr. Justice Brennan: The Great Conciliator*. New York: Birch Lane, 1995.

Davis, Hunter D., and Hunter R. Clark. *Thurgood Marshall, Warrior at the Bar, Rebel on the Bench*. New York: Birch Lane, 1992.

Davis, Sue. *Justice Rehnquist and the Constitution*. Princeton, NJ: Princeton University Press, 1989.

Douglas, William O. *The Court Years, 1939–1975: The Autobiography of William O. Douglas*. New York: Random House, 1980.

———. *Go East, Young Man: The Early Years—The Autobiography of William O. Douglas*. New York: Random House, 1974.

Eisler, Kim Isaac. *The Last Liberal: William J. Brennan and the Decisions That Transformed America*. Washington, DC: Beard Books, 2003.

Epstein, Lee, and Joseph F. Kobylka. *The Supreme Court and Legal Change: Abortion and the Death Penalty*. Chapel Hill: University of North Carolina Press, 1992.

Epstein, Richard A. "Substantive Due Process by Any Other Name: The Abortion Cases." *Supreme Court Review* (1973): 159–186.

Faux, Marian. Roe v. Wade: *The Untold Story of the Supreme Court Decision That Made Abortion Legal*. New York: Cooper Square, 2000.

Forsythe, Clarke D. *Abuse of Discretion: The Inside Story of* Roe v. Wade. Jackson, TN: Encounter Books, 2013.

Friedman, Leon, and Fred L. Israel, eds. *The Justices of the Supreme Court: Their Lives and Major Opinions*. New York: Chelsea House, 1997.

Funston, Richard Y. *Constitutional Counter-Revolution? The Warren Court and the Burger Court: Judicial Policy Making in America*. New York: Wiley, 1977, 66–73.

Gallup, George H. *The Gallup Poll: Public Opinion, 1972–1977*. Wilmington, DE: Scholarly Resources, 1978.

Garnett, Richard W. "Religion, Division, and the First Amendment." *Georgetown Law Journal* 94 (2006): 1667–2035.

Garrow, David J. *Liberty and Sexuality: The Right to Privacy and the Making of* Roe v. Wade. New York: Macmillan, 1994.

Gibson, Larry S. *Young Thurgood: The Making of a Supreme Court Justice*. Amherst, NY: Prometheus Books, 2012.

Goldstein, Stephen R. "Interdistrict Inequalities in School Financing: A Critical Analysis of *Serrano v. Priest* and Its Progeny." *University of Pennsylvania Law Review* 120 (1972): 504–544.

Graglia, Lino A. *Disaster by Decree: The Supreme Court Decisions on Race and the Schools.* Ithaca, NY: Cornell University Press, 1976.

Greenhouse, Linda. *Becoming Justice Blackmun: Harry Blackmun's Supreme Court Journey.* New York: Times Books, 2005.

Gunther, Gerald. "The Supreme Court, 1971 Term: Foreword—in Search of Evolving Doctrine on a Changing Court: A Model for a Newer Equal Protection." *Harvard Law Review* 86 (1972): 1–48.

Gupta-Kagan, Josh. "*Stanley v. Illinois*' Untold Story." *William & Mary Bill of Rights Journal*, http://papers.ssrn.com/s013/papers.cfm?abstract_id=2663356.

Haines, Charles G. *The American Doctrine of Judicial Supremacy.* New York: Russell and Russell, 1959.

Heise, Michael. "The Story of *San Antonio Independent School Dist. v. Rodriguez.*" In *Education Law Stories.* Edited by Michael A. Olivas and Ronna Schneider. New York: Foundation, 2007.

Herda, D. J. Furman v. Georgia*: The Death Penalty Case.* Lawrence: University Press of Kansas, 2010.

Horwitz, Morton J. *The Warren Court and the Pursuit of Justice.* New York: Hill and Wang, 1998.

Hull, N. E. H., and Peter Charles Hoffer. Roe v. Wade: *The Abortion Rights Controversy in American History.* Lawrence: University Press of Kansas, 2010.

Hutchinson, Dennis J. *The Man Who Once Was Whizzer White: A Portrait of Justice Byron R. White.* New York: Free Press, 1998.

Jeffries, John C., Jr. *Justice Lewis F. Powell, Jr.* New York: Scribner's, 1994.

Jenkins, John A. *The Partisan: The Life of William Rehnquist.* New York: Public Affairs, 2012.

Jones, Jeffrey M. "Americans' Support for Death Penalty Stable." http://www.gallup.com/poll/178790/americans-support-death-penalty-stable.aspx.

Kahn, Ronald. *The Supreme Court and Constitutional Theory, 1953–1993.* Lawrence: University Press of Kansas, 1994.

Kalk, Bruce H. "The Carswell Affair: The Politics of a Supreme Court Nomination in the Nixon Administration." *American Journal of Legal History* 42 (1998): 262–287.

Kalman, Laura. *Abe Fortas: A Biography.* New Haven, CT: Yale University Press, 1990.

Kamisar, Yale. "The Warren Court (Was It Really So Defense-Minded?), the Burger Court (Is It Really So Defense-Oriented?), and Police Investigatory Practices." In *The Burger Court: The Counter-Revolution That Wasn't.* Edited by Vincent Blasi. New Haven, CT: Yale University Press, 1983, 62–92.

Katz, Wilbur G. "Radiations from Church Tax Exemption." *Supreme Court Review* (1970): 93–108.

Kellett, Christine H. "The Burger Decade: More Than Toothless Scrutiny for Laws Affecting Illegitimates." *University of Detroit Journal of Urban Law* 57 (1980): 791–811.

Lamb, Charles M., and Stephen C. Halpern, eds. *The Burger Court: Political and Judicial Profiles.* Champaign: University of Illinois Press, 1991.

Lee, Francis Graham. *Neither Liberal nor Conservative: The Burger Court on Civil Rights and Liberties.* Malabar, FL: Robert E. Krieger, 1983.

Lockhart, William B., and Robert C. McClure. "Liberty, the Law of Obscenity, and the Constitution." *Minnesota Law Review* 38 (1972): 295–396.

Mackay, Robert B. *Reapportionment: The Law and Politics of Equal Representation.* New York: Twentieth Century Fund, 1965.

Maltz, Earl M. *The Chief Justiceship of Warren Burger, 1969–1986.* Columbia: University of South Carolina Press, 2000.

———. "Illegitimacy and Equal Protection." *Arizona State Law Journal* (1980): 831–851.

Mandery, Evan. *A Wild Justice: The Death and Resurrection of Capital Punishment in America.* New York: Norton, 2013.

Marion, David E. *The Jurisprudence of Justice William J. Brennan, Jr.: The Law and Politics of Libertarian Dignity.* Lanham, MD: Rowman and Littlefield, 1997.

Mayeri, Serena. *Reasoning from Race: Feminism, Law, and the Civil Rights Revolution.* Cambridge, MA: Harvard University Press, 2011.

———. "'When the Trouble Started': The Story of *Frontiero v. Richardson.*" In *Women and the Law Stories.* Edited by Elizabeth Schneider and Stephanie M. Wildman. New York: Foundation, 2011.

McMahon, Kevin, *Nixon's Court: His Challenge to Political Liberalism and Its Political Consequences.* Chicago: University of Chicago Press, 2011.

Michelman, Frank I. *Brennan and Democracy.* Princeton, NJ: Princeton University Press, 1999.

———. "Super Liberal: Romance, Community, and Tradition in William J. Brennan, Jr.'s Constitutional Thought." *Virginia Law Review* 77 (1991): 1261–1332.

———. "The Supreme Court, 1968 Term: Foreword—on Protecting the Poor through the Fourteenth Amendment." *Harvard Law Review* 83 (November 1969): 7–59.

Morgan, Richard E. "The Establishment Clause and Sectarian Schools: A Final Establishment?" *Supreme Court Review* (1973): 57–98.

Murphy, Bruce Allen. *Fortas: The Rise and Ruin of a Supreme Court Justice.* New York: Morrow, 1988.

———. *Wild Bill: The Life and Legend of William O. Douglas.* New York: Random House, 2003.

Obermayer, Herman J. *Rehnquist: A Personal Portrait of the Distinguished Chief Justice of the U.S.* New York: Threshold, 2009.

Pfeffer, Leo. *Religion, State, and the Burger Court*. New York: Prometheus Books, 1984.

Powe, Lucas, Jr. *The Warren Court and American Politics*. Cambridge, MA: Belknap Press of Harvard University Press, 2000.

Read, Frank T. "Judicial Evolution of the Law of School Integration since *Brown v. Board of Education*." *Law and Contemporary Problems* 39 (1975): 7–49.

Rehnquist, William H. "The Notion of a Living Constitution." *Texas Law Review* 54 (1976): 957–994.

Rowan, Carl T. *Dream Makers, Dream Breakers: The World of Justice Thurgood Marshall*. Boston: Little, Brown, 1993.

Saltzburg, Stephen A. "Foreword: The Flow and Ebb of Constitutional Criminal Procedure in the Warren and Burger Courts." *Georgetown Law Journal* 69 (1980): 151–209.

"School Desegregation and Equal Educational Opportunity." http://www.civilrights.org/resources/civilrights101/desegregation.html.

Schragger, Richard. "*San Antonio v. Rodriguez* and the Legal Geography of School Finance Reform." In *Civil Rights Stories*. Edited by Myriam Gilles and Risa Goluboff. New York: Foundation, 2008.

Schwartz, Bernard. *The Ascent of Pragmatism: The Burger Court in Action*. Reading, MA: Addison-Wesley, 1990.

———, ed. *The Burger Court: Counter-Revolution or Confirmation?* New York: Oxford University Press, 1998.

———. *Swann's Way: The School Busing Case and the Supreme Court*. New York: Oxford University Press, 1986.

———, ed. *The Warren Court: A Retrospective*. New York: Oxford University Press, 1996.

Schwartz, Herman, ed. *The Burger Years: Rights and Wrongs in the Supreme Court, 1969–1986*. New York: Viking, 1987.

Shapiro, David L. "Mr. Justice Rehnquist: A Preliminary View." *Harvard Law Review* 90 (1976): 293–357.

Simon, James F. *Independent Journey: The Life of William O. Douglas*. New York: Harper and Row, 1980.

———. *In His Own Image: The Supreme Court in Richard Nixon's America*. New York: David McKay, 1973.

Smarick, Andy. "Can Catholic Schools Be Saved?" *National Affairs* (Spring 2011): 113–130.

Smith, J. Douglas. *On Democracy's Doorstep: How the Supreme Court Brought "One Person, One Vote" to the United States*. New York: Hill and Wang, 2014.

Sracic, Paul A. San Antonio v. Rodriguez *and the Pursuit of Equal Education*. Lawrence: University Press of Kansas, 2006.

Stenger, Robert L. "The Supreme Court and Illegitimacy: 1968–1977." *Family Law Quarterly* 11 (1978): 365–405.

Stern, Seth Ross, and Stephen Wermeil. *Justice Brennan: Liberal Champion.* Boston: Houghton Mifflin Harcourt, 2010.

Sunderland, Lane V. *Obscenity: The Court, the Congress, and the President's Commission.* Washington, DC: American Enterprise Institute for Public Policy Research, 1974.

"The Supreme Court, 1971 Term." *Harvard Law Review* 86 (1972): 52–306.

"The Supreme Court, 1972 Term." *Harvard Law Review* 87 (1973): 55–309.

"Supreme Court Statistics." *Harvard Law Review* 82 (1968): 306.

"Supreme Court Statistics." *Harvard Law Review* 83 (1969): 278.

"Supreme Court Statistics," *Harvard Law Review* 87 (1973): 303.

Sutton, Jeffrey S. "*San Antonio Independent School District v. Rodriguez* and Its Aftermath." *Virginia Law Review* 94 (2008): 1963–1986.

"Symposium: Thurgood Marshall—His Life, His Work, His Legacy." *Howard Law Journal* 52 (2009): 507–708.

Tribe, Laurence H. "The Supreme Court, 1972 Term: Foreword—Toward a Model of Roles in the Due Process of Life and Law." *Harvard Law Review* 7 (1973): 1–53.

Tushnet, Mark V. "'. . . And Only Wealth Will Buy You Justice': Some Notes on the Supreme Court, 1972 Term." *Wisconsin Law Review* (1974): 177–197.

———. "The Burger Court in Historical Perspective: The Triumph of Country-Club Republicanism." In *The Burger Court: Counter-Revolution or Confirmation?* Edited by Bernard Schwartz. New York: Oxford University Press, 1998, 203–215.

———. *Making Civil Rights Law: Thurgood Marshall and the Supreme Court, 1936–1961.* New York: Oxford University Press, 1994.

———. *Making Constitutional Law: Thurgood Marshall and the Supreme Court, 1961–1991.* New York: Oxford University Press, 1997.

———, ed. *The Warren Court in Historical and Political Perspective.* Charlottesville: University Press of Virginia, 1993.

———, ed. *Thurgood Marshall: His Speeches, Writings, Arguments, Opinions, and Reminiscences.* Chicago: Lawrence Hill Books, 2001.

Van Alstyne, William. "The Demise of the Right-Privilege Distinction in Constitutional Law." *Harvard Law Review* 81 (1968): 1439–1464.

Wasby, Stephen L., ed. *"He Shall Not Pass This Way Again": The Legacy of William O. Douglas.* Pittsburgh, PA: University of Pittsburgh Press, 1990.

Wasby, Stephen L., and Joel B. Grossman. "Judge Clement F. Haynsworth, Jr.: New Perspective on His Nomination to the Supreme Court." *Duke Law Journal* (1990): 74–80.

Wechsler, Herbert. "Toward Neutral Principles of Constitutional Law." *Harvard Law Review* 73 (1959): 1–35.

Wilkinson, J. Harvie, III. *From* Brown *to* Bakke*: The Supreme Court and School Integration, 1954–1978.* New York: Oxford University Press, 1979.

Williams, Juan. *Thurgood Marshall: American Revolutionary.* New York: Times Books, 1998.

Woodward, Bob, and Scott Armstrong. *The Brethren: Inside the Supreme Court.* New York: Simon and Schuster, 1979.

Yarbrough, Tinsley E. *Harry A. Blackmun, the Outsider Justice.* New York: Oxford University Press, 2008.

Zelden, Charles L. *Thurgood Marshall: Race, Rights, and the Struggle for a More Perfect Union.* New York: Routledge, 2013.

Index